BEYOND PATRIARCHY

The Images of Family in Jesus

by
D. Jacobs-Malina

Diane Jacobs-Malina

PAULIST PRESS
New York/Mahwah, N.J.

Cover concept by Diane Jacobs-Malina.

ACKNOWLEDGEMENTS

The Publisher gratefully acknowledges the use of material quoted from *The Untouched Key* by Alice Miller. Copyright © 1990 by Alice Miller. Used by permission of Doubleday, a division of Bantam Doubleday Dell Publishing Group, Inc.

Library of Congress Cataloging-in-Publication Data

Jacobs-Malina, Diane, 1948-
    Beyond patriarchy: the images of family in Jesus/Diane Jacobs-Malina.
    p.   cm.
    Includes bibliographical references.
    ISBN 0-8091-3421-7
    1. Jesus Christ—Political and social views. 2. Jesus Christ—Views on the family. 3. Feminist theology. 4. Patriarchy—Religious aspects—Christianity. 5. Family—Biblical teaching. 6. Family—Middle East. I. Title.
BT202.J27   1993
261.8'3585'09015—dc20   93-24501
                                                                          CIP

Published by Paulist Press
997 Macarthur Boulevard
Mahwah, New Jersey 07430

Printed and bound in the
United States of America

TABLE OF CONTENTS

Contents

For Barbara Reardon Heaney
with love

ACKNOWLEDGEMENTS

The "feminine" as I had first experienced her was neither trustworthy nor likeable. The domestic domain provided the environment in which I learned the intricate complexities of survival. The limitations of my own early experiences were not helped in my formal education by the negative images of women and nature that religious and secular traditions promulgated as "authoritative." Nature was viewed as antithetical to social development, and nurture was considered to be optional. Neither early experiences nor later theory predisposed me to write this book. The people to whom I am most indebted are those who changed the original image of the feminine that I had internalized along with the understanding of nature that flowed from it.

My greatest debt of gratitude goes to Barbara Reardon Heaney. Her instinctive way of knowing, loving and giving to me profoundly altered my image of the feminine and nature. From Barbara I received the unconditional gift of life, a gift that did not come at birth. I would also like to thank Sr. Barbara Markey whose critical thinking, humor and friendship have influenced and supported me since adolescence. To my sister, Lisa Jacobs-McCusker, I am grateful for the continuous loving relation that began at her birth, gathered momentum and passed on to the next generation with the birth of Kyle Thomas McCusker this year. For more than a quarter of a century, each of these three women has been restructuring and reconstituting the feminine within me.

There are four men to whom I owe debts of gratitude as well. The first is Nicholas Gage, a Greek immigrant to this country whom I have never met. He wrote a powerful book about his own mother, *Eleni*. His personal story became for me the parable which generated a new understanding of the life and death of Jesus. Next I wish to thank Halvor Moxnes of the University of Oslo, Norway. He not only gave me the impetus to begin writing this book but timely support and friendship when most needed. Musa Al-Hindi arrived from Beirut eight years ago and became part of our family. Muslim and Palestinian, the quintessential "Other" and "Outsider," Musa's combined warmth and patience wore down the reserves of animosity and intolerance that I had unconsciously assimilated toward his world and his religion. Without his patience, perspective and friendship, an important window on the world of Jesus would have remained closed to me.

Finally, I want to thank my husband, Bruce J. Malina, for his commitment to understanding the social worlds of the Bible in order to interpret its words; for introducing me to sources that supported and expanded my thesis; for streamlining my writing and research with his computer expertise; for volunteering to read each of the last three drafts; and for patiently seeing this project through to publication.

Easter, April 19, 1992
Omaha, Nebraska

INTRODUCTION

PATRIARCHY AND THE DOMESTIC DOMAIN [1]

Jesus lived in a patriarchal social system. This system designated the father/husband as the head of the family. The father was recognized as such by the law and was accepted as a participating member within the city/state or kingdom. The status enjoyed by the male as patriarch rested on the assumption that the male seed alone provided everything necessary to form his offspring. It was believed that the female provided nothing beyond a place for the seed's growth until birth, followed by nurture and care for the male's offspring after birth. Flowing from this interpretation of human reproduction was an ordering of society which gave the male a position superior to that of the female. This superior position was symbolized by "honor" which was ascribed to each male at birth. Unlike the male whose gender made him whole and complete, the female was raised with a sense of shame which made her as dependent on the male for her own "completeness" as she was dependent on him for children, support and honor. The woman whose modesty and strictly controlled behavior in public manifested this sense of shame brought honor on the males to whom she was attached.

The honor (or shame) of the patriarch was extended to the name of his family. Since the father provided the seed, that is "everything" but incubation and nurture which the woman provided, all children belonged to him. When it came to the children of sons and daughters, the children of sons belonged to the paternal family while the children of daughters belonged to the family of the daughter's husband.[2] The title, Son of God, means that Jesus received his "everything" (life, identity and role) from God. Since Jesus received "everything" from God, those who received "everything" from Jesus acknowledged God as the original and ultimate source. Replicating the social understanding that children of sons belonged to the paternal family, those attached to Jesus became members of his Father's household.

The tribe was the larger social unit which joined families based on extended kinship. The honor of the tribe was as dependent on the honor of each individual family as the family was dependent on the honor of each male. This replication of the importance of honor throughout every level of society made honor the central concern. Thus the maintenance, defense, loss and restoration of honor due to males provided the matrix out of which social

1

values and customs arose governing the behavior of both sexes. Furthermore, there is a corollary between the centrality of honor and the disparity and separation between the genders. This separation and disparity between male and female as created and maintained within traditional patriarchal perception became the basic analogy for understanding the ordering of the universe: God is to man as man is to woman; man is to nature what man is to woman; the master is to slave as man is to woman; the emperor is to his people as man is to woman; the teacher is to his pupil as man is to woman, etc.

The superiority of the male as well as the unbridgeable distance between the male and female was emphasized continuously through these replications. Thus, the central axiom was stringently upheld that a man who "acts like a woman," that is who does anything which was assigned to the female as part of her role, crossed the most rigorously maintained of all boundaries. Such a boundary violation cost a male his honor. Fully aware of how the social world of Jesus viewed honor and the crossing of gender boundaries, it is not surprising that analogies for his behavior have been limited to male roles. So while Jesus called himself "Son of man" and was called "Son of God," the idealized role of son as imagined in a patriarchal social world does not account for the multiple roles Jesus played. Many would argue that it is not necessary for Jesus' words and actions to be explained through any single role. Yet there was a commonly known role that does unify the multiple dimensions of Jesus as he is presented in the gospels.

It is the thesis of this book that the image of Jesus presented in the gospels finds as its closest analogy the idealized role of the wife/mother as it was established in the world of Jesus. Making it quite clear that he was authorized to carry out his role, Jesus taught his followers to call God, Father. Acting on behalf of the Father "who was in heaven," Jesus' primary role was to create and to maintain the household of God on earth. Thus it is possible to be even more specific and assert that Jesus' role was most like that of the "wife of the absent husband."

The Idealized Role of Woman as the Wife/Mother—There are some profound insights to be gained into the actions of Jesus from understanding the role of the woman as the idealized wife/mother in the patriarchal world of the first century Mediterranean. Let us spend some time to focus on the dimensions of that role.

The social group expected the woman to integrate all the facets of her life and personality into a single identity revolving ultimately around the domestic world. Initially this embraced the private domain of her father, and subsequently that of her husband. The months that followed the wedding provided ample opportunity for the husband's family to test the new wife in order to see the extent to which she belonged to them to the exclusion of all others.

The first test was passed when physical evidence of the bride's virginity (blood on a cloth from the marriage bed) was witnessed by the groom who showed it to his mother or publicized it in some other way to the honor of the bride and her family. The months that followed were an important transition period where "training" alternated with testing the young wife. This preceded the birth of children to whom the mother would be the most important socializing agent on behalf of the husband's family and the larger society.

The wife's place in the traditional, patriarchal household totally defines who she is and circumscribes her behavior as she becomes both functionally and symbolically associated with it. That is, all of her actions and identity are intimately linked with her husband's household.[3] In that role, the woman's most important achievements are those that lead to the creation and nurturing of children. Marriage and motherhood authorize the wife to act and speak on behalf of her husband in the process of social reproduction which she fulfills: 1) by the introduction of new members within an environment where the young are allowed to grow and mature; 2) by socializing children to fulfill their roles as adults to the honor of their family and expectations of society; 3) by contributing to the renewal and regeneration of older members whose interactions with the outside world leave them personally depleted.[4]

Social reproduction, which includes procreation and socialization of the new generation as well as the renewal of the present generation, makes communication and interpersonal relations of primary importance in the lives of women. In addition to verbal communication centered on concrete behavior in the physical world, the mother teaches how actions and example also communicate at a symbolic or abstract level. For instance, her example of suffering communicates to her children how to struggle well, how to cope with the need to work hard in a world that is relentlessly demanding, while resisting the personal erosion that comes from inevitable and necessary suffering.[5]

Her second most important duty is to change the animals and produce that enter the house into food. Because food is the general idiom which symbolizes bonds and relationships among those on the inside, it is an integral part of every woman's responsibilities. The significance of meals extends beyond the household to include outsiders who enter into relations with the family.[6] The kind and amount of food the family eats, its preparation, the quality and quantity served to outsiders, symbolize how the family sees itself in relation to outsiders.

The move from the outside of the house to the inside totally changes the quality of social relationships among household members as well as the self-image of each. All members, including men, should be able to experience the security and freedom to be oneself. The private sphere represents both the hidden and secret dimensions of its members as well as those who are weaker, dependent, subordinate and in need of care.[7] It is within this setting that the ambiguity of the woman's role as primary socializing agent is clearly seen when she "binds up the social and psychological wounds" that the public inflicts on members of her household so that they may be sent out only to suffer again.[8] Similarly, she must "toughen" (a masculine aspect of her role) new members of society so that they will be able to live and function in a society which demands that all of them be sacrificed to some degree, for family and/or group gain and solidarity. This aspect of socialization splits the woman who is expected to act against the personal interests of herself, her children and her husband when the interests of the larger group demand it.

Within the household if nowhere else, it is also the wife's job to see that her husband has a central position. This necessitates that the wife subordinate herself to her husband even though the domestic domain is her proper sphere. She becomes the weak one so that he can be the stronger member. Her obedience to her husband suppresses the limits which the world outside places on him. She turns his public impotence into her own private impotence, obscuring his social weakness within his private sphere.[9] Thus, the ideal wife/mother in the traditional, patriarchal household achieves her status by self-expenditure on behalf of those above her as well as those who rank below her in the social hierarchy.

The woman is in charge of the economic functions of the household which include food, clothing and other objects required for multiple household duties. In the same way, she is responsible for those goods which the family might produce to exchange or sell in the marketplace. This link to the public necessitates that women act as mediators between the privacy of the household and the public. Both symbolically and physically, the wife/mother replicates the relationship between the inside of the house and the outside, as well as the inter-penetrations of the private and public spheres. The social and economic isolation of each household is "symbolized by the woman as a social figure, communicated by her as a social participant and re-created by her as a social actor."[10]

She is not only servant in the house but its most vigilant sentry, guarding the domestic domain against alien influences and outside intrusion. Another dimension of this role as sentry is the transformation of raw materials or unacceptable influences from the outside into forms socially acceptable and useful for the inside. Examples of transforming raw materials include cooking, spinning, weaving, sewing.[11] Thus she makes socially acceptable dimensions of nature that were considered unacceptable by cultural standards.[12] In this way, she exerts power over various aspects and manifestations of nature. Rearing children is the human replication of this responsibility where infants are raised and socialized to manifest socially acceptable behavior both in private as well as in public.

There is no indication, however, that the woman enjoys any power or privileges because she is expected to be the moral symbol of her house in public. This expectation endows her with no real power as defined in the world of men.[13] Unlike them, the woman's "power" is limited to how much influence she can wield. But when she is denied what she considers to be her due, either in the domestic or public spheres, the woman may seek to exercise her influence in "illegitimate" ways. She may disrupt or subvert normal social relationships or cause trouble, agitating until she gets what she needs. This kind of "power" that flows through influence is not limited by the social rules that normally circumscribe the legitimate use of power.

One of the best descriptions to be found of the woman's roles as it existed in biblical times that reiterates the description just given is found in Proverbs 31:10-31:

> A good wife who can find?
> She is far more precious than jewels.
> The heart of her husband trusts in her,
> and he will have no lack of gain.
> She does him good, and not harm,
> all the days of her life.
> She seeks wool and flax,
> and works with willing hands.
> She is like the ships of the merchant,
> she brings her food from afar.
> She rises while it is yet night
> and provides food for her household
> and tasks for her servant girls.
> She considers a field and buys it;
> with the fruit of her hands she plants a vineyard.
> She girds her loins with strength
> and makes her arms strong.
> She perceives that her merchandise is profitable.
> Her lamp does not go out at night.
> She puts her hands to the distaff,
> and her hands hold the spindle.
> She opens her hand to the poor,
> and reaches out her hands to the needy.
> She is not afraid of snow for her household,
> for her household are clothed in scarlet.
> She makes herself coverings;
> her clothing is fine linen and purple.
> Her husband is known in the gates,
> when he sits among the elders of the land.

She makes linen garments and sells them;
she delivers girdles to the merchant.
Strength and dignity are her clothing,
and she laughs at the time to come.
She opens her mouth with wisdom,
and the teaching of kindness is on her tongue.
She looks well to the ways of her household,
and does not eat the bread of idleness.
Her children rise up and call her blessed;
her husband also, and he praises her:
"Many women had done excellently,
but you surpass them all."
Charm is deceitful, and beauty is vain,
but a woman who fears the Lord is to be praised.
Give her of the fruit of her hands,
and let her works praise her at the gates.

This description from Proverbs corresponds exactly to what was expected of women in the first century.[14]

Patriarchal cultures foster the belief that male presence is necessary to keep the woman from bringing shame on her family. Indeed, betrothal in the post-exilic religion of Israel was referred to as that stage in the marriage where the husband "sanctified" his bride.[15] At all times, the wife was expected to act according to her absent husband's wishes, orders, expectations, goals and in his best interests. When the husband was absent, social scrutiny of the wife/mother intensified. Because she was left unsupervised and authorized to act on his behalf, the wife was held to even more strenuous standards of propriety than when the husband was present. So, despite his absence, the husband was ever present in his wife, both to his children as well as to others who might try to usurp what belonged to him.[16] This role, with its rights and obligations, its values and activities, provides the most adequate analogy, the best model for understanding the role which Jesus played in the gospels in his relation to God as well as in his relation to his own followers and outsiders.

THE GOSPELS: THE AUTHORIZED IMAGE OF GOD-IN-JESUS

A unified image of Jesus—Despite their separate origins and unique features, Mark, Matthew, Luke and John consistently present an image of Jesus which bears a striking resemblance to the above role. As women relied on their male family members to maintain and/or restore their honor, so did

Jesus depend on God for the maintenance and restoration of his honor. The kingdom of God as revealed by Jesus found the life-giving and nurturing roles of women to be equally appropriate for men because it best reflected God's commitment to the care of his children. This was the central concern of the kingdom of God, not the preservation of honor through the maintenance of rigid gender roles. God himself and those obedient to him replaced the public as the arbiter of honor and substituted forgiveness for revenge because that is how he acts toward human beings.

This radical alteration of the male role invites a closer look at each gospel from the domestic standpoint, the world of nature and nurture. From this perspective, God's testing of Jesus, Jesus' complete loyalty to the Father who authorized him, the unique role Jesus enjoys as he brings children into the household of God, his role of socializing these "children" as well as meeting their physical needs, Jesus' example of hard work and suffering in order to maintain the household according to the will of the Father, and Jesus' designation of his own body and blood as food are but a few examples of activities that Jesus performed as part of his unique role in the household of God. The role of the eldest son in a patriarchal family is quite different from the multiple roles just described.

The title Jesus used most frequently for himself was "son of man," a human being. Within the limitations of those languages which are gender based, that is designating all nouns as masculine or feminine (or neuter), the title "son of man" minimizes the issue of gender and implies no religious or ethnic superiority. The social understanding of what it meant to be a human being in Jesus' world integrated the physical dimensions of the human body with knowing, loving, communicating and acting. Not surprisingly Jesus chose the concrete language of parables that relied on the common humanity of his audience and their shared needs. There was nothing about nature, human needs or the physical world which resisted the activity of God's Spirit. Nature and domestic settings provided analogies for the kingdom of heaven and disclosed the absent Father whose household Jesus helped create and maintain. The miracle stories affirm that no aspect of nature was unresponsive to God's activity in Jesus. The same cannot be said of human beings where culture intervenes with interpretations of reality (nature included) which resist God's ongoing activity on behalf of his creation. While Jesus found nothing in the processes of nature that was alien to the mind of God, many of the customs and values of his social world required radical change before they could reflect the designs of God as Father.

Organization and goals—The primary goal of this book is to recover the image of Jesus, that of God as Father as well as that of the believer as a child of God. These images arise with clarity and consistency whether portrayed by Mark, Matthew, Luke or John. Jesus not only revealed that God is

Father but his own words and actions clarified for the first time **how** God fathers. As the wife reflects her husband so did Jesus reflect God who is without the ambiguities of the God revealed by Moses or Muhammad. As children reflect their parents and **the parenting they experienced,** so do those who are attached to Jesus replicate in their behavior the fathering of God. But human life and experience begin with human parenting.

Styles of human parenting are created and maintained by the social system. The example of Jesus clarified how the patriarchal social system as embodied in Israel was at odds with the values of the kingdom. This discrepancy between the kingdom and Israel began with human beings at birth, in the household with those people whose main work was the care and nurture of children. The fissure between the kingdom and the social system only broadened as the child became more enculturated. Human parenting did not reflect the care and nurture of God as Father because the social system did not reflect the values of the kingdom of God. The changes that Jesus advocated began in the private life, in the domestic domain, and require that perspective for adequate interpretation and appreciation.

The next five chapters set out to accomplish three goals: first, to enable the reader to view the parables and activities of Jesus from the perspective of the domestic model given in this introduction; second, to discover the image of God that Jesus sets out to reveal through his own words and works; third, to understand how the domestic perspective changes the identity and role expectations of those who follow Jesus. The image of God, of Jesus and that of the believer are consistently presented in each gospel regardless of the situation in the gospel community or the various traditions used by each evangelist. Exploring these images from the perspective of the submerged and subordinated social world of women in patriarchal society makes the nineteenth century western debate over the Jesus of history vs. the Christ of faith irrelevant to the discussion within this book.

Since the Markan image of Jesus is accepted by Matthew and Luke, the gospel of Mark will be presented in Chapter I as far as the last supper. Viewed from the perspective of the creation and maintenance of a household, the Markan image of Jesus emerges with clarity and consistency. The analogy of the wife/mother unifies the relations, words and actions of Jesus without limiting him to multiple roles that are no longer meaningful to an audience not rooted in the religion of Israel (e.g. prophet, Messiah, son of David, king of Israel, high priest, sacrificial lamb, suffering servant, etc.).

Chapter II examines the role of the Spirit, Jesus' use of the term "son of man" as well as his parables to confirm the positive role that nature enjoys in God's household. The kingdom of God/heaven dominates Chapter III as the larger social group which eclipsed Israel's hold on those who joined the household Jesus established. The additions and expansions of Matthew and

Luke in no way diminish or undermine the unity and integrity forged by the Markan image of Jesus which both gospels incorporate. In Chapter IV, the gospel of John follows its own course in creating an image of Jesus which likewise arises from domestic analogies. The distinctive approach of the fourth gospel includes the vertical boundaries which Jesus crossed, time as the eternal "present," the use of repetition, and the cosmic cycle of God's activity set amidst competing worlds. The last supper, passion, death and resurrection accounts from all four gospels will be reviewed together in Chapter V. The sixth chapter will introduce Pauline analogies, values and goals which were compatible with the patriarchal social system but incompatible with the standards of the kingdom as presented in the gospels. The seventh chapter initiates an understanding of Jesus which arises from a consideration of the similarities that exist between Islam and Judaism. The pervasiveness of social systems as the interpreter of reality is examined. The image of nature, which is also controlled by social systems, is re-examined from a perspective that is aligned with the understanding of nature promulgated by Jesus' words and actions.

As the patriarchal strata of each society are replaced by less rigid gender roles, equality between the sexes, a guarantee of human rights for all, a more comprehensive understanding of the impact of one's childhood on adult life, etc., the more urgent will be the task of finding a viewpoint which yields more than outdated wisdom dependent upon irrelevant analogies. For example, the Hebrew epic, Greek philosophy and Roman law which are so intricately interwoven and dependent upon a patriarchal perspective will become less and less relevant to growing numbers of Christians. This book focuses on the domestic side of patriarchy which was totally organized around nature, the demands of nurture and the encouragement of optimum human development. These are concerns which transcend time and culture. Because of this, the standards and goals of the gospels will continue to be relevant for human behavior long after the demise of patriarchy. The standards of the kingdom of God as manifested by Jesus continue to provide the criteria against which all following social systems are to be evaluated.[17]

I.

THE MARKAN IMAGE

INTRODUCTION

As we shall see, the Markan image of Jesus arose from the private side of man's life and was based on analogies flowing from familial relations and roles that were common within a household.[1] Every gospel reveals something of the community out of which it emerged. Mark, the oldest written gospel, emerged out of a community mixed with Gentiles. Various Jewish customs were unknown and had to be explained to the audience, e.g. on the washing of hands and vessels (Mk 7:3,4), as well as reapplications of Jesus' teachings to fit Gentile situations, e.g. divorce was forbidden to Gentile women (Mk 10:12) who were free to sue for divorce unlike Jewish women. Thus, Gentiles were present in the Markan community but there is no evidence that their presence was not accepted by Jewish-Christians. Similarly, the Markan community reflected none of the hostility from unbaptized Jews that is evident in the other three gospels.

HOUSEHOLD BEGINNINGS (1:1-20)

Jesus, "the beloved"—The earliest gospel begins with John the Baptist, a prophet who lived his adult life outside the spaces civilized by man. He appeared in the wilderness "preaching a baptism of repentance for the forgiveness of sins" (1:4). Among those drawn to John's call for conversion was Jesus of Nazareth. He joined others in baptism as an outward manifestation that they were "plunged or drenched in a change of heart for their release from the wrong path or direction"(1:4).[2] Jesus emerged from the Jordan river to hear a voice from heaven call him Son, the beloved, the one who pleased God. Following this, Jesus was subsequently driven by the Spirit into the wilderness where his allegiance to God was tested. As confirmation that Jesus was well-anchored in the household of God, angels ministered to his needs after his attachment to God proved to be unshakable.

The first members—Following John's arrest, Jesus returned to Galilee proclaiming that the time was fulfilled and the kingdom of God was at hand.

Jesus had responded to John's words with a complete change in his life and urged others to respond similarly. Passing two fishermen, Simon and his brother Andrew, Jesus called them and immediately they followed him. Next, another set of brothers are described as mending their nets when they are called. Once again, the response is immediate as the brothers leave their father and hired servants behind to go with Jesus.

There is an analogy from the domestic world which provides the context in which to understand the kind of discipleship expected. The invitation that Jesus extended to Simon, Andrew, James and John replicates the invitation he accepted at his own baptism where he presumably left everyone and everything behind. Such behavior is that of the bride who leaves her family. The disciples trusted Jesus and his arrangements for them as the girl trusts those who arrange for her marriage even though she might not meet the groom until her wedding. On that day, she leaves behind father and family to join a procession[3] which takes her to a new life in the house of her husband's family. While theologians have described the kind of discipleship expected by Jesus of his followers as "radical," it was no different from the behavior expected of young brides for centuries.[4]

Analogies based on marriage, wedding feasts, brides and bridegrooms rise and fall throughout all the gospels. It is not unlikely that Jesus' own personal commitment flowed from an analogy based on the wife's role in a marriage since it was one of the traditional ways Israel understood itself in relation to God.[5] This analogy provided Jesus with the standard for group commitment expected of those who joined him as the household of God began to expand. The degree to which the ideal wife was expected to demonstrate commitment to her husband is the degree to which both male and female believers are expected to commit themselves to God, as witnessed in their words and actions.

SOCIALIZATION WITHIN THE NEW HOUSEHOLD

Service with propriety, without publicity (1:21-45)—Three themes develop before the end of this first chapter: 1) the amazement of people at the authority with which Jesus teaches and acts; 2) the question of **who** authorized and empowered him—which evil spirits inappropriately reveal (only to be silenced); 3) Jesus' insistence on no publicity from those who are healed. The propriety of God's household demanded that the activity of Jesus not make him a public spectacle. Nevertheless, his reputation spread because of his teachings, healings and casting out (not destroying) those evil spirits who inhabited human beings.

Leaving the synagogue, Jesus went with Andrew, James and John to

Simon's house. His mother-in-law was sick with a fever, upsetting the order and routine of a house where hospitality required serving the guests. Jesus took her by the hand and lifted her up; the fever left her and she served them. The sabbath ended with the city gathered at Simon's door as Jesus' continued service to guests paralleled that initiated by Peter's mother-in-law at the beginning of the passage.

The next day Jesus got up while it was still dark and left to pray, only to be pursued by Simon who announced that everyone was looking for him. Jesus responded that they must go to the other towns "...that I may preach there also; for that is why **I came out**." They journeyed throughout Galilee preaching in synagogues and casting out evil spirits. The cure of a leper followed by Jesus' stern charge to say nothing about it was uncharacteristic behavior for men whose honor was normally gained, augmented or lost in public settings.[6] Touching the leper pointed to Jesus' disregard of ritual purity restrictions.[7] Throughout Mark Jesus was more concerned with the impropriety of his name and actions gaining publicity than he was with purity prohibitions. Because the "outside," the public square, was a male arena, the female had to be concerned with propriety and unassuming behavior in public. Becoming the object of public attention could readily dishonor the males in whom she was embedded, e.g. father, brother or husband.[8] Jesus' actions were not circumscribed by purity restrictions but by the possibility of detracting from the honor due to God.

Authorized by the absent Father (2:1-12)—**Inside** his home in Capernaum, Jesus was teaching visitors who extended beyond his door when four men removed roof tiles and lowered a paralytic in need of healing. Despite the irregular entry, their faith indicated that they belonged inside with Jesus. Calling the paralytic, "child," he told him that his sins were forgiven. This declaration made **within** Jesus' home caused the scribes to question **within** their hearts if Jesus was not usurping some privilege that belonged to God alone. Not a word was spoken as Jesus perceived **within** his spirit what they questioned **within** themselves. Responding to what went unspoken, he assured them that as the Son of man, he had been authorized both to forgive sins as well as to heal.

The private or domestic spaces are replicated by: 1) the setting **within** the house; 2) questions that remained **within** the person; and 3) Jesus' response **within these "interiors"** to the paralytic and the other visitors. His example was one of propriety as he continued to reveal nothing of a personal nature about the One on whose authority he acted. With that, he told the paralytic to pick up his pallet and go home.

Food as the main idiom of the household (2:13-28)—Departing to the seashore, Jesus continued to do "outside" what he did "inside." His actions were not limited by the physical walls of a house, the familial walls of kinship nor by the social walls of group boundaries. He met Levi whom he called away from his tax table to follow him. Once again, everyone ended up at Jesus' house where the meals included those beyond the household who entered into relations with the growing family. This is the first of three successive episodes where the scribes and Pharisees have problems with: 1) the people with whom Jesus eats; 2) the fact that Jesus' disciples are eating and not fasting; 3) and how the disciples obtain their food on the sabbath.

Since food was the general idiom which symbolized bonds and relationships, it was an integral part of Jesus' responsibility. What, with whom, when and how one ate revealed the character of the family or household. Jesus responded that sinners belong at his table; that his presence precluded fasting by those attached to him; and that as lord of the sabbath, he was authorized to see that members of his house ate whatever food was available without sabbath requirements restricting how it was obtained.

Jesus as servant and sentry of the household—Thus far, Jesus has acted as servant to people in their needs for healing, teaching and food. Previously, forgiving sins had been the prerogative of God alone, yet Jesus announced the forgiveness of sins as though he knew the mind of God and claimed that "the son of man" had been authorized to forgive sins. Similarly, the sabbath had been considered sacred time allocated to God alone, yet Jesus declared that the sabbath was made for man and then announced himself as lord of the sabbath. Thus Jesus also acted as sentry authorizing within the household of God the unprecedented passage of the boundaries of sacred time and assuming prerogatives that had belonged to God alone. What was implicitly being revealed by Jesus' actions as servant and sentry was the identity of the One on whose behalf he acted and the character of his household.

Abundance manifested by Jesus arouses envy among outsiders (3:1-12)—One of the most moving episodes in Mark takes place when Jesus enters a synagogue and sees a man with a withered hand. The question of behavior appropriate to time and person continued as Jesus asked whether it was lawful on the sabbath "to do good or to harm, to save life or to kill." The instinctive response Jesus had to alleviate suffering was not shared by the synagogue members. No one answered his question and Jesus was "grieved and angry at their hardness of heart," a condition which made them impervious either to pity or to reason.[9] "Hardness of heart" often appears in the Old Testament but never with such frequency as when Pharaoh refused to listen to Moses despite the mounting sufferings of his fellow Egyptians with each additional plague. Similarly, none of the men present with Jesus in the synagogue were moved with pity at the condition of their fellow member. Finally Jesus asked the man to stretch out his hand and then healed him.

The Pharisees responded to this action by plotting with the Herodians to destroy Jesus. Such a response might have been prompted by envy, an emotion directed against someone that "stems from the desire to acquire something possessed by another person." Envy is not to be confused with jealousy which is "rooted in the fear of losing something already possessed."[10] Envy can galvanize a group just as forcibly as challenges to family honor or charges of religious violations. The members of highly cohesive groups tend to hover unconsciously at the same level. Those who rise above this accepted level become the target of those around them.[11] While some responded to Jesus' words and actions with belief and repentance, there were others who responded with envy. Jesus reacted to this by "withdrawing" (quite literally) to the sea with his disciples where great multitudes from Galilee, Judea, Jerusalem, Idumea, Tyre and Sidon followed him because of his growing reputation for responding to their physical needs. The press of people continued as they sought to touch Jesus and be healed. It is not surprising that by the next passage Jesus is authorizing disciples to share his work.

THE HOUSEHOLD EXPANDS

Authorizing the next generation (3:13-19)—Jesus took his disciples from the sea to a mountain where he appointed twelve to stay with him. They were authorized to preach as well as to cast out demons. Within the Israelite epic, the mountain is God's space, the place to which Moses had been called and commissioned to establish a new law and covenant between God and Israel. This was the third boundary belonging to God that Jesus had crossed. The first boundary was crossed when Jesus had been authorized to share what had been God's singular prerogative to forgive sins against him; the second boundary marked off sacred time over which Jesus announced himself to be lord of the sabbath; now Jesus empowers others on space made sacred by its association with God's commissioning to Moses.

Loyalty to the Master and his household (3:20-35)—The following three segments witness Jesus' temptation to place the honor of his biological family before that of God's household. Once again the scene is set within the domestic space of a house where **outsiders** made it impossible for those **inside** to eat. His family arrived after hearing that he had lost his mind, while the scribes from Jerusalem arrived proclaiming that he was possessed by the prince of demons. Jesus first responded to the charge that his master is the prince of demons by asserting that a kingdom or household divided within cannot stand. Similarly, if Satan has risen up against himself, then his house is coming to an end. Without naming his master, Jesus goes on to point out that what is more likely to happen is that the house is beset by **outside** forces who invade with the intention of binding the strong man so they can plunder his house.

Jesus answered their accusation that one may neither give nor ascribe to the prince of demons what belongs to God alone. It is clear from the passage that no one knows for sure who has empowered Jesus to teach and act as he does. The Pharisees' claim that Beelzebul is the one who had empowered Jesus deprives God of what Jesus had been doing in his name, thus handing everything over to the wrong person. This is the equivalent of plundering the house of God as Beelzebul is credited with or given what belongs to God. Ultimately, those same authorities will penetrate God's house, bind and kill Jesus in an attempt to steal those who belong to God.

Then Jesus deals with the arrival of his mother, brothers and sisters. Their family honor is at stake in the accusations being made against the presumably eldest son. In this account, the family is on the **outside** of the house asking the crowd to relay word of their presence to Jesus who is on the **inside**. Upon hearing that his family was outside, Jesus asked who his mother and brothers might be. Looking at those **inside** around him, he answered his own question: those who do the will of God are mother and brother and sister to him. This passage has been frequently misunderstood by audiences who remain unaware of analogies based on a wife's absolute commitment to the household of her husband. Her identity is radically altered within this new set of relations that take precedence over the family of her birth. Just as the wife gives evidence of her new identity by allegiance to her husband's family, so also does Jesus give evidence of his primary allegiance to God when he openly declares that now those surrounding him who do the will of God are mother, brothers and sisters to him.

Jesus' life radically changed after his baptism when he publicly transferred his primary allegiance to God. When norms arising from the public domain of the male are applied here, Jesus' words are interpreted as being anti-family as though the domestic life is incompatible with public commitment to God. In a culture where women and children cannot live apart from male authority, this interpretation fostered the denigration of women and children. It further confirmed the social and religious positions that women and children were antithetical to male holiness. Using the norms characteristic of a wife, Jesus is publicly showing himself to be securely embedded within his new family. Thus, the choice is not between domestic allegiance and God. Jesus' example **redefined** family and based kinship on **doing** the will of the Father who is God. One analogy dismisses the family while the other analogy reorganizes that family membership around **God** as head, necessitating major role changes for the biological husband/father of each family.

Having answered the charge of the Jerusalem scribes, Jesus first clarified that he did not belong to the household of Beelzebul. Jesus then went on to identify who else (based on their belief and actions) belonged within his house. This account affirmed that he could no longer be relied on to place the interests of his family before those of God's household. Or, stating this another way, his relation to his family of birth was contingent on its members reorganizing themselves around the will of God as patriarch or primary "male'" in the household.

Household members are to bear fruit in abundance (4:1-20)—In the next scene, Jesus is sitting outside in a boat on the sea where he tells the parable about the sower planting seeds. The focus is on how the word-within-the-seed is affected by its surroundings. Of the four different environments in which the seed may fall, only one produces fruit. A digression is introduced here which lets us know that the secrets of the kingdom have been revealed to those **on the inside** while "for those **outside** everything is in parables; so that they may indeed see but not perceive, and may indeed hear but not understand; lest they should turn again, and be forgiven."

This appears to be a strange position for any teacher unless one realizes that: 1) while this saying originates in Israel's Bible when Isaiah volunteered to be God's messenger to the house of Israel, the writing of that passage **followed** Israel's rejection of proper covenant behavior; 2) similarly, the gospels were written after Jewish rejection of Jesus was well known. In the earlier situation, God tells his messenger that the people will neither see, hear, understand nor be converted. Isaiah asks how long this will last and God's response is: until only the stock remains, for the stock is a holy seed (Is 6:5-13). The seed in this passage and the setting in which it can grow and bear fruit are understood within the context of Isaiah.

ONE STANDARD FOR BOTH MEN AND WOMEN

Acceptable behavior cuts across gender lines (4:21-25)—The parable of the lamp on the stand proceeds from the assumption that lamps are placed so that their light dispels darkness making everything visible. Jesus goes on to say that there is nothing hidden except that it be exposed and no secret except that it be made clear. The boundary between public space and private space is erased in God's house because he sees what happens in private as well as what happens in public. "If anyone has ears to hear, let him hear," is followed immediately by a second warning to listen. Both admonitions precede the declaration that "The measure you give out will be the measure you receive and still more. For the one who has will receive more while the one who has not will lose everything."

This was the axiom applied to women in that culture whose status was acquired by self-expenditure on behalf of others while

> ...the superiority of the man is based on the belief that he is, by
> nature, in a certain relationship with the divine world that woman
> has to strive endlessly to create for herself. Thus whatever the
> stature of woman in this society...it is achieved on the condition
> that she remains loyal to her husband and obedient to the spiritu-
> al principle embodied in him.[12]

For the woman to have withheld herself or to have limited her giving was not
only to lose what status was to be gained at that moment, it was to risk losing
the status that she might have earned up to that time. There was no point
where the status of a non-elite woman was secure and she could stop giving;[13] those situations only existed for men. Indeed, situations existed where
male society dictated that men **must** refuse to give and/or forgive in order to
defend, regain or augment their honor.[14] The axiom that "the measure you
give will be the measure you get" applies equally to men and women where
status continues to be earned in the household of God.

Earth analogies for the kingdom (4:26-34)—The next parable compares the kingdom of God to the process by which the seed is planted, and
the earth provides everything necessary for the grain to ripen and ultimately
to be harvested. The following parable compares the kingdom of God to the
process by which the mustard seed grows until the birds of the air can make
nests in its branches. These analogies do not interpret God's rule to be like
the kingdoms of men. There is nothing in either analogy based on culturally
created political abstractions. Instead the analogy is between the kingdom of
God and processes in nature. Traditionally, the social world of men has represented civilization while woman, as tied to nature, was considered inferi-
or.[15] Thus, the social group (culture) determined that women could not be
fully participating members because they had no phallus to circumcise and
their reproductive cycle was judged as making them "unclean" for a good
part of their lives. Yet, in this parable, the earth and its natural processes
became the analogy by which the reign of God was described through an
inevitable process where it persisted and grew, in ways man "knows not
how."

The Father who empowered Jesus: welcomed or rejected? (4:35-
6:13)—Five different stories follow where the power that Jesus manifested
on behalf of those present was interpreted variously. The first account is the
calming of the sea which began in the evening when Jesus and his disciples
were in boats crossing to the other side. A great wind arose creating waves
that threatened to fill the boat while Jesus slept. In a panic, the disciples
woke Jesus who rebuked the wind and calmed the sea. His question as to
why they were afraid was not meant to suggest the incompatibility of fear
and manliness, but the incompatibility of fear and belief in Jesus.

His words and actions attempted to resocialize the disciples regarding new relations that called for different emotional responses. Situations which had previously evoked fear were now to evoke trust from those members within the household. Thus, Jesus' dealings with nature went beyond food and healing. His interactions with nature extended to the elements around him which responded to his word as readily as demons who were dispelled, diseases which were eradicated and bread that was multiplied. Nature was viewed as alive and readily responsive to the words of Jesus. However, this cannot be said about the group whose vested interests made them unwilling to change.

Finally having reached the other side of the sea, Jesus and his disciples were met by a man with an unclean spirit who lived amid the tombs. While attempts had been made by others "to meet force with force," the chains and fetters had always been broken as the man continued to harm himself. Two additional pieces of information testify to the strength of the spirit and the overwhelming distress that had gripped the man. The spirit's name was "...Legion; for we are many" and when allowed to possess a herd of two thousand swine, all of them rushed down a steep bank into the sea where they drowned. Recognized by the unclean spirits as "Son of the Most High God," Jesus had manifested such power as to evoke fear among the inhabitants. While the group begged Jesus to leave, the healed man begged to be allowed to join Jesus. Instead, Jesus commissioned him to go home to his friends and tell them how much God had done for him. The author adds that the man spread the news of how much Jesus had done for him throughout the Decapolis and all men marveled (5:1-20).

Crossing by boat to the other side of the sea, Jesus was met by a synagogue official, Jairus, who begged Jesus to attend his little daughter who was at the point of death. The crowd that followed them included a woman whose flow of blood had not stopped for twelve years.[16] Coming up behind Jesus, she touched his garment with the expectation of being cured, and she was not disappointed. But Jesus immediately turned and demanded to know who had touched him. Not realizing that Jesus had just negotiated emigration for a legion of unclean spirits at the Gerasene tombs, she knew she was guilty of making this Jewish man ritually unclean. Trembling and afraid, the woman came forward and confessed. Addressing her as daughter, Jesus informed her that her faith had made her well and told her to go in peace. Before he had even finished talking to her, Jesus overheard the news that Jairus' daughter had died and that the Teacher was no longer needed. Telling the official not to fear, but to believe, Jesus took Peter, James and John with him to the house where he put everyone out of the girl's room except for his disciples and her parents. Taking the girl by the hand, he told her to get up and she walked to the amazement of everyone present. Jesus strictly charged the insiders to tell no one on the outside.

Arriving in Nazareth, Jesus and his disciples went to the synagogue where Jesus' teaching astonished many of his former neighbors who judged his wisdom and mighty works to be incompatible with their memories of him. He had only been a carpenter, nothing more than the son of Mary, the brother of James and Joses and Judas and Simon, whose sisters lived among them. The public consensus was not a grant of honor—"And they took offense at him." The author notes that he could do no mighty works there and marveled at their unbelief (6:1-6).

Each of these five stories describes a variety of responses to the power that Jesus used on behalf of others. The three individuals whom Jesus healed responded positively to his power. Once healed, the Gerasene demoniac wanted to follow Jesus. The woman with the hemorrhage was as grateful and as amazed as Jairus had been at the cure Jesus worked for him. Out of the three groups who had witnessed Jesus' power only one had accepted him. The community of the Gerasene demoniac rejected Jesus because it could not tolerate the imbalance of power between itself and an "outsider." The members of Nazareth's synagogue rejected Jesus out of envy because as an "insider" he had risen too high above the level where most community members located themselves. Only the disciples received Jesus' action on their behalf and remained with him.

Following these last episodes, Jesus sent the twelve out in twos to preach repentance and to heal. Propriety in representing God demanded that they take nothing for their journey except a staff, sandals and the tunics they were wearing. Members of God's household did not travel with the same style as those from the households of wealthy men and kings. Once they arrived at their destination, they were to stay in the same house until they left. Should they be refused hospitality or rejected, they were to shake the dust from their feet as a testimony. It is clear that Jesus' disciples were to continue in his modest and unpretentious style while preaching repentance, casting out demons and healing the sick. When meeting with rejection they were not to engage in behavior inappropriate to the Father they publicly represented (6:7-13).

THE STRUGGLE CONTINUES TO RESOCIALIZE
MEMBERS OF THE HOUSEHOLD

A sign of rejection: the death of John the Baptist (6:14-29)—The next section informs us that news of Jesus had even reached King Herod who was considering the possibility that Jesus could be John the Baptist raised from the dead. For, while Herod had recognized John as a righteous and holy man and had protected him, Herod's concern for his honor and public opinion forced him to act against his internal beliefs. This split between personal convictions and public expectations was the fissure that Jesus tried to heal by placing the expectations of God before the demands of the group. In the previous passage, Jesus had shown himself to be working against this submission to the outside when the disciples were sent out with the **internal** power to fulfill their duties to the exclusion of **external** show for winning public approval.

Household duties amid difficulties (6:30-52)—Jesus' disciples returned and told him everything that had happened. This is a wonderful glimpse into the social reproduction which Jesus carried out by contributing to the renewal and regeneration of his disciples. He encouraged them to get away from the crowds who gave them no time even to eat. One of the ambiguous roles of women is to repair at home the wear and tear of public intercourse in order to send the family members back out into the public.[17] The author of this gospel portrays the public as people with basic human needs that are not being met by anyone. Jesus sees that they are like sheep without a shepherd, and his response in this passage is to restore them by teaching.

Finishing at a late hour, Jesus is prepared to feed the crowd. Once again he turns outside space into domestic space[18] and allows food to be the medium which transforms strangers into household members or "friends of the family." Assuming responsibility for the needs of those following him, Jesus invites people to eat and satisfies their needs with food left over in abundance. However, still concerned about his disciples, Jesus made them leave by boat while he sent the people away. Following that, Jesus went up on the mountain to pray.

A strange episode follows where Jesus "sees" that his disciples are struggling painfully with rowing the boat because the wind is against them. About the fourth watch in the night Jesus came to them walking on the sea, but, the author informs us, it was his intention to pass them by. When they all saw him, they thought it was a ghost and cried out in terror. Immediately Jesus spoke, then got into the boat with them, the wind ceased, and they were utterly astonished. Only after the winds have been calmed and the situation restored are we told that the disciples had not understood about the loaves because their hearts were hardened. While they had been empowered by Jesus and returned successful from their mission, hardness of heart made them unable to understand the feeding of the multitude. The wind against them coupled with Jesus' intention to pass them by mirrored their condition. Nevertheless, Jesus did not abandon them, "Take courage, it is I; have no fear."

Of the healings recounted thus far, belief did **not** precede the healing of the unclean spirit 1:21ff; healing Simon's mother-in-law nor the subsequent healings at Simon's house 1:29ff; the man healed with the withered hand 3:1ff; the stilling of the storm 4:35ff; the Gerasene demoniac 5:1ff; the accounts of the twelve returning from healing 6:7ff; the feeding of the five thousand 6:35ff nor in the general accounts such as that in 6:54. Faith is recounted as being present only in the healing of a leper 1:40ff; healing of the paralytic 2:1ff; healing of Jairus' daughter and the woman with the internal hemorrhage 5:21ff. The author mentioned that Jesus could do no mighty works in Nazareth 6:1ff but marveled at their unbelief.

The Markan Jesus manifests the need to continue working on behalf of people with no indication that he expects them to reciprocate or make a personal return to him. This is the situation of women in general and mothers in particular whose status is earned by giving freely. Males who give to others outside the family initiate a relation governed by balanced or generalized reciprocity (*quid pro quo*). In the situation with males nothing is given freely.

Explaining boundaries within the household (7:1-24)—In the following sequence, the author gives us an insight into the very elementary areas that fell within Jesus' role. A mother functions as the first and primary socializing agent of her children. She represents to the child what is to be expected of boys as well as of girls. The mother embodies both the female role of nurture as well as the male role of discipline.[19] Jesus acts as the primary socializing agent in his household. His teaching makes it clear that he is acting on behalf of an absent Master whose household is not to be run according to the norms of the house of Israel.

When criticized by scribes and Pharisees from Jerusalem because his disciples did not wash their hands before they ate, Jesus pointed out that there is nothing outside a man which by going into him can defile him. Only the things which come out of a man can defile him (and this did not refer to bodily functions). The important or decisive space is man's interior as opposed to the external or public space. This viewpoint is completely at odds with patriarchy which sets the highest priority on honor. Honor is gained or lost by males and their families **in public** on the basis of how closely their behavior conforms to societal expectations. Jesus moved the focus of influence from the public to the private or interior space. The outside should not create or control the inside. Rather it is the inside or heart of human beings which creates the outside or the public. The primary focus is not social control but personal conversion to the designs of God. Thus, the personal space must be taken care of first before the public can reflect the standards of the kingdom.

Removing boundaries that prohibit membership (7:24-30)—Jesus traveled to the prominent Hellenistic regions of Tyre and Sidon where he secretly entered a house. His arrival was discovered by at least one woman who had heard of his reputation and begged that her daughter be released from possession by an unclean spirit. Jesus answered this Gentile woman with a proverb declaring that the children (house of Israel) must be fed first, for it is not right to throw their bread to the dogs (Gentiles). The determined mother stays within that proverb and answers that even dogs under the table (she and her daughter) can eat the crumbs (good things Jesus brings) that fall from the table. Her words prompted him to cross another major boundary: being a member of the house of Israel had now become an optional condition for membership within God's household. **Anyone** who received from Jesus could gain access through him into the household of God.

Evidence of unlimited abundance: healing and feeding (7:31-9:1)— The feeding of the four thousand (8:1-10), the demand by the Pharisees for a sign (8:11-13) and Jesus' warning about the leaven of the Pharisees and Herod (8:14-21) are introduced by the healing of a deaf and dumb man (7:31-37) and concluded with the healing of a blind man in Bethsaida (8:22-26). After the blind man was given sight, Jesus asked his disciples two questions: who do others say that Jesus is and who do the disciples say that he is (8:27-30)? The sequence is noteworthy because the demand of the Pharisees for a sign followed both the healing of the deaf and dumb man as well as the feeding of the four thousand. After that, Jesus warned his disciples about the leaven or influence of the Pharisees who appeared to be blind themselves. But the disciples were so preoccupied with the fact that they had only one loaf of bread in the boat that they also appeared to be blind.

The Pharisees had witnessed the first miraculous feeding but had still asked Jesus for a sign from heaven. Immediately after this exchange with them, Jesus left in a boat with his disciples. When they appeared to be preoccupied with the fear that they had not brought along enough bread, Jesus cautioned them to beware of the leaven of the Pharisees and Herod. They did not understand Jesus' use of leaven as an analogy because their concern for bread ruled out anything but concrete, physical concerns. At that point, Jesus accused the disciples of having eyes that did not see, ears that did not hear and hearts that were hardened. They had shown themselves to be "outsiders" for whom the parables were stumbling blocks that revealed their lack of common ground with Jesus. Following that sequence, Jesus healed the blind man with the same remedy that he had used on the deaf-mute, saliva and the touch of his hand.

Later, Jesus asked his disciples, "Who do men say that I am?" The answers ranged from John the Baptist to Elijah or one of the prophets. When he put that same question to the disciples, Peter answered that he was the Christ and Jesus forbade them to tell anyone (8:27-30). Subsequently Jesus talked about his approaching suffering, death and resurrection. In front of the disciples, Peter's response was to rebuke, that is to attempt to deprive Jesus' words of their power, making his prediction of suffering only so much air. In calling Peter, "Satan," Jesus declared him to be antithetical to the action of God, not because he was on the side of Satan, but because he was on the side of men, the **group**. There was no place for dishonorable suffering and humiliation in the idealized roles that men carved out for themselves. However, the roles that society carved out for women left little chance of escaping suffering and humiliation and no chance of having it regarded as heroic. The new wife was often regarded as little more than a slave to be ordered about by men and older women in the family. The woman who risked her life or who died in childbirth was considered neither heroic nor courageous while the woman who bore no sons was consigned to a life of shame.[20]

As the primary socializing agent, Jesus goes on to instruct his disciples, as many mothers instructed their daughters before marriage, that suffering was an inevitable part of their role. This is an important analogy because it is based on hardship that is inevitable for giving and sustaining life—not suffering imposed artificially with the desire to toughen, to harden or to render a person insensitive. Jesus' death was inevitable because he could not abdicate his responsibilities even when threatened by members of the larger group who envied him and sought his destruction. That threat could not exempt him from fulfilling the obligations which were necessary for the expansion and maintenance of God's household.

For men who had not grown up with the understanding that the male role **necessarily** involved bearing humiliation in the way that the woman's role did, these were bitter pills to swallow. But should his listeners misunderstand, Jesus continued that those who are ashamed of him and his words will be the focus of Jesus' own shame when he comes in the glory-of-his-Father with the holy angels. Many parents similarly admonished young brides not to behave in a manner which would make the parents ashamed.

Jesus: acknowledged as the new symbol and focus of God's house (9:2-13)—After six days, Jesus took Peter, James and John up to a high mountain apart by themselves. There he was transformed before them and was seen speaking with Moses and Elijah. The declaration of Jesus' identity, the revelation of God holding him dear and the admonition to listen to him is a three part response to the disciples (and Mark's readers) about everything that Jesus had been doing and saying. As **beloved of God**, he was going to suffer humiliation at the hands of men and die on a cross. The admonition to listen to Jesus carried with it complete affirmation of Jesus' words, including those on the inevitability of suffering in carrying out their roles.

Jesus charged the three disciples to say nothing about what they had seen until the Son of man was raised from the dead. But they did ask him why the scribes said that Elijah must come first. Jesus told them that Elijah was to come and to restore all things. To this answer he added the question, "How can it be that the Son of man should suffer many things and be treated with contempt?" He answered his own question by saying Elijah had come and "they" did to him whatever they pleased "as it is written." In the former prophets it was written that Elijah had run away when the news came that he was to be killed like the rest of the prophets (1 Kgs 19:9ff). The word of the Lord found him in a cave and asked what he was doing there. Elijah answered that the house of Israel had forsaken the covenant, thrown down the altars and slain the prophets with the sword. He alone remained, and he was hiding lest they kill him as well. Jesus clearly intimated that Elijah had returned as John the Baptist. He had been killed as a party favor granted to a young girl to save Herod's honor. If this was how Elijah was treated when he returned in John, then the situation looked very bleak for Jesus. Because the word of God had been eroded by the precepts of the group, not only had the death of John been inevitable, but the death of Jesus would be as well.

A question of belief (9:14-29)—The four left the mountain and returned to the disciples who were surrounded by a crowd where they argued with some scribes. A man in the crowd had brought his son, possessed by a brutal spirit, to the disciples who had failed to cast it out. Having listened to this explanation, Jesus understands immediately that belief is completely absent. There is no one who is securely attached to God with the confidence that this relation brings. Calling the crowd a faithless generation, Jesus wondered aloud how long he must put up with them. Asking that the boy be brought to him, the spirit saw Jesus and immediately convulsed the boy. The listener is able to determine the strength of this spirit by the answers the boy's father gives to Jesus' question, "How long has he had this?" Since childhood, this spirit had sought to destroy the boy by throwing him into fire and water. Gripped by desperation, the father of the boy asked Jesus to help if he could. Jesus repeated the man's final words, "**if** you can" and restated that all things are possible to him who **believes** (in God). The father cried out that he did believe but to help his **unbelief**. Seeing that a crowd was about to form, Jesus rebuked the deaf and dumb spirit who left the boy after a great convulsion where he lay like a corpse. Taking the boy by the hand, Jesus lifted him to his feet.

Jesus was the one person in that situation who was securely attached to God. This attachment enabled Jesus to reflect the loving fidelity which had characterized God's activity in his own life. When later asked by the disciples why they had failed, Jesus answered that only prayer could drive out that kind of spirit. The admission of utter dependence which lies at the heart of all prayer reflects more than the condition of inequality that exists between a master and slave. The prayer of Jesus testified to a God whose fidelity never wavered and whose loving-kindness was unswerving. Such faith is the outcome of a relation where God is accessible, personally involved with the one who is faithful, the one who believes.

Throughout Galilee Jesus continued to teach his disciples that he would have to be delivered into the hands of men, to be killed and after three days to rise. While they did not understand, they were afraid to ask. This was not like their previous question when they asked why they had not been able to heal the boy. That was a question that dealt with power they wanted to possess. The question they now left unasked pertained to suffering, with nothing promised beyond weakness and humiliation as his followers.

STATUS: EARNED NOT ASCRIBED IN GOD'S HOUSEHOLD

The greatest in the household (9:33-41)—Subsequent to the discussion on suffering, the disciples became involved in an argument over which of them was the greatest. The disciples were anticipating a title or some rank which would testify to their status. Jesus sat down as he tried again to resocialize them. The one who wanted to be first must demonstrate that status by being **last of all and servant of all**. In the family, the men and guests ate first, the children were fed next and the women would eat what was left. The ideal woman was the servant of all and last to be considered. This was the behavior that earned status for the woman.

Jesus then went a step further and introduced something else about the one who had authorized and empowered him. Taking a child in his arms, Jesus told his disciples that whoever receives one such child in his name receives him, and whoever receives Jesus receives the one who sent him. The child was the responsibility of the mother. Other women looked after one another's children "for your mother" or "to help her out," a matter that didn't concern the father as this was not his responsibility. But in the house of God, the action of receiving a child in Jesus' name—not controlling or correcting, but **receiving**[21] a child—was an action that linked the receiver first to Jesus and ultimately to God.

This is completely at odds with the belief that children must be taken from an "animal state" and socialized to the group's approval so they can become human beings. Woman has been consistently declared inferior to man because her body, mind and energies have revolved around child bearing and child rearing. Yet this saying declares the child to be more "kingdom worthy" than fully enculturated adults. The time and effort people have spent becoming socialized has quite possibly made them **less** prepared for the kingdom if not ineligible altogether.

In the next passage, the disciples had forbidden a man to cast out demons in Jesus' name because he was not a member of their group. The opinion was that power should reside only with insiders. But the decision of Jesus once again erased the boundaries separating his commissioned disciples from this non-commissioned believer. If mighty works were done in his name, then evil was not involved. The man in question was in no way against them or the direction that Jesus took. He went further and declared that anyone along the way, whether insiders or outsiders who extended even the smallest gesture such as a cup of water, this person would not lose his reward. Within the house of God no one would be left out, not even strangers whose only interaction has been through a gesture on behalf of someone who belonged to the household. The believer who received from the outsider or stranger bound the giver to some share in the abundance of God's household.

Hardness of heart: a disease that kills (9:42-10:45)—The next section continues, "Whoever causes one of these little ones who believe in me to sin, it would be better for him if a great millstone were hung around his neck and he were thrown into the sea." This is the strongest saying in Mark, and it continues to escalate with the declaration that if a person's hands or feet cause one to sin, it should be destroyed before causing the entire body to be destroyed in hell.[22] Evil excludes God, and members of the household are totally dependent on God's actions as Father. If a hand or leg must be cut off to save the rest of the body, how much more dangerous is sin which can sever the life-giving relation between God and his family?

Following this is the Pharisees' question as to whether or not it is lawful for a man to divorce his wife. Jesus inquires about the law of Moses and is told that Moses allowed the husband to write a certificate of divorce to put his wife away. Jesus answered that their hardness of heart was the reason for this because it had not been that way from the beginning. Hardness of heart had aroused Jesus' anger each time it manifested itself, even with the disciples. Like the men in the synagogue who were not moved by the plight of the man with the withered hand, those who divorced their wives were similarly not moved by the situation this created for the wife.

While Moses may have accepted hardness of heart as an inevitable situation, Jesus did not. He attempted to restore the condition created by God where man was joined to his wife and the two became **one flesh**. The thrust of the Jewish law was separation so that men could observe the rules governing ritual purity. Purity boundaries were erected to separate female flesh, blood, pregnancy and childbearing from men. Because those aspects of the female could not be kept fully within boundaries, they had been considered antithetical to the holy, to God. If hardness of heart resulted in men separating what God had joined together, that separation had begun when the culture organized itself around the phallus with circumcision interpreted as divine affirmation of male status.

When the holy space of a religion is sacred for male sexuality (as
in the marking of the covenant upon the male phallus in circumcision), and sacred for blood sacrifice presided over by males;
and when that same holy space is contaminated by female blood
and female fertility (as in menstruating and in giving birth), we
are dealing with a male fertility cult, no matter what its other
lofty spiritual insights may be.[23]

Interpreted to be at odds with the male's access to God, estrangement
between the sexes escalated when the female's body and blood were
declared unclean as opposed to the blood shed at circumcision or that spilled
in animal sacrifice. Forty percent of the woman's year until menopause was
lived in "banishment."[24] While God had intended that man and woman be
one **flesh**, hardness of heart had already interpreted their biological differences to be the basis for a "natural" estrangement. The option of divorce was
not surprising where men saw women as dangerous, threatening both male
honor and sanctity. The teaching of Jesus placed men under the same restric-
tion which the group had devised for women who could not sue for divorce.
The next two verses prohibiting women from suing for divorce were adapted
to fit situations in other cultures where women can act like men and sue for a
divorce.

The last part of this sequence describes a scene where children are
being brought to Jesus when the disciples reprimand those involved in bringing them. The disciples can always be counted on to reflect the rules governing public norms of behavior, not expecting that Jesus will act as though he
were within his own house. Socialization within the household of God
required that men receive the kingdom like a child. This is an activity at odds
with the central values of power, force, domination and control. Children are
not told "to grow up" and boys are not told to "act like men." Rather, men
are told to be like children, those who are in the position of receiving everything from the parents to whom they are bound. This is the proper posture of
every member of the household to God as the Father and provider.
Furthermore, childhood was the only stage in life where gender restrictions
did not separate males from females.

This children-divorce-children sequence is very important. The ultimate threat is directed against those who cause children to sin, that is, those
who raise them in such a way that they are ineligible for the kingdom. Once
inside his household, everyone belongs to God—children **by virtue of being
children.** But the others must be salted first (just as every grain offering that
comes from the ground must be salted before it is burned to God in the temple). "Have salt in yourselves and be at peace with one another" (9:50).
Believers have salt in themselves because they belong to God. But if the salt

has lost its saltiness, how will it be restored? What happens to those who "fall outside" God's rule?

Wealth (not women) as an impediment to members (10:17-31)— Preparing to resume his journey through Judea, a man came up and asked Jesus what was required to inherit eternal life. After some discussion the man stated that he already kept the commandments. Jesus looked "upon him and loved him," then told the young man to sell what he had, give it to the poor and follow him. The man went away sorrowful **because** he had great possessions. Jesus' response was to look at those gathered and tell them that it is hard for those who have riches to enter the kingdom of God. Jesus continued to demonstrate that nature was not the barrier to God which culture had imagined. However, this could not be said about all cultural creations, particularly not about wealth. The disciples had been socialized into seeing the antithetical relation between holiness and women, between holiness and various manifestations of nature but not between holiness and wealth.

In this context, the disciples inquired what they, who had left everything behind and followed Jesus, would receive. Ordinarily when men left home it was to seek wealth and/or honor, both of which had been criticized by Jesus. What benefit did the kingdom of God offer? This was an easy question for Jesus to answer because he understood whose house they had entered. They would receive a hundredfold, houses and brothers and sisters and mothers and children and lands with persecution, and all of this would be followed by eternal life. There was nothing jolting about either reversals or suffering because they were simply inevitable parts of human life.

Jerusalem's claims on the household (10:32-52)—By this time, the disciples and Jesus were on the road going up to Jerusalem when he began to tell the twelve that the Son of man was to be delivered over to the chief priests and scribes where he would be mocked, spat upon, scourged and killed, and then in three days he would be raised. The first time he had told them this, it had elicited a major rebuke from Peter which ended in sharp words. The second time they were too afraid to say anything. This third prediction of the passion was graphic, but nonetheless James and John were not to be deterred in asking for a guarantee that each of them would sit at his right and left when Jesus entered into glory! This competition for status caused a major falling out with the other disciples and once again Jesus tried to explain that greatness is not ascribed, it is acquired. The great one is the servant and the first place is held by the one is who slave to all. "For the Son of man had come to serve and to give his life as a ransom for many" (10:35-45). Ransom effects redemption or liberation and restores social unity. The recipient of this ransom (price of manumission, freedom) is yet to be made clear in Chapter V.

The last event occurring before Jesus reached Jerusalem was the healing of the blind beggar, Bartimaeus. Thus far in Mark, he is the only person who calls out to Jesus as "son of David"' that is, heir to the promises made to David. Hearing the man calling out, Jesus stopped and asked that he be brought to him. Bartimaeus sprang up, threw off his mantle and ran to Jesus who healed him, saying that his faith had made him well. This newly healed man joined the procession that went with Jesus to Jerusalem (10:46-52).

JERUSALEM: CONFRONTATION BETWEEN JESUS AND THE ELITES WHO MAKE CLAIMS ON GOD'S HOUSEHOLD

Omens that accompany Jesus' arrival (11:1-12:12)—Jesus' entry into Jerusalem is on a non-war animal as he is greeted by the crowds with "Hosannas" ("Save us!") and recognized as the one who comes in the name of the Lord. Accompanying that is "Blessed is the kingdom of our father David that is coming." As symbol of God's household on earth, Jesus came to the city that was the heart of power and authority in the house of Israel. Jesus went straight to the temple but "it was already late" so he returned to Bethany with the twelve. In the morning before they left for the temple, Jesus was hungry. Seeing a fig tree in the distance, he went to see if he could find anything on it. The author points out that it was not the season for figs. Nonetheless, Jesus cursed the tree. Not dependent on the seasons of man or nature, God's time had come but the tree bore no fruit for Jesus to harvest.

Arriving in Jerusalem, Jesus began his activity with no illusions as to the shortcomings of either the temple or the Judean leadership. He first expelled from the temple those authorized to sell the animals that were needed to fulfill the temple's rituals. Isaiah is quoted, calling the temple a "house of prayer for **all the nations**," while Jeremiah was quoted condemning those who had made the temple into a **"den of robbers."** These were the inaugural actions and words that Jesus directed at the center of Israel's life, the temple. The response of the chief priests and scribes to this public challenge by Jesus was to meet and discuss a way to destroy him. The crowds were astonished at his teaching and the leaders did nothing out of fear of the people. On the following morning, the disciples noticed that the fig tree had withered from Jesus' curse. He used the barren and cursed tree to teach them that only faith in God would consistently yield whatever they needed, regardless of the "season" or situation. Both faith and the forgiveness of others are linked to the Father's actions on their behalf.

Overall, the situation in Jerusalem does not bode well: the season of the fig tree does not correspond with Jesus' arrival; the temple in Jerusalem does not correspond with God's intentions that it be a place of prayer for all the nations; the fig tree withered overnight and produced no more fruit because its time did not correspond to God's time. Yet, the disciples had been reminded that God would take care of all their needs. Once again at the temple, the chief priests, scribes and elders came to Jesus and demanded outright to know from where his authority came. Jesus' answer was that they should first tell him whether John's baptism was from heaven or from men. For the second time, afraid of the people, they would not answer, and Jesus in turn refused to answer as well.

The gospel continues to darken with the parable of the wicked tenants who refused to give the absent landlord some of the fruit of the vineyard. This bleak tone intensifies as many servants are sent but each in turn is beaten or killed. Finally the landlord sends his own son who is killed so that they might keep the inheritance that was to be his. Theft is possible once the strong man is overcome and envy offers powerful motivation to strip the strong man of everything. But Jesus concludes the story by declaring that the owner of the vineyard will find other tenants. He ends with the lines from Psalm 118 where the stone which the builders rejected would be the head of the corner, this is the Lord's doing and it is "marvelous in our eyes." The animosity from the Jerusalem authorities continued to grow as they perceived the parable to have been about themselves.

The Jerusalem leadership (12:13-44)—Following the responses of the chief priests, scribes and elders, the author now tells how the priests induced the Pharisees and the Herodians to test Jesus. They begin by noting that Jesus neither looks for nor concerns himself with the "face" of men but teaches the way of God. In this instance, "face" means the honor that can be granted men in public. The question that followed this observation was whether taxes should be paid to Caesar. Jesus asked for a coin and presented it to the people with the question, "Whose likeness and inscription is this?" They responded that it was Caesar's. Jesus declared that they should give to Caesar what belonged to him but also to give God what is God's. The issue of taxes was not in conflict with the demands of the kingdom of God.

The author of Mark brings in the Sadducees at this time with the mocking question of whose wife would the widow of seven husbands be in the resurrection. Jesus' response is to underscore their culpable ignorance by questioning aloud where they had gone wrong. His own answer was that they knew neither the scripture nor the power of God. Then he was approached by a scribe who wanted to know what was the most important commandment of all, and Jesus answered with the creedal prayer that he recited daily, "Hear, O Israel: The Lord our God, the Lord is one; and you shall love the Lord your God with all your heart, and with all your soul, and with all your mind, and with all your strength," and then he added a second, "You shall love your neighbor as yourself. There are no commandments greater than these."

The scribe agreed and added that these were much more than all the burnt offerings and sacrifices. The author writes that Jesus saw the scribe had answered wisely and declared that the man was not far from the kingdom of God.

Recalling the title, son of David, by which Bartimaeus the blind beggar had addressed Jesus, he asked those around him in the temple how the Christ could be the son of David when according to Psalm 110, David himself called the Christ his Lord. How then is the Christ his son? Apart from the voice at his baptism and the transfiguration, and the identity disclosures of the evil spirits, these statements are among the few passages in Mark that deal, though indirectly, with the disclosure of Jesus' identity (as Son of God). As son of David, he is heir to the promises made to his forefather but the question remains in this gospel, is he also the one whom David called Lord?

The next passage criticized the scribes for their concern for the acquisition of honor from men while in private they devoured the houses of widows while pretending to fool God by making long prayers. The story of the widow's penny stands in contrast both to the public example of the scribes who sought honor from men, as well as to the example of rich people who donated a large sum to the temple treasury from their abundance. Having put in everything, the widow contributed more than the others. Once again, the criteria by which God judges are not those of men. The standard unit when dealing with God is "everything," an amount that society routinely expected of a woman who was wife and mother. Specific amounts might be important in the world of male honor, but they were totally irrelevant in the household of God.

Behavior appropriate for the end (13:1-14:11)—The prediction of the temple's destruction begins the section where the signs of the end include the presence of the Holy Spirit active in believers, as well as the admission that neither the angels nor the Son knows either the day or the hour when the Father will transform the world. In the closing section, Jesus admonishes his disciples three times in four sentences that the only adequate preparation is to be watchful.

Two days before the Passover, the chief priests and scribes have not stopped trying to find ways to have Jesus arrested and killed. At the same time Jesus was back in Bethany in the house of Simon the leper where Jesus sat at table. While each gospel includes a variation of this story, Mark places the woman anointing Jesus between the desire of the chief priests and scribes to kill Jesus and the deal that Judas worked out to betray his master. The author wrote that Jesus received her activity as a beautiful thing done to him, "...the anointing of his body before burial." Tended by this woman before his death, Jesus promised that what she had done would be told in memory of her. So much for the Markan gospel now. In Chapter V we will survey the last supper, passion and resurrection accounts of each gospel.

Within the Markan perspective, Jesus' relations, words and actions appear coherent and integrated when interpreted from the perspective of the wife/mother's role in a household. Since the one who has authorized and empowered Jesus is God, it is God's household over which Jesus takes charge. In this role, he both symbolizes the house and serves as its focus. Thus, his actions set the example of how God cares for his children. Jesus' concern for propriety rather than publicity in carrying out the numerous required tasks is a concrete reminder that honor is bestowed by God alone, no one else. The Markan author makes no attempt to hide either the domestic orientation of Jesus' work or the utter inability of his disciples to understand what he was doing.

Jesus disrupted leaders at all levels within the house of Israel because their teaching and actions were detrimental to his household. He had arrived in Jerusalem to find that the situation in the capital city was as far from the kingdom of God as every other place had been. While he tried to subvert the influence these leaders exerted over those who followed him, Jesus was powerless to change them. The changes, additions and expansions found in Matthew and Luke do not alter this tireless image of Jesus who was relentless in his efforts on behalf of the household. Rather, each subsequent gospel included additional sources which confirmed the original image of Jesus found in the oldest gospel.

II.

GOD'S SPIRIT AND
THE SON OF MAN

God's Spirit and the Creation of God's Household—In each gospel, the action of God is signaled by the presence of the Holy Spirit. All the gospels include the presence of the Spirit at Jesus' baptism and declare that Jesus will be the one who baptizes with the Spirit (Mk 1:8//Mt 3:11//Lk 3:16//Jn 1:33). This designation implies that God has both authorized and empowered Jesus to act on his behalf. Matthew and Luke begin with birth accounts to establish the initiative of God in the conception of Jesus. Both gospels begin in the domestic domain of those who accepted God's initiatives in their lives.

1. The infancy narratives—Passages from the Hebrew scriptures are woven into the Lukan infancy narrative (Lk 1–2). The new activity of God's Spirit is described in the events that surrounded the birth of Jesus and John the Baptist.

a) The angel Gabriel ("God's power") announced to an elderly priest serving his turn in the temple that he and his barren wife would have a son who would be filled with the Holy Spirit from the mother's womb (Lk 1:15). Thus, neither age (fetal, infancy, childhood), nor physical inclusion in the woman's body, nor natural processes prohibited the actions of God's Spirit, contrary to what a patriarchal culture might expect. And just as nature did not hamper the actions of the Spirit, so too John stayed in the wilderness, apart from the cultivated spaces of humans, until his time to inaugurate the beginning of the end times.

b) Mary, an unmarried woman, was told that the Holy Spirit would come upon her, and she would bear a child whose conception was to be attributed to the initiative of God alone. Leaving her honor in God's hands, another woman was receptive to the designs of God, and this child would be called Son of God (Lk 1:35//Mt 1:18-22).

c) Mary's visit to Elizabeth found the aged woman to be filled with the Holy Spirit (Lk 1:41). The words the author chose for Mary (Lk 1:46-56) have roots in well over a dozen passages from Israel's Bible. The new order is characterized by the activity of God on behalf of the weak and lowly while the arrogant are scattered in the "thinking of their hearts" (emotion-fused

34

judgment); the mighty are pulled down while those of low degree are raised up; the hungry are filled while the rich are sent away empty. Thus, the activity of God's Spirit is characterized by reversing what culture values and replacing it with the standards of the kingdom of God.

d) Zechariah, John's father, was filled with the Holy Spirit at the birth of his son (Lk 1:67). His prophecy is likewise an eloquent gathering of scripture texts that are recast in a Lukan formula recognizing that John will turn "many of the sons of Israel to the Lord their God, and he will go before him in the spirit and power of Elijah, to turn the hearts of the fathers to their children..." (Lk 1:17).

e) At Jesus' presentation in the temple, the Holy Spirit was upon Simeon, a devout man from Jerusalem who was inspired to visit the temple and eloquently declared that Jesus would be "a light for revelation to the Gentiles and for glory to thy people Israel" (Lk 2:25-35). And finally there was the aged widow Anna, who recognized in Jesus the one who would redeem Jerusalem.

This impassioned eloquence about the visitation of God assumes that nothing in nature is alien to its creator, including his manifestation in a human being. The Lukan account of Jesus' birth finds no wise men from the east (Mt 2:1-12), but there are fields with shepherds who keep watch over their sheep throughout the night. The author fills the night sky with angels announcing to humble shepherds that an infant was born who is Christ the Lord. The shepherds went to see "this thing that has happened" and, finding Mary and Joseph, told them what they had just heard. All these events were kept in the hearts of those who witnessed the beginning of events which they did not completely understand (Lk 2:1-20).

2. The Spirit in the lives of John the Baptist and Jesus: The difference—The public life of John the Baptist in Luke begins with an elaborate introduction,

> In the fifteenth year of the reign of Tiberius Caesar, Pontius Pilate being governor of Judea, and Herod being tetrarch of Galilee, and his brother Philip tetrarch of the region of Ituraea and Trachonitis, and Lysanias tetrarch of Abilene, in the high-priesthood of Annas and Caiaphas, **the word of God came** to John the son of Zechariah in the wilderness (Lk 3:1-2).

Before John, "the word of God came" to Moses, Samuel, David, Solomon, "the man of God," Ahijah, Jehu, Zimri, Joshua, Elijah, Elisha, Isaiah, Jeremiah, Ezekiel, Osee, Joel, Amos, Jonah, Micah, Zephaniah, Haggai, Zechariah, Malachi and other servants and prophets of God. No such formula introduces Jesus in any gospel. Instead, John the Baptist announces that the one following him will not baptize with water, but with the Spirit. The Spirit descended on Jesus at his baptism, and he was called "Son" by the voice from heaven (Mk 1:10-11//Mt 3:16-17//Lk 3:22).

Jesus did not quote what God had told him nor what God had said. Prophets invariably did so as part of their declarations. Jesus knew this was the traditional way of talking on behalf of God and yet he did not imitate it. A different relation is implied between Jesus and God as compared to that between God and previous prophets. Jesus never disclosed what God said to him apart from his own actions and parables. The first language of the household in which Jesus addressed his followers was parables. That was the language he chose to teach "what has been hidden since the foundation of the world" (Mt 13:35).

3. Continuation of the Spirit's activity in the ministry of Jesus— "And Jesus, full of the Holy Spirit, returned from the Jordan, and was led by the Spirit for forty days in the wilderness, tempted by the devil" (Lk 4:1-2//Mt 4:1-11//Mk 1:12). After that period of temptation, "Jesus returned in the power of the Spirit into Galilee…" (Lk 4:14). He went to Nazareth and was given the book of Isaiah from which he chose the reading, "The Spirit of the Lord is upon me…" (Lk 4:18).

Later, the seventy disciples who had been commissioned to preach returned to share with Jesus the joy they felt at their successes where even demons were subject to them in Jesus' name. "In that same hour he rejoiced in the Holy Spirit and said, 'I thank thee, Father, Lord of heaven and earth, that thou hast hidden these things from the wise and understanding and revealed them to babes; yes, Father, for such was thy gracious will'" (Lk 10:21//Mt 11:25). Overturning the priorities set by man is the activity of the Holy Spirit.

Jesus understood the important role of the Spirit. He observed that if those who are evil know how to give good things to their children, "…how much more will the heavenly Father give the Holy Spirit to those who ask him!" (Lk 11:13). Within the household, the Spirit is absolutely essential for every member. That is why Jesus said in another context that anyone "who blasphemes against the Holy Spirit will not be forgiven" (Lk 12:10//Mt 12:32//Mk 3:28).

Jesus: The Son of Man/Human Being—The term, "son of man," simply means a male human being. In the gospels, this title is used exclusively by Jesus of himself with greater frequency than any other title. When he referred to himself as "son of man," it was in two vastly different roles. The one role that has been discussed thus far finds its closest analogy in the idealized role of those who create and maintain households. This role seems to have inspired Jesus: 1) to form his identity-in-relation with God and not with the group; 2) to add new members, taking charge of the nurture and socialization of "the young"; 3) to advocate service to others as a core value; 4) to introduce new members through his actions and parables to their Father; 5) to organize and direct the household so that it reflected the glory of God to insiders as well as to outsiders; 6) to meet everyone's needs according to what the Father had provided for them; 7) to conduct himself in public in such a way that he reflects the glory of God; 8) to leave the defense of his honor in God's hands; 9) to give his life to protect God's household which he both reflects and symbolizes.

In contrast to the role described above, the "son of man" who had no place to lay his head while living among men was to sit at the right hand of God. The "son of man" who taught in parables was the same "son of man" who was to return and judge according to the standards he set. The "son of man" who was betrayed, tortured and killed by men was the same one who was to be raised by God. The "son of man" who was powerless against his own rulers was the one who was to return in the clouds of heaven with great power and glory to judge his judges. This contradictory image that Jesus accepted for himself aroused fear and incomprehension in those who knew him best. The ambiguity which split his self-image arose from man's rejection of God. It did not originate as the result of some flaw in human nature. The model of a human being presupposed by Jesus was as integrated and whole as God had intended.

Over thirty years ago Bernard de Geradon published an article discussing a three zone model of human beings that was subsequently reintroduced to English speaking audiences by B. Malina in 1981.[1] This model is pivotal in understanding how Jesus and his contemporaries thought about themselves as human beings. A human being is an integrated being whose emotion-fused thought is centered in the heart. Perception, how things are "seen," depends on the "soundness" of the eyes. Together the eyes/heart perceive, reflect, think and judge. Self-expressive speech arises from the heart and is communicated through the mouth to be received by the ears of others. Thus, the mouth/ears convey the thoughts of the heart and is one of the main ways that people come to know each other. However the thoughts and desires of the heart often go beyond communication and demand action. Hands and feet reveal what is in the heart and communicate through action more forcefully than a look or even a word. The gospels frequently describe Jesus pointing to his actions (as opposed to abstract ideas), as evidence of the One who authorized him.

This understanding of how people perceive is very close to what Margaret Miles calls "carnal knowing." She defines her usage of the term as "an activity in which the intimate interdependence and irreducible cooperation of thinking, feeling, sensing and understanding is revealed. Carnal

knowing is both embodied and social; it includes the most private and intimate experiences as well as the most public and social experiences."[2] Both of
these models of perception presume that the body is an integral part of all
dimensions of being human—not an option or the enemy as western philo-
sophical/religious traditions have so often portrayed it. Thus the body is
undivided, the spiritual and physical dimensions intertwined. This model is
neither gender nor age specific, it applies to men and women, adults and
children equally.

While human beings learn to have immediate and first-hand awareness
of themselves, how they **interpret** these various aspects is dependent on
social conceptions or the meaning assigned by the group. Members who
accept and receive that interpretation or those meanings bind themselves to
the group and show themselves to be its members. Thus, the person who was
understood and discussed in the gospels was an integrated unity of emotion-
fused thought (eye/heart), whose mouth/ears manifested the heart in communication, and whose hands/feet acted out the directives of the heart.

Sin according to the gospel model of being human—Jesus taught
that the conditions which impair access to God do not arise from ethnic origins, gender, nature, sickness, food or any biological function of the human
body. Rather, *hearts* produce evil thoughts, murder, adultery, fornication,
theft, false witnessing and slander (Mt 15:18-20; Mk 7:14-23) and *eyes* give
rise to sin, that is, words and actions incompatible with God.

1. This eye/heart zone of emotion-fused judgment receives a good deal
of attention because all words and actions proceed from the way a person
"sees" a situation before making the decision which comes from the heart:

> If your right *eye* causes you to sin, pluck it out and throw it away
> (Mt 5:29//Mk 9:47).

> Your eye is the lamp of your body; when your eye is sound, your
> whole body is full of light; but when it is not sound, your whole
> body is full of darkness (Lk 11:34//Mt 6:22). If then the light in
> you is darkness, how great is the darkness (Mt 6:22).

> Why do you see the speck that is in your brother's *eye*, but do
> not notice the log that is in your own *eye*? Or how can you say to
> your brother, "Let me take the speck out of your *eye*," when
> there is the log in your own *eye*? You hypocrite, first take the log
> out of your own *eye*, and then you will see clearly to take the
> speck out of your brother's *eye* (Mt 7:3//Lk 6:42).

> But I say to you that everyone who *looks* at a woman lustfully
> has already committed adultery with her in his *heart* (Mt 5:28).

(The look reveals the judgment of the *heart* even before the action is carried out.)

For where your treasure is, there will be your *heart* (Mt 6:21//Lk 12:34).

But Jesus, knowing their thoughts, said, "Why do you think evil in your *hearts*?" (Mt 9:4). When Jesus perceived their questionings, he answered them, "Why do you question in your *hearts*?" (Lk 5:22//Mk 2:8).

You brood of vipers! How can you speak good, when you are evil? For out of the abundance of the *heart* the mouth speaks (Mt 12:34).

When any one hears the words of the kingdom and does not understand it, the evil one comes and snatches away what is sown in his *heart*; this is what was sown along the path (Mt 13:19).

This people honors me with their lips, their *heart* is far from me (Mt 15:8).

But what comes out of the mouth proceeds from the *heart*, and this defiles a man (Mt 15:18).

But he [Jesus] said to them, "You are those who justify yourselves before men, but God knows your *hearts*; for what is exalted among men is an abomination in the sight of God" (Lk 16:15).

So also my heavenly Father will do to everyone of you, if you do not forgive your brother from your *heart* (Mt 18:35).

He said to them, "For your hardness of *heart* Moses allowed you to divorce your wives, but from the beginning it was not so (Mt 19:8). But take heed to yourselves lest your *hearts* be weighed down with dissipation and drunkenness and cares of this life" (Lk 21:34).

And he said to him, "You shall love the Lord your God with all your *heart*, and with all your soul, and with all your mind" (Mt 22:37//Lk 10:27).

And he told them a parable, to the effect that they ought always to pray and not lose *heart* (Lk 18:1).

Jesus touched eyes, healed eyes, opened eyes and ultimately judged that Israel's "*heart* has grown dull, and their *ears* are heavy of hearing, and their eyes they have closed" (Mt 13:15).

2. The second zone is that of communication where the ears can be "unsound" in much the same way as the eyes. *How* a person interprets what is heard affects the judgment made by the heart. The outcome will be apparent in either the verbal response or by the action or inaction that follows.

> Hear and understand: not what goes into the *mouth* defiles a man, but what comes out of the *mouth*, this defiles a man (Mt 15:11).

> But what comes out of the *mouth* proceeds from the heart, and this defiles a man (Mt 15:18).

> ...for out of the abundance of the heart his *mouth* speaks (Lk 6:45).

> I tell you, on the day of judgment men will render account for every careless word they utter (Mt 12:36).

> Whoever insults his brother shall be liable to the council, and whoever says, "You fool!" shall be liable to the hell of fire (Mt 5:22).

> But I say to you, Do not swear at all...(Mt 5:34).

> ...for by your words you will be justified, and by your words you will be condemned (Mt 12:37).

Jesus repeats, "He who has *ears* to hear, let him hear" (Mt 13:9), as well as "Blessed are your eyes, for they see, and your *ears* for they hear" (Mt 13:16).

3. The third zone is that of activity where the hands/feet "enact" or make concrete and visible the judgments of the heart.

> And if your right *hand* causes you to sin, cut it off and throw it away; it is better that you lose one of your members than that your whole body go into hell (Mt 5:30).

> But when you give alms, do not let your left *hand* know what your right *hand* is doing (Mt 6:3).

> And if your *hand* or *foot* causes you to sin, cut it off and throw it away; it is better for you to enter life maimed or lame than with two *hands* or two *feet* to be thrown into the eternal fire (Mt 18:8).

> I was hungry and you gave me food, I was thirsty and you gave

me drink, I was naked and you clothed me, I was sick and you visited me, I was in prison and you came to me (Mt 25:35ff).

I was hungry and you gave me no food, I was thirsty and you gave me no drink, I was a stranger and you did not welcome me, naked and you did not clothe me, sick and in prison and you did not visit me (Mt 25:42-43).

Truly I say to you, as you did it not to one of the least of these, you did it not to me (Mt 25:45).

Jesus stretched out his hand to heal lepers, laid his hands on the sick, took children into his arms, rescued Peter from sinking into the sea, and gestured with his hand to indicate that his disciples were his family. A synagogue audience in Mark 6:2 exclaimed, "What mighty works are wrought by his hands!" He knew that his betrayer dipped his hand into the same dish with him, and that others would lay hands on him and he would suffer at the hands of men. But in the end, the sheep would take their place at his right hand with the goats on his left. Ultimately the Son of man would sit "at the right hand of the Power, coming on the clouds of heaven."

The gospels promulgate an understanding of the person quite different from the philosophical model that was later accepted within Christianity. The standpoint of the gospels presumes the image of person as reviewed in this chapter. The axiom that "All theology is analogy" incorporates the belief that everything is standpoint-dependent. It is not surprising then that the gospel image of God includes facets of being that are compatible with the image of human beings we have just reviewed: the Father who sees and judges is **like** the eye/heart zone of emotion-fused thought; Jesus was **like** the mouth/ears of God that communicated the Father's emotion-fused thought; and the Spirit whose activity concretizes the heart of God is **like** the third zone of activity (hands/feet). Thus, the analogy concludes that human beings and God relate because they share a drive toward emotion-fused judgment, communication and action—all the dimensions necessary for interpersonal relations. Jesus used parables to reinforce this belief in the accessibility of God and in the "naturalness' of humans relating with him.

Parables: Verbal Imagery with a Range of Meanings—As mentioned earlier, actions which disclose what is in the heart of God signal the presence of God's Spirit. Since speech is also an activity, words which communicate what proceeds from God's heart are also the work of the Spirit. Matthew states that Jesus said nothing to the crowds without a parable: "this was to fulfill what was spoken by the prophet, 'I will open my mouth in parables, I will utter what has been hidden since the foundation of the

world'" (Mt 13:34-35). Mark says simply, "With many such parables he
spoke the word to them, as they were able to hear it; he did not speak to them
without a parable, but privately to his own disciples he explained everything"
(Mk 4:33-34). The parable used verbal imagery to highlight the individual
and experiential insights of Jesus as opposed to proverbs which conveyed the
wisdom of the group.

Speaking in parables presumes that there is common ground between
the speaker and the audience which prompts the listener to reflect on common concerns and familiar situations. Such personal reflection evokes emotion and stirs the imagination. New possibilities, connections and relations
can be seen that have immediate relevance to the personal experiences under
consideration. It is the essence of parables "to provoke discussion and
demand interpretation through multiple, diverse and successive commentaries."[3] Thus, the outcome is a personal evaluation that begins with a concrete visual image of life and leads to behavioral choices rather than a moral
axiom or abstract ethical principle.

As figures of speech, parables range from one line to stories, dialogues
and discourses. All forms share two things in common: 1) something more or
something else is meant by the saying or literary piece; 2) this something
more or something else is to be arrived at by the listener in his or her own
concrete circumstances. The listener must participate and engage the inner
eye to find the meaning within and beyond the concrete descriptive scene.
Parables can embody a full story with beginning, middle and end, e.g. the
parables of the prodigal son, the tenants and vineyard, the Good Samaritan,
or they might be no more than a single sentence.

The vocabulary of parables is derived from the tangible world which is
available to the senses and cultural interpretation. Take for example something as common as a stone and see the multiple meanings it can acquire
within this language. Stones play various roles in the world of Lukan symbols: God is able to raise up children for Abraham from stones (Lk 3:8/Mt
3:9); the devil first charged Jesus to command that the stones become bread
(Lk 4:3/Mt 4:3), and then challenged him to throw himself down from the
temple since the angels would guard the Son of God lest he strike his foot
against a stone (Lk 4:10-11/Mt 4:6); the stones in Jerusalem would have cried
out if the people were silenced at Jesus' entry (Lk 19:40); once he entered the
city, Jesus wept over it saying that not one stone would be left on top of
another (Lk 19:41-44); in the parable of the wicked tenants (Lk 20:9-18/Mt
21:33-46/Mk 12:1-12), the stone rejected by the builders became the head of
the corner. Unique to Luke is the additional phrase, "Everyone who falls on
that stone will be broken to pieces; but when it falls on any one it will crush
him." Jesus was in the temple when his attention was called to the noble
stones from which the temple was built. He repeated that no stone would be

left on top of another, nothing would be left that was not thrown down (Lk 21:5).

The language of parables allows stones to be transformed into mental images out of which could come children, bread, cries and shouts, the house of God, retribution and utter destruction. Jesus did not choose abstract, philosophical language to talk about the kingdom of God. Because ideas were not given superiority over images in Jesus' teaching, the gospels require an approach that differs from those which concentrate on words as the carrier of ideas. It is not the relation between the biblical text and the image which requires examination. The relation that demands attention is the one which Jesus creates between the images he chooses and the beholder.

Blessings, curses and laments—Beatitudes are figurative or poetic sayings that express attitudes, conduct or a condition that were valued by the culture. Jesus took this form and applied it to what was valued in the Kingdom, e.g. "Blessed are the poor in spirit...the merciful, the pure in heart, the peacemakers"; "Blessed is he who takes no offense at me"; "Blessed are your eyes, for they see, and your ears, for they hear." In its most elemental form, a blessing was the acknowledgement of some communication of life from God. Life is the basic requirement from which comes more life or fertility, strength, vigor and, above all, success and prosperity.[4]

God could bless groups, nations, households and/or individual people, those who blessed others, lands, cities, animals, activities, goals, food and special days. Man responded by blessing God, that is by recognizing what he had received, accepting it, being thankful and living according to God's desire. This state or condition of being blessed could be passed on until the impetus that began with God extended to all "the blessed of God" who lived from his generosity under his rule. As blessing brought people into the circle of life, so it was believed that curses brought people into the circle of shame, sorrow, loss, grief and everything that is antithetical to the life that flows from God and those attached to him.

Like the blessing, the curse necessarily takes a concrete form. Both forms testify to the power of the spoken word which is endowed with a dynamism that quite literally pursues its object. Any person or thing which can be blessed can likewise be cursed, e.g. God, men and women, land, trees, activities, etc. In Matthew, the Son of man who returns to judge human beings will say to those at his left hand, "Depart from me, you cursed, into the eternal fire prepared for the devil and his angels..." (Mt 25:41); Peter began to curse himself when accused of being one of Jesus' followers (Mt 26:74//Mk 14:71); the fig tree that was cursed with barrenness withered at once (Mt 21:19//Mk 11:14,21).

There is another form that is found more frequently in the gospels than the curse and that is the lament as a form of social protest. Laments were poetic forms of language that belonged equally to women and men alike. This form was used to mediate between the living and the dead and between seemingly disparate or antithetical types of experiences.[5] The speaker was one who represented the voice of the "weak, marginal, or downtrodden."[6] The lament as folklore can be used to "dramatize conflict, to encourage dissent, to cause disunity, and to rouse people to activism and even to press for revolutionary changes in the social system."[7] Juxtaposition of antithetical situations or positions is often, though not always, included within the style of the lament. Margaret Alexiou says that "Antithetical style is a fundamental and integral part of the structure and thought of the lament, though by no means exclusive to it."[8] The best known gospel examples of this are found in Luke, "...woe to you that are rich, for you have received your consolation. Woe to you that are full now, for you shall hunger. Woe to you that laugh now, for you shall mourn. Woe to you, when all men speak well of you, for so their fathers did to the false prophets" (Lk 6:24-26). There are numerous examples of this form not only in the Hebrew scriptures but in Greek literature as well. "Since antiquity, laments have commented on, protested against and affected social change."[9]

Thus, the figurative language of parables is rooted in the physical world as opposed to the abstract; the world of experience as opposed to that of explicit pure theory; the world of men and women with no gender distinctions. The title, son of man, the understanding of human being already described and this concrete language of parables make a direct appeal to the human heart dismissing all additional categories of gender, nationality or status as non-essential. The images that Jesus chose to reveal God as Father subverted the image of God as revealed in the Hebrew scriptures. Images, not ideas, changed how God was projected on the human heart.

1. God must be at least as good as...—Jesus often told stories where he tried to correct the traditional image of God. This image that had come to reflect a tyrant or political despot, "eccentric and unpredictable, at one moment lavishly generous, affectedly fraternizing with the common people, and then again ferocious and tyrannical."[10] By highlighting good activity that is possible among the very worst people, Jesus hoped to move his audience to believe that God must be **at least** as good as outrageous human beings when it suits them. Jesus told the parable about the widow who appealed to a judge who neither feared God nor regarded men. Only because she gave him no peace did he finally see that justice was done in her case. The parable ends, "And will not God vindicate his elect, who cry to him day and night? Will he delay long over them? I tell you, he will vindicate them speedily" (Lk 18:1-8). The parable of the pound (or talents) is another parable pointing out that God must be at least as good as evil men. The account found in Matthew 25:14-30 is somewhat different from the Lukan account which begins with a nobleman who leaves for a far country where he is officially to be given a kingdom to rule. Stressing how evil this man is, the author writes that people sent a delegation to stop him from being promoted ruler. In the meantime, those who had been given charge of his money increased the amounts he had left in their care except for one man who did not want to risk losing the little he had been given.

The man returned as ruler despite the efforts of the delegation. The ruler rewards those who were able to extort the maximum amount using what he had given them. To those who had made money for him in his absence, rewards were forthcoming "...for those who are faithful in little things" will be faithful in larger matters. But one intimidated man who had hoarded his coin for safekeeping had it taken away and handed over to the most successful (possibly the least ethical) of the three. The narrative does not allow the cruelty of the ruler to recede into the background. The ruler gave the order that those involved with the delegation against him were to be slain in front of him (Lk 19:11-27). The familiar lines come shortly before the order of execution is given, "I tell you, that to every one who has will more be given; but from him who has not, even what he has will be taken away." If such an utterly heartless despot was capable of rewarding those who acted as he did, would God do less?

Thus, as a minimal standard for an image of God, Jesus introduces stories with real life rulers or kings. They are invariably harsh and yet know how to reward those who imitate them. The parable of the talents is doubly significant in Matthew because of the passage that follows it describing the return of the Son of man whose standards are juxtaposed with those of the master in the parable. He returned to inquire how much interest his **money** had made in his absence while the Son of man will return to inquire how **people** were treated in his absence. "As you did it to one of the least of these my brethren...you did it to me" (Mt 25:45). While cultures declare that the need to please elites eclipses the concerns for those who are poor, outcast, powerless, etc., caring for others is the kingdom's standard against which all will be judged by the Son of man.

Another set of parables point to "those who are evil" yet who know how to give good things to their children. Such passages are found in both Luke 11:5-13 and Matthew 7:9-12, "If you then, who are evil, know how to give good gifts to your children, how much more will your Father who is in heaven give good things to those who ask him!" (Mt 7:11). Moving higher up the ladder, Jesus talks about exemplary fathers like the one in the prodigal son where God must be at least as good as the overjoyed father who welcomed his wayward son with no reservations, no desire for revenge and no need to punish the penitent man (Lk 15:11-32).

There is another class of parables meant to reflect both the care of God and the value of human beings: (1) There are shepherds who look for their lost sheep; God must be at least that good and people surely have at least as much value as sheep. (2) People lose possessions, e.g. coins, sheep, or find objects, e.g. the pearl, and rejoice when they find them; God must be at least that diligent and people must have at least that much value. (3) God, who takes care of the grass and flowers of the field, the birds, counts the hairs on the head, etc., must be at least that concerned about people whose value in his eyes must at least equal that of grass, flowers and birds.

2. Neighbors, a reflection of God—Jesus is asked by a lawyer what he should do to inherit eternal life. The lawyer recites the two main commandments of loving God above all and the neighbor as himself. But then follows the question of who is his neighbor? The cultural answer based on Israel's scriptures is fellow Israelites. Jesus answers with the parable of the good Samaritan where a despised outsider takes action which reflects the heart of God while Israel's religious leaders reflect correct public behavior expected of elites. This parable is only found in Luke and its conclusion is that the one who shows mercy to the man in need is the only person acting like a neighbor. The final line is, "Go and do likewise" (Lk 10:25-35).[11] By adjusting what is considered acceptable behavior by elites, the popular image of God which people have internalized from the examples of elites around them is also subject to change.

3. Continuity: God's mercy was never limited to Israel—In the Lukan account, Jesus began his public life in the synagogue at Nazareth where his fellow villagers question his claims. In response he talked about Elijah and Elisha, two prophets who had been sent by God to two Gentiles despite the needs of the house of Israel. He reminds them that Elijah had been sent to a Sidonian widow while Israel was suffering from famine; and despite the fact that there had been many lepers during the time of Elisha, he was sent to cleanse Naaman the Syrian. Those who sat in the synagogue were insulted at his attempts to adjust their attitudes toward outsiders based on how the prophets treated Gentiles. Their response was one of rage and the desire to silence him permanently as they wanted to push him off a cliff, "But passing through the midst of them he went away" (Lk 4:16-30).

Luke accepted the Markan Jesus as one whose role encompassed aspects of both servant and sentry. The value of existing boundaries between Jew and Gentile is questioned at the beginning of Jesus' public life in Luke, starting in his own town among the people who knew him best. One of the many streams of traditions that are included in the Hebrew Bible, the one most frequently quoted or alluded to in the gospels as being particularly applicable to Jesus and his mission, was that which highlighted God's mercy to the Gentiles. Jesus' occasional use of the Hebrew scriptures, his parables and his own experiences with those few Gentiles who came to him out of need reflected the tradition where God had always been active among the Gentiles.

4. Forgiveness without punishment—The prodigal son (Lk 15:11-32) was mentioned previously in relation to the image of the father. Equally important in the parable is the image of the son who left home with his inheritance and lost everything on wild living. He returned with nothing but desperation, eager to live out a life with the most meager living accommodations and food as one of his father's servants. However, the father's joy upon his son's return was such that instead of meting out punishment, the father gives a banquet.

The third character in this parable, the first born son, refused to join the celebration because he who had always behaved properly never received a celebration like the kind that greeted his wayward younger brother. The elder son is important because with his protest, the listener discovers that the father had been as generous with the obedient son, "...all that is mine is yours," as he is determined to be with the disobedient son **who repented and returned.**

Jesus reveals a God at odds with the punitive, exacting divinity who appeared in the Hebrew scriptures and lives on in Christianity. The fact that this distinction has not been embraced and incorporated as central to Christianity is because the image of the Father that Jesus revealed continues to be the unimagined image of God. In its place is a familiar image traditionally cast in the limitations that both culture and personal experience incorporate into the image of father. This distorted image of God bolsters and sanctions the abuse which frequently accompanies human parenting.

5. God sees the heart—Jesus told a parable of a Pharisee who stood and thanked God that he was not like other men who were extortioners, unjust, adulterers or even like the tax collector who stood praying far away. Not only did this Pharisee avoid doing bad things, but on the positive side he fasted, prayed and gave tithes of all that he acquired. Jesus next draws a contrasting picture of how the tax collector prayed, very simply declaring himself a sinner and asking for God's mercy. "I tell you, this man went down to his house justified rather than the other; for everyone who exalts himself will be humbled, but he who humbles himself will be exalted" (Lk 18:9-14). A desire to control God based on self-perfection and separation from sinners is not supported by the gospels where Jesus' response to sinners is to bring them back and to forgive them without reserve.

6. The Father is the provider—Much can be learned about the Father in the prayer that Jesus taught his disciples, the Lord's Prayer. The kernel of this prayer can be found in Mark 11:25. Its expanded form is the Lukan version (Lk 11:2-4/Mt 6:9-15). The prayer begins by calling God Father. Yet, believers do not lose sight of who their Father is: as creator of the worlds and

Lord of the universe, he cannot be used, manipulated or fooled ("hallowed be thy Name"). The prayer expresses the desire for God to fully inaugurate his kingdom ("thy kingdom come") and carry out his designs on earth ("thy will be done on earth as it is in heaven"), so that everyone can live secure in the knowledge that God is their Father. Their daily bread, that is, their share in the kingdom, is God's to distribute ("Give us this day our daily bread"). Likewise, forgiveness is God's to give ("and forgive our debts") as long as we forgive the debts of others ("as we forgive our debtors"). Finally God is appealed to that he might save the petitioner from the test of loyalty in face of the forces of evil which could sever relations with God ("And lead us not into temptation, but deliver us from evil").[12]

The heavenly Father is one who shows mercy (the determination to save, not out of obligation but out of abundance) and expects to see this same determination replicated by the members of his household who draw from his abundance. Similarly, God forgives and expects to see that mirrored in the behavior of his children. Those who receive are bound to **reflect** what they have received from him, the physical needs of life as well as forgiveness. "An eye for an eye" was a step forward for mankind to keep revenge in check. The teachings of Jesus go further and replace justice with mercy because that is what people receive from God.

Dimensions of the Father Revealed by Jesus' Actions—The One who sent Jesus, the One who authorized and empowered him, becomes apparent not only in Jesus' words, but in his actions as well. The following qualities which are exemplified in the actions of Jesus are taken from the Lukan account. In most instances, examples can be found in the other gospels which likewise confirm the values discussed below. This list of values is not complete and will continue to expand in the following chapters.

1. Abundance—The people were pressing around Jesus when he saw two boats by the lake (Lk 5:1-11). When he finished speaking, he told Simon to put out his nets even though Simon protested that he and his partners had fished all night in vain. The efforts of the fishermen at Jesus' request were rewarded with a catch so enormous that both boats were nearly sinking. Jesus tells Peter, James and John not to be afraid because from now on they would be catching men, "And when they had brought their boats to land, they left everything and followed him." The social rule that insisted on balanced reciprocity among equal males in public gave way to God's action in Jesus as one of unlimited generosity—the primary value from man's private side to be witnessed in familial situations and settings.

2. Concern for those who fall between the cracks—The Lukan account of the cure of the centurion's slave (Lk 7:1-10) includes some important social insights that shed light on the resuscitation account that follows it. A centurion asks Jewish elders (who are in his debt because he built their synagogue) to approach Jesus about healing his servant. The Jewish elders understood not only the rules of reciprocity but the social necessity of mediators who establish contact between unknown parties. The centurion knew that Jesus might be more favorably disposed to grant requests made by his own people on behalf of outsiders. The elders described to Jesus how the centurion both respected Israel and acted on behalf of it—thus making him "worthy to have you do this for him."

On the way to the centurion's house, they are all met by other friends dispatched to tell Jesus that the centurion had declared himself unworthy to have Jesus in his house. The centurion understood the rules of social hierarchy where orders are given by those in higher positions to be carried out by those below them. So he sent friends to deliver his word to Jesus. The centurion realized that his request cast Jesus in a role above his own and judged himself not worthy to have Jesus enter his house. The centurion's friends requested that Jesus merely say the word and the slave would be made well. Since neither distance nor nature was an impediment to the word of Jesus once activated on behalf of someone, the slave was well by the time the delegation of intermediaries returned. Jesus responded, as he did in Matthew 8:10, that he had not found such faith in all of Israel.

The next passage reveals the reason for Luke's placement of the cure of the centurion's slave. It is located within a complex network of reciprocity followed by the account of a widow of Nain. Jesus and his disciples were leaving the town of Nain when a man who had died was being carried out. He was the only son of his mother, and she was a widow. As mentioned earlier, women didn't exist alone in the world of Jesus. Their lives were necessarily dependent on some male relative. The woman in this story was probably left socially indigent with the death of her son. She asked for nothing from Jesus, and no one came forward on her behalf. He saw her need and restored the life of her son. With that, the people exclaimed, "God has visited his people!" It is clear that at times Jesus operated beyond the social boundaries of acceptable public behavior when he saw people in need. He could act within that system when it worked (e.g. the centurion), but he was free to catch those who fell between the cracks, like this widow for whom the social system had nothing more to offer (7:11-17). Jesus continues to act according to rules from the private domain where members of the household give and receive help without the complex set of limitations that controlled relations between those from different households in public. Values that governed behavior among family members are more in keeping with the designs of God than are those declared appropriate for males among non-relatives in public.

First, the main goal or organizing principle is "right relations" or righteousness. Second, from the perspective of the kingdom, everyone is related to God because he **gives to everyone,** both good and bad people without discrimination. Third, emotion-fused thought (eyes/heart) is re-formed in believers to see this connectedness and reflect the nurture and care they experience from God in their relations to others. Fourth, the acceptable manifestation of power is that those who have more serve those who have less.

Taking the negative approach as to what the gospel is **not** saying, members of his household are not to organize their lives around culturally revered values such as honor, revenge, power, segregation, goodness, exclusivity, impersonalism or emotional detachment. Neither are the restrictive social categories of gender, race, religion, wealth, age, status, sickness or health adequate for governing or directing human behavior. All these categories inhibit the activity of God on behalf of his children.

3. Loving forgiveness cancels punishment—In face of the efforts of John and Jesus, hard-heartedness inhibited many listeners from responding to either man. Luke follows this observation about men's inability to respond with the story of the woman who anoints Jesus' feet with ointment, tears and kisses, before she wiped them with her hair (Lk 7:36-50). Jesus was at dinner with a Pharisee when this woman of the city found him. The host could tell that Jesus was no prophet, or he would have known the kind of woman who touched him (and to maintain his honor, he would have shunned her). So Jesus answered his host's unspoken observations with a parable about the creditor who forgave the debts of two men: one owed five hundred denarii and the other owed fifty. Jesus asked his host who loved the creditor more. The Pharisee answered that the one for who was forgiven more, loved more.

Jesus points out to the man giving the dinner that he had failed in his role as host but this "sinful" woman had taken care of everything. Consequently she was forgiven everything because "she loved much" while those who love little are forgiven little. With that he declared her sins forgiven by God. Apparently, punishment, in addition to repentance, restitution and change, is a human requirement, not a divine one.

4. Women are included—The Lukan account of Martha and Mary (Lk 10:38-42) revolves around a domestic dispute where Martha asks for help, while her sister, Mary, sits listening to Jesus (usually the prerogative of men). Martha is upset and complains, asking that Jesus tell Mary to help serve (which is, after all, the woman's role). Jesus supports Mary in her role of listening and learning, a role he will not take from her (Lk 10:38-42). This story, unique to Luke, establishes the value of women sitting at Jesus' feet just like men and learning from him. While the service of women is acknowledged by Jesus, they too must adapt their roles (independent of society's expectations) to the demands of a household organized around **God** in whom each member, male and female, is embedded.

Another Lukan passage that acknowledges a variation in gender roles is the one where he narrates that Jesus and his disciples went through cities and villages bringing the good news of the kingdom of God while being "provided for" out of the means of some women who accompanied them (Lk 8:1-3). While the patronage of wealthy women was not new to the culture, its inclusion in this gospel signifies acceptance of women who provide the economic and physical security for men to participate in activities on behalf of the kingdom which otherwise would be impossible.

5. Women, too, take precedence over the sabbath—The parable of the woman afflicted with a spirit of infirmity for eighteen years is told only in Luke 13:10-17. Much to the indignation of the synagogue ruler, Jesus saw her and his response was to heal her in the synagogue as he had healed the man with the withered hand (Lk 6:6-11). Having "made her straight," the synagogue ruler turns to the people and says, "There are six days on which work ought to be done; come on those days and be healed, and not on the sabbath day!" Then Jesus denounces them as hypocrites who untie their animals and lead them to water but have no sympathy for this woman bound by Satan for eighteen years. Even if Jesus could move them to regard each other with the same concern they show their animals, he would be gaining ground. But those watching were not happy to see the woman cured at the cost of their honor.

There is one more healing event which took place on the sabbath while at dinner in the home of a Pharisee (Lk 14:1-6). Jesus asked again if it was lawful to heal on the sabbath (this is the third time the question has arisen in Luke). No one said anything, so Jesus healed the man of dropsy. His argument was similar to the other times, "Which of you, having a son or an ox that has fallen into a well, will not immediately pull him out on a sabbath day?" No matter what approach he tried, he was unable to inspire in them a response even to their fellow members that equaled the concern they showed for their animals. They were unable to see in Jesus' words and actions God's activity in their midst.

6. "Outsiders" receive good things from God—Material unique to Luke further includes the story of the ten lepers who are cured somewhere on the road to Jerusalem between Galilee and Samaria. Only one of the ten returned after seeing that he had been healed along the way. He fell at Jesus' feet and gave him thanks. Then the text says, "Now he was a Samaritan. Then Jesus said, 'Were not ten cleansed? Where are the nine? Was no one found to return and give **praise to God** except this foreigner?' And he said to him, 'Rise and go your way; your faith has made you well'" (Lk 17:11-19). The abundance of God is available not only to Jews and Gentiles, but also to this Samaritan who was considered an apostate by the house of Israel. The only criterion for God's action in a person's life seems to be that the person be willing to receive such action.

Both Matthew and Luke accept and incorporate the Markan image of Jesus whose words and actions are infused with the Spirit. Calling himself "son of man," Jesus accepted his basic humanity as the common ground which linked him to his listeners. He understood the power of those private images of God, self and the neighbor which all human beings carry inside. For this reason, Jesus chose parables which would allow the very concrete elements and relations that characterized people's lives to recreate their internalized private images of God, self and others. At odds with these images which Jesus created were social forces which created and maintained other images to act as internal referents which would reinforce the social order.

III.

THE HEART: LOCUS OF GOD'S KINGDOM

The Kingdom of God/Heaven—"The kingdom of heaven is at hand." This was the message of John the Baptist that called Jesus from obscurity and joined him publicly and immutably to God. This total and unrestricted fidelity necessitated changes in Jesus' life. The example of Jesus' conversion showed the heart to be the locus of God's kingdom. The long, slow process of healing and changing one heart at a time is the way the kingdom of God expands. And if indeed it was by the "finger of God" (Lk 11:20) or the Spirit of God (Mt 12:28) that Jesus cast out demons, then the vital process of rooting out whatever stands between God and the human heart received a decisive impetus with Jesus. Those who attached themselves to him were healed and brought into a household where they were able to reflect in their relations with others the love and acceptance they experienced within God's household if nowhere else.

The relation that exists between the public which seeks to control group members and the privacy of the household has often been problematic. Frequently the best interests of the domestic domain have been sacrificed to meet the needs of elites who rule the public arena. Not surprisingly the domestic world of concrete needs and specific relations has frequently opposed culture's "superimposed network of alliances and relationships."[1] It was precisely this relation between the Father's household and Israel's influence as the wider, social group that Jesus found objectionable.

The Son of man and the eclipse of Israel's influence—Like every other human being, Jesus was born of a particular woman, at a precise time, in a concrete place, and grew up in a specific culture. In the gospels Jesus is called a Galilean. Galilee lies at the northern end of Palestine separated from Judea in the south by Samaria.[2] From the viewpoint of the Judeans, "Galilean" was a derisive epithet more emotionally related to "Samaritan" than to "Judean." So while Jesus called himself "Son of man," he was identified as a Galilean by the Judeans, and a Jew by the rest of the world. The word that has come to be translated "Jew" derives from the word "Judean." So while Jesus was from the region of Galilee and was considered a Galilean by the Judeans, outside the country he was called a Judean because that was popularly regarded as the center of the house of Israel, his *ethnos* or the group to which he belonged by birth.

Groups in competition for allegiance—Jerusalem was the city in Judea which was regarded as the center of Israel's political or religious polity and the various groups to which its members belonged. The Pharisees considered themselves to be a group apart from the main body of Israel as such. But as a group, the Pharisees were representative of Israel's legal orientation toward fulfillment of the law in every detail. What isolated and earned for them the name "Separate" (Pharisee) was the extreme degree to which they practiced separation and avoided "mixture." They avoided anyone who was suspected of lower standards in maintaining ritual purity laws. In order to know precisely what the law required involved knowing the interpretation and commentary on the Torah. Both interpretation and commentary came to be known as the oral Torah. Pharisees believed it was impossible to be upright in matters of the law without being equally committed to the oral Torah.[3]

The Sadducees formed a much smaller group composed of aristocrats and wealthy families associated with the priesthood as well as the high priestly families. Prosperity and security had made conservatives of the Sadducees in whose best interests it was to keep things stable and preserve the past rather than support changes. They held fast to the written Torah of Moses and refused to accept the oral Torah as binding. The Sadducees regarded the Pharisees as a group who wanted to limit Sadducean hereditary, judicial and doctrinal authority. They did not believe in resurrection, personal salvation or retribution in some future life for the actions of this life since these were not in the written Torah.

The high priestly families were attracted to this party because it was far more favorably disposed to accommodating not only foreign rulers but foreign culture as well. Under the Persians and Greeks, the high priest had been cast in the dual role of being the political focus of the people as well as fulfilling his singular duties of high priest. These roles were often viewed as mutually exclusive where the fulfillment of one led to the demise of the other. Inevitably it was the religious role which suffered. Hellenism was widely accepted by the aristocrats whose position required good relations with rulers. The more the priesthood became influenced by outside groups, the more the people turned to scribes, those who interpreted the Torah.[4]

This split in the loyalties of the controlling priestly families moved the Torah experts, the scribes, into key roles. The Sadducees achieved position by inherited wealth, the controlling priests held power by hereditary right and the scribes gained power by learning. As a group, these experts in Torah were criticized by Jesus for their love of esteem and the prestige which they were accorded in public. Since their honor obliged them not to charge for teaching Torah, they worked in various professions to earn a living or had benefactors, e.g. the scribes of the Sadducees. The "lawyers" referred to in the gospels were members of this group whose specialties were studying and teaching the legal aspects of the law.[5]

The high priestly families claimed to be the descendants of the Levites of the house of Zadok in Jerusalem. They are not to be confused with the Levites in general who were considered second rate ministers and forbidden since the time of Ezra (mid 400s BC) to officiate at sacrificial worship because they were suspected of participation in alien rituals. The Levites performed functions in the temple such as guards and butchers of the animals that were to be sacrificed.[6] The high priestly family alone could offer sacrifices and mediate between the people and God. As such, they were a necessary group for the fulfillment of the individual and national religious duties. Thus, their role was secure regardless of the growing influence of the scribes, and despite the people's suspicions of the extent to which the priestly family was influenced by the outsiders with whom they dealt on behalf of the people.[7]

Along with those previously mentioned, the elders were powerful men of status and the heads of families who were a conspicuous component in public leadership.[8] By the time of Jesus, the great sanhedrin in Jerusalem was presided over by the high priestly aristocracy surrounded by distinguished Israelites. As such it was not a council of scholars but a representation of the elites.[9] Nevertheless, a moral weight was attached to the decisions of the sanhedrin which extended to members of Israel living outside Palestine. The Jerusalem sanhedrin was considered a final tribunal for decisions or questions connected with Jewish law on which lower courts could not agree.[10]

Israel and the standards of the kingdom—It had become increasingly obvious to Jesus that his household members had no external or larger group whose values, goals, customs, etc. were aligned with the mind of God. Despite Israel's claim to be the kingdom or place where God ruled, each group within Israel was judged by Jesus according to the standards of the kingdom and found to be lacking: the elders, scribes, Pharisees, Sadducees and ultimately the priests who ran the temple. As one who lived away from the center of power in Galilee, that part of Palestine judged harshly by the standards of Jerusalem orthodoxy,[11] Jesus had expected the Judean leadership to reflect the glory and will of God in Jerusalem if nowhere else.

Jesus' experiences in Jerusalem culminated in a very different realization. His generation was not open to the initiatives of God. The leaders and the temple were not aligned with the mind of God. The city was not receptive to the rule of God. Jesus found his generation to be evil and adulterous (Mt 12:39; 12:45; 16:4) as well as faithless and perverse (Mt 17:17//Lk 9:41). Mark called that generation adulterous and sinful (Mk 8:38); faithless (Mk 9:19); Luke used evil as well (Lk 11:29). All these terms, used to describe Israel in the past, are based on the analogy of marriage where Israel is like the wife and God is like the husband. Thus, Jesus is like the faithful wife and those who follow him are to be like faithful daughters according to the role created within the patriarchal world of Jesus' time and place.

Criticized by the leaders as disruptive, Jesus continued to cry out against the leaders for betraying the very households which formed Israel. In laments, the literary form that belonged equally to women as well as to men, Jesus represented the masses, the large body of Israel as he cried out against the leaders who marched their followers into the pit they had dug out for themselves.

> Woe to you scribes and Pharisees, hypocrites! because you shut the kingdom of heaven against men; for you neither enter yourselves, nor allow those who would enter to go in (Mt 23:13).

> Woe to you, scribes and Pharisees, hypocrites! for you traverse sea and land to make a single proselyte, and when he becomes a proselyte, you make him twice as much a child of hell as yourselves (Mt 23:15).

> Woe to you, blind guides, who say, "If anyone swears by the temple, it is nothing; but if any one swears by the gold of the temple, he is bound by his oath" (Mt 23:16).

> Woe to you scribes and Pharisees, hypocrites! for you cleanse the outside of the cup and of the plate, but inside they are full of extortion and rapacity (Mt 23:25).

> Woe to you, scribes and Pharisees, hypocrites! for you are like whitewashed tombs, which outwardly appear beautiful, but within they are full of dead men's bones and all uncleanness (Mt 23:27).

> Woe to you, scribes and Pharisees, hypocrites! for you build the tombs of the prophets and adorn the monuments of the righteous...Thus you witness against yourselves that you are the sons of those who murdered the prophets (Mt 23:29-31; Lukan woes 11:37-52).

Shocked and appalled at the condition of the Jerusalem leadership who believed itself to be the standard by which others were judged, Jesus' pain and disillusionment reached its climax in his lament over Jerusalem.

> O Jerusalem, Jerusalem, killing the prophets and stoning those who are sent to you! How often would I have gathered your chil-

dren as a hen gathers her brood under her wings, and you would not! Behold your house is forsaken and desolate. For I tell you, you will not see me again, until you say, "Blessed is he who comes in the name of the Lord" (Mt 23:37-39/Lk 13:34-35).

His lament stood in the tradition of others who had mourned the loss of Jerusalem in the past. There was no way the city would survive in light of the leadership and the elite of his generation. Like the prophets who had lamented the ancient cities which had defied the activity of God in the past, Jesus' laments extended to the cities of Bethsaida, Chorazin (Mt 11:21//Lk 10:13) and Capernaum (Mt 11:23/Lk 10:15) as well as all the cities which rejected the message that the kingdom was at hand, "Truly, I say to you, it shall be more tolerable on the day of judgment for the land of Sodom and Gomorrah than for that town" (Mt 10:15; Lk 10:12). The destruction of the temple was predicted after Jesus announced that the house of Israel was forsaken and desolate.

Written into the very core of the gospel is the mandate to change. The values and standards of human beings are very often not those of God. A complete change involves a total reorientation for all who follow Jesus. Regardless of the family into which a person is born, the culture or time in which the person lives, or the "religion" to which a person belongs, change is the central premise and ongoing activity of those who follow Jesus. The demands of life in God's household are different from life in other households. The demands of social life in the kingdom are different from those esteemed by most cultures. Because of these sharp differences, Jesus changed the boundaries to clearly delineate activity appropriate to the children of God as influenced by the kingdom of God.

What can be known from the gospels about the kingdom of heaven that competes with Israel for the loyalty of each household? Regarding the location of the kingdom, it was clear to Jesus that **the kingdom was close** at hand (Mt 3:2//Mk 1:15). At times the kingdom actually came upon some people (Mt 12:28; Lk 11:20), it existed in their midst (Lk 17:21). The kingdom of heaven/God was as near as the other "kingdoms" which competed for the allegiance of Jesus' followers.

The **kingdom of God belonged:** to children (Mt 19:14); to those who were like children (Mt 18:3; Mk 10:14); to those whose spirit (force of life) was characterized by the deprivation of essentials necessary for life (Mt 5:3); to those who fed, housed, clothed and cared for those in need (Mt 25:34f); to those whose actions were governed by the designs of God (Mt 7:21); to those who were persecuted for the sake of righteousness (proper interpersonal relations—Mt 5:10); to those who produced the fruits of the kingdom (Mt 21:43); to those who came from all directions (Lk 13:29); to sinners who repented (Mt 21:31). But the **greatest in the kingdom of heaven** is someone who becomes "like a child" (Mt 18:4).

Those for whom **entering the kingdom** is difficult are those who have riches (Mk 10:23//Mt 19:23//Lk 18:24). Those who are **excluded from the kingdom** are: those who claim that God is in charge when they say, "Lord, Lord" but do not live according to the will of God (Mt 7:21); those whose righteousness is no better than that of the scribes and Pharisees (Mt 5:20); those who after laying their hand to the plow "look back" (Lk 9:62); those who do not respond to the needs of the poor, powerless, hungry, etc. (Mt 25:41ff); all those whose actions are evil, that is, against the designs and will of God (Mt 13:41).

Those who inherit the kingdom are the ones who responded to the needs of others as though they were responding to Jesus.

> When the Son of man comes in his glory, and all the angels with him, then he will sit on his glorious throne. Before him will be gathered all the nations, and he will separate them one from another as a shepherd separates the sheep from the goats, and he will place the sheep at his right hand, but the goats at the left. Then the King will say to those at his right hand, "Come, O blessed of my Father, inherit the kingdom prepared for you from the foundation of the world; for I was hungry and you gave me food, I was thirsty..." (Mt 25:31-46).

The final line is, "Truly, I say to you, as you did it not to one of the least of these, you did it not to me." This statement ends any doubts about the relation between Jesus, the members of the household and their relation to God. The very concrete, physical needs that tie everyone to nature are not to be neglected, minimized or glossed over in favor of "higher" goals. Those that are cast out of the kingdom are the ones who never ministered to those in need.

Thus, the kingdom of God/heaven is manifested by those whose words and actions are directed by God's own Spirit. The heart was the focus of Jesus' words and healing activities. Adherence or attachment to God is the outcome of a personal decision or choice. Despite God's limitless power, it is never used to coerce or control human behavior. The revelation of Jesus made it manifestly clear that God's rule was extended by invitation, accepted through individual conversion, and sustained in a relation where choice was never violated. There has never been a government that ruled in God's name which has accepted the limitations that God accepts in dealing with human beings. Thus there are no parables that describe the kingdom to be anything like what people commonly experience with rulers whose power controls the external behavior of those forced to live according to public demands.

Instead, many of the parables that describe the kingdom are based on individual scenarios and individual choices.

The kingdom of heaven is as irresistible as the pearl was to the merchant who sold everything he had to buy it (Mt 13:45-46), as desirable as the field in which was hidden a treasure (Mt 13:44). Not everyone finds the kingdom of God to be desirable because individual responses to God's Spirit are so varied. The parable of the sower (Mk 4:2-9/Mt 13:3-9/Lk 8:4-8) finds that in some cases, evil carries the word away. In others, people who hear it have "no root" while in other cases some people are more delighted by riches and the desire for things than for the kingdom. Only one group out of the four in that parable bears fruit. That is, only one in four hears the word and accepts it.

Additional parables compare the kingdom to the wheat that grows up alongside weeds (Mt 13:36-43). This condition is not to be altered by destroying the weeds out of fear of rooting up the wheat. Thus, both live side by side until the harvest. Only then will the Son of man send the angels to gather out "all causes of sin and all evildoers." Similarly, the kingdom can be compared to the fish net that brings in all kinds of fish (Mt 13:47-50) which are only sorted out after it is full. At "the end of the age" the angels will be sent to separate the righteous from the evil. Likewise, only when the Son of man comes in glory will he separate the sheep from the goats (Mt 25:31-46). It is manifestly clear that human beings in this life are not trusted "in God's name" with either judging or punishing those who do evil.

Jesus teaches that the kingdom grows like the seed in ways not understood by men (Mk 4:26-29). It begins like the mustard seed which grows from the smallest of seeds to a tree where birds build nests (Mk 4:30-32). Those who belong to the Kingdom affect the competing social world around them as leaven affects flour (Mt 13:33/Lk 13:20-21). None of these analogies are derived from the world of government or politics where the external social forces are to control the individual members. None of these parables project a social order where man is to rule in place of God. While the kingdom of heaven might be called the rule or reign of God, that reign depends on conversion or changing the human heart where trust and attachment to God result in performing good deeds that go unpublicized. From these beginnings, goodness expands in society as a manifestation of God's Spirit and a faithful reflection of God's own mercy.

THE GOSPEL DILEMMA: ISRAEL'S REJECTION OF JESUS

The Jewish-Christian crisis—The house of Israel had traditionally viewed itself as one people and the rest of the world as a single people, "the (other) nations." Within the perspective of the house of Israel, Israel's own superiority and uniqueness constituted self-evident reality,[12] a position commonly held by most groups about themselves. However, those who followed Jesus from the house of Israel were severely shaken in their exclusive and high regard for their group. Those members who were expelled experienced the confusion, uncertainty and disorientation that arise when group membership totally determines individual identity. While Jewish-Christians supported one another, they were apprehensive about the inclusion of Gentiles who had traditionally been outsiders.

Matthew reflects a community riddled with problems. Its members had been rejected by the house of Israel for accepting Jesus as Messiah and subsequently excluded from the synagogues.[13] Those excluded were known as the minim,[14] the heretics who were despised with a special animosity reserved for those insiders who turn against the consensus of strongly cohesive groups. The conflicts that Jesus faced with the leaders of Israel were more meaningful to this community than to the Markan community where there remains little evidence of active Jewish rejection or hostility.

The gospels of both Matthew and Luke accepted the Markan image of Jesus as well as material from a source which is not included in either Mark or John. In addition to these shared sources, both gospels have material that is unique to each. They also share a heavy reliance on the Hebrew scriptures to interpret: 1) the life of Jesus; 2) his rejection by the house of Israel; and 3) the inclusion of the Gentiles.

The evolution of Jesus' image for Jewish-Christians: The role of John the Baptist—John the Baptist is a difficult figure for many Christians to appreciate because his significance to the Jewish-Christian for whom the gospels were written is dependent on understanding the role of Elijah as it developed within Israel's religion. Each Passover celebration to this day continues to anticipate the return of Elijah. Thus, the impact of declaring that Elijah **had** returned as John the Baptist is lost on audiences that do not share Israel's symbols or epic traditions. Nevertheless, the baptism of John publicly bound Jesus to the imminent arrival of God's kingdom. John's message was both accepted and promulgated by Jesus, "Repent (change), for the kingdom of heaven is at hand." John's criterion was also adopted by Jesus, "Bear fruit that befits repentance" (or "concretely manifest change for the better in your actions").

Fulfillment—For Jewish-Christians, John's role as Elijah testified to the inauguration of a new age where God's activity in Jesus was interpreted as the fulfillment of the law and the prophets. This fulfillment pattern interpreted the life and death of Jesus as a natural progression of God's activity with Israel. Events in the story of Jesus or those touching on the life of Jesus are interpreted as the fulfillment of prophecies fifteen times in Matthew (only twice in Mark and eight times in Luke). The Matthean infancy narrative begins this pattern when Joseph is told that Mary has conceived of the Holy Spirit (Mt 1:22); Joseph takes his family to Egypt for their safety and returns after Herod's death (Mt 2:15); Herod orders the infants killed in hopes of destroying Jesus (Mt 2:17); and Joseph settled his family in Nazareth (Mt 2:23)—all to fulfill scripture.

Jesus' baptism by John is the next fulfillment (Mt 3:15), followed by Jesus' inauguration of his ministry in Capernaum (Mt 4:14). He proclaims that his role is to fulfill the law and the prophets (Mt 5:17). His active life of healing fulfills the prophecy of Isaiah (Mt 8:17) and his ministry to the Gentiles similarly fulfills yet another prophecy by Isaiah (Mt 12:17). Just as the inclusion of the Gentiles is according to Hebrew scriptures, so is the rejection by the house of Israel (Mt 13:14). Jesus' teaching method relies heavily on the use of parables which fulfills another prophecy (Mt 13:35).

Jesus enters Jerusalem according to what the prophets had said (Mt 21:4). Both his arrest and the flight of his disciples are according to scripture (Mt 26:54,56). The amount of money that Judas was paid for his betrayal fulfilled the words spoken by Jeremiah (Mt 27:9). The theme of fulfillment ends with Jesus fulfilling what he himself had declared earlier, "He is risen as he said" (Mt 28:6). A number of the significant aspects of Jesus' life are interpreted as the fulfillment of prophecies, a strategy aimed at showing the Jews who knew their own scriptures that God was at work in the life of Jesus. Despite the unexpected way Jesus went about fulfilling his role, Jewish-Christians believed that Jesus was the one in whom the promises made to Israel were fulfilled.

As mentioned in the last chapter, Mark inaugurates the public life of Jesus after John's arrest when "Jesus came into Galilee, preaching the gospel of God, and saying, "The time is fulfilled, and the kingdom of God is at hand; repent, and believe in the gospel"" (Mk 1:15). Obviously an audience that did not share belief in Israel's folk epic would find a theme on the fulfillment of time more meaningful than the fulfillment of unaccepted scriptures. Luke begins the public ministry of Jesus in the synagogue of Nazareth where he formally began his role with a passage from Isaiah 61:1,

> The Spirit of the Lord is upon me,
> because he has anointed me to preach good news to the poor.
> He has sent me to proclaim release to the captives
> and recovery of sight to the blind,
> to set at liberty those who are oppressed,
> to proclaim the acceptable year of the Lord.

After he was finished reading this text, Jesus declared that the "scripture" was being fulfilled as they listened. The fulfillment theme in Luke appears again when Jesus speaks of an age to come (Lk 21:22) and again at the last supper when Jesus affirms that he will not participate in another passover until "it is fulfilled in the kingdom of God" (Lk 22:16). Both Mark 14:49 and Luke 22:37 portray Jesus' awareness at this arrest that his death fulfills scripture. At the very end of the Lukan account when Jesus appeared to his disciples after the resurrection in Jerusalem, he tells his disciples that "'These are my words which I spoke to you, while I was still with you, that everything written about me in the law of Moses and the prophets and the psalms must be fulfilled.' Then he opened their mind to understand the scriptures…" (Lk 24:44-45).

The shadow of Moses in the life of Jesus—Israel's interpretation of Moses made much that Jesus taught by word and example unacceptable. The author of Matthew used principal settings and symbols that were dominant in the traditions about Moses to demonstrate that Jesus was his successor. Thus the beginning of Jesus' life is linked with Egypt and a scripture passage; the sermon on the mount recalls Moses and the Torah on Mount Sinai; the covenant at the last supper in Jesus' blood was set within the context of Passover; as Moses lifted the yoke from the shoulders of the Israelites in Egypt, so does Jesus promise a yoke that is easy and a burden that is light.

Reversals—But the Jewish-Christians realized that fulfillment themes and associations with aspects from the life of Moses could not account for everything that Jesus did and taught. There were changes that Jesus introduced which were not explained either by the fulfillment or successor motifs. Reversals were an obvious dimension in the teachings and example of Jesus who revoked or changed much that had been previously accepted as being of religious and/or social value. Included among these reversals was acceptance of Gentiles who followed Jesus:

a) the wise men from the east who saw the star and came west to worship Jesus (Mt 2:1ff);

b) Egypt as a safer dwelling for Joseph's family than Judea, the center of their own people;

c) Capernaum, Galilee of the Gentiles about which Isaiah 9:1-2 spoke, "…the people who sat in darkness have seen a great light, and for those who sat in the region and shadow of death, light has dawned";

d) the centurion whose faith was declared by Jesus to be without equal even in Israel as he predicted that many would come from the east and west and sit at the table with Abraham, Isaac and Jacob, while the sons would be thrown out (Mt 8:5-13);

e) the Canaanite woman whose great faith in Jesus was rewarded with the health of her daughter and his praise of her (Mt 15:21-28);

f) the centurion at the crucifixion who recognized Jesus as Son of God (Mt 27:54).

But this inclusion of the Gentiles who followed Jesus was no more drastic than being taught that concern for honor should not dominate one's life.

Israel's religion was so utterly interwoven with and dependent upon a patriarchal social system that its survival is dependent upon the sanctification of those values and gender roles promulgated within that social system. The reversals found in Jesus' life and the events bordering on it encompass a variety of values, behaviors and customs. This motif begins in Matthew with the infancy narrative (Mt 1:1-2:23) and continues throughout the entire Gospel. The angel's announcement to Joseph dispelled his concerns about honor which had prompted him to think about quietly divorcing Mary. When he learned that this infant whom she carried had been conceived by the very decision and action of God himself, Joseph acquiesced and left the matter of his honor in God's hands (Mt 1:18-25).

Gentiles arrived from the east in the form of magi who followed a star to the west which they interpreted as an omen of great significance for the house of Israel. These outsiders alerted the Judean king, Herod, who subsequently looked for the child, not to receive him but to kill him. No longer safe among their own people, Joseph took his family to Egypt where they found safety among outsiders who had been traditionally characterized as oppressive enemies of Israel. In the meantime, the Judean king ordered the killing of his own subjects in an attempt to destroy the child spoken of by the wise men.

Matthew leaves no doubt that **because** Jesus was of the house of Israel, he must have come first and foremost to benefit the members of his own group (Mt 10:5-15). It is not surprising that Jesus' disciples were sent on their first mission to members of their own group. But since the house of Israel could no longer be trusted as representing the will of God, belief was not forthcoming. First, the Pharisees, Sadducees, Herodians, scribes and lawyers were repudiated by Jesus. Second, the temple and priests were criticized for their deviance from God's will. Third, Jesus upbraided the cities, e.g. Chorazin, Bethsaida, Capernaum and Jerusalem, for their refusal to accept him. Fourth, Jesus condemned this "generation" who were unable to repent and believe. Yet, everything happened according to the will and plan of God who knew that Israel would hear but never understand, see but never perceive (Mt 13:14-17). For it honored God with lips while its heart was far away, proclaiming as doctrine the teachings of men (Mt 15:7).

Israel's rejection of its covenant responsibilities was legendary. A basic element in its own tradition included the murder of prophets sent to

them (Mt 23:37-39). In strong group societies, personal identity is inseparable from group affiliation. How the group conceives of itself is replicated in
the individual lives and personal choices of its members. Israel believed that
regardless of its infidelities, God would always keep them in a superior position in relation to other nations. Punishments such as wars, famines and sickness were considered the standard disciplinary actions of God. These along
with religious sacrifices were expected to keep in repair the covenant relation
that Israel had accepted. Jewish-Christian belief that "the kingdom of God
will be taken away from you and given to a nation producing the fruits of it"
(Mt 21:33-46) must have been traumatic to their sense of group identity.

Along with the highly conflicting images of God and Israel, the
Hebrew scriptures also portray "the nations" (Gentiles) in opposing categories. They are simply the various peoples who live around Israel (Lev
25:44); they are the enemy (Neh 5:9); they are the ones who strike Israel
with the sword of God (Lev 26:38); they are those whom Israel defeats (Deut
8:20); they are the people whose lands are to be taken by Israel (Deut 12:29);
they are also ruled by God (2 Chr 20:6; Ps 47:8); they are witnesses of what
God does with Israel (Neh 6:16); they are disdained by God (Ps 59:8); they
are the ones who are to follow Israel's example (Is 49:6); Israel is not to follow their example (Jer 10:2); Israel is to be small and despised among the
nations (Jer 49:15); etc. Minimally stated, the consistent category for "the
nations" in the Hebrew scriptures is that of "outgroup."

The early Jewish-Christians were caught in a vise: non-believing Jews
were hostile and rejecting on one side while Gentile-Christians were accepting yet "invasive" on the other. The question of who qualified for group
membership was but one more area irrevocably altered by accepting Jesus.
The gospels resolve this problem of Jewish-Christian acceptance of Gentile-
Christians by forging an image of Jesus which fulfilled, surpassed or
reversed traditional customs, values and expectations. From the perspective
of Gentile-Christians, belief in Jesus linked them to Jewish-Christians. And
while the early Jewish-Christians understood Jesus from within the perspective of their own group identity as it had been formed by their scriptures, the
interpretation that grew out of that perspective is not meaningful to those
who do not resonate with the Hebrew epic, heroes, values and symbols.

Understanding Jesus from the domestic perspective of his own social
world minimizes those religious elements which are not meaningful to
Gentiles and no longer relevant to Christians. At the same time, the vital
issues of family, human health, interpersonal relations and gender roles can
be illuminated by the words and example of Jesus. In reconstituting the family around God as Father, Jesus challenged not only the existing gender roles,
but what each culture esteems as desirable and valued among its members as
well. There is every reason to believe that Israel's rejection of Jesus was

necessitated by the maintenance of a patriarchal social system which would have deplored Jesus' negation of male honor as the central social value, his summons to service rather than to control, and his unflagging criticism of Israel's purity laws which maintained discrimination and segregation as the will of God.

Values of the Kingdom Reinforce Human Development—Jesus revealed that children are "kingdom worthy" just by virtue of being children. This means that written into human nature is a process which unfolds or evolves according to the designs of God. Parenting and socialization are important components in human growth and development which are to facilitate this "natural" development. More often than not, however, both influences undermine and distort the direction and inclinations which God has placed within each human being. Most human beings come to be lost at some point in their lives. Because this is such a frequent occurrence, "change" is a necessary component before human beings can reorient themselves as God had originally intended. The gospels have much to say about interpersonal relations because that is the first area to be impaired by human experiences of pain and anxiety.

"Blessed are you..."—The Matthean beatitudes (5:2-12) express attitudes and conduct which can be seen as having directed Jesus' life and which are likewise appropriate for both males and females who follow him. Despised and disowned by the elites in society, the poor and meek who experience social powerlessness are to live with complete openness to God and utter dependence on him because they belong to his kingdom. Members of the household who hunger, thirst and mourn for righteousness live in visible protest against all that militates against God's desires for the proper care of his creation. Purity of heart pertains to that eye/heart zone where one's emotion-fused judgment remains uncluttered and uninfluenced by anti-God values and positions. Similarly, the peacemakers and those persecuted for the sake of righteousness find their model in the actions of Jesus whose life was bound up with the kingdom of God. He was not part of the cycle of revenge and violence that is promulgated by cultures as each man's "right."

Matthew 5:43-48 represents a significant reversal not only of what Moses taught, but, more significantly, of the image of God that is part of the Moses epic. Consider, for example, this Matthean passage:

> But I say to you, Love your enemies and pray for those who persecute you, so that you may be sons of your Father who is in heaven; for he makes his sun rise on the evil and on the good, and sends rain on the just and on the unjust. For if you love those who love you, what reward have you? Do not even tax collectors

do the same? And if you salute only your brothers, what more
are you doing than others? Do not even the Gentiles do the
same? You, therefore, must be perfect, as your heavenly Father
is perfect (Mt 5:44-48).

Compare this with the account taken from Exodus 20:5 which precedes the
giving of the law where Yahweh reminds his people:

I, Yahweh your God, am a jealous God and I punish the father's
fault in the sons, the grandsons and the great-grandsons of those
who hate me; but I show kindness to thousands of those who
love me and keep my commandments.

The passage from Exodus cited above (also Num 14:18) reflects a God who
is no different from any other powerful "patriarch" for whom blood vendet-
tas and revenge set one family against another for generations. While jealousy and revenge might be common among human beings, it was imperative
that Jesus correct all false images of God which had created him in the image
and likeness of the elites who ruled. With this in mind, Luke 6:27-36 and
Matthew 5:38-48 establish that treatment of enemies must follow the example of God so that human beings reflect the Father who allows the sun to rise
and set and the rain to fall on both the just and the unjust. This is a radically
different revelation of God than that found in either Judaism or Islam.

The problem that arises with "resisting evil" is the corrosive effect it
has on the hearts of good people. It is not unusual for individual innocence
and goodness to be lost during a struggle which began with noble aspirations. This appears as a common theme in entertainment and military actions
where the hero wins out over the forces of evil by initiating a greater level of
violence in order to defeat the enemy. Often, the only difference between
good and bad people in such scenarios is not the actions but the motives that
drive the actions, and those are often highly ambiguous. The personal trans-
formations that take place during this intimate involvement with evil can neither be predicted nor controlled. Good people place themselves and "the
enemy" at high risk of being permanently damaged when their response to
evil is not in line with the gospel standard for proper interpersonal relations:
love your neighbor as yourself.

Following the parallel but briefer Lukan beatitudes (and woes—Lk
6:20-26) which begin his sermon on the plain are nine verses (Lk 6:27-36)
describing appropriate behavior and attitudes toward enemies: love them; do
good to those who hate you; bless those who curse you and pray for those
who abuse you. If called to defend one's honor by the slap to the face, offer
the other cheek and let God worry about your honor; if your coat is taken do

not withhold your shirt—God knows what you need. Give to everyone who begs and don't ask for the return of property that is stolen. This behavior is required **because** believers are children of the Most High who is kind to the ungrateful and the selfish. Children of God are those whose actions reflect to other human beings the manner in which they have been fathered by God (Lk 6:27-36).

The disadvantages of wealth—The majority of people lived a "hand to mouth" existence or in what is called a subsistence economy. There was no abundance, no left-overs, no affluence and nothing for free in public exchanges. Relations were kept balanced so that no one owed interpersonal debts outside the family beyond what could be paid. Given this social perception that **all** good things are limited, the unspoken charge throughout the gospels is that those in control who are wealthy, secure, content and socially accepted enjoy a short-lived prosperity because it has been gained at the expense of the poor, the hungry, those who mourn and those who are reviled as social outcasts. This is the social condition which inspires the Lukan laments: for those who are rich now have received their consolation; for those who are full now shall hunger; for those who laugh now shall mourn and weep; for those about whom all men speak well—their fathers spoke well of the false prophets (Lk 6:20-26).

Jesus tells a parable (unique to Luke) demonstrating that a man's life does not consist in the abundance of his possessions. A rich man who lived and accumulated the produce of the land, building larger barns, was suddenly called to God before he could enjoy his stored-up wealth and the security it promised. Since his life had been organized around the acquisition of wealth, he had done nothing of value in God's eyes. "God said to him, 'Fool! this night your soul [life] is required of you; and the things you have prepared, whose will they be?' So is he who lays up treasure for himself, and is not rich toward God" (Lk 12:16-21). What is such a person according to the standards of the kingdom? A fool. Following this parable is the admonition, "Therefore I tell you, do not be anxious about life, what you shall eat, nor about your body, what you shall put on..." (Lk 12:22-34//Mt 6:25-34). The message is twofold, "seek first the kingdom and all else shall follow"; and "where your treasure is, there will be your heart."

In Luke there are numerous references, sayings and parables that highlight the situation of the poor as well as the dangers that accompany wealth. One such parable is that of the unjust steward (Lk 16:1-8) whose shady dealings had cheated his master on what was rightfully coming to him. This man was not strong enough for manual labor nor was he prepared to beg, and yet he would be left with nothing. So he called on everyone who owed his master and reduced their debts so that he could gather a large sum quickly. The master commended the steward on his shrewdness: "...for the sons of the world are more shrewd in dealing with their own generation than the sons of light." If a steward who is threatened with losing his job can be so adept at bringing his situation into proper order, how much more serious is the situation of wealthy believers who face ultimate sanctions when death cancels out all hope of change.

The Lukan chapter continues with the belief that those who are faithful in small things will be faithful in much; those honest in small things will be honest in larger matters.

> If then you have not been faithful in the unrighteous money or riches, who will entrust to you the true riches? And if you have not been faithful in that which is another's, who will give you that which is your own? No servant can serve two masters; for either he will hate the one and love the other, or he will be devoted to the one and despise the other. You cannot serve God and mammon (Semitic word for money or riches) (Lk 16:10-13)

The "something else and other" which enables the listener to understand this parable is that these two masters, God and wealth, are mutually exclusive. The demands of God cancel out the demands of wealth and vice versa. The focus is not on the steward who could theoretically serve two or three other masters whose demands did not exclude service to others. The focus is on the **Master**, whose service necessarily **excludes** the possibility of wealth. The Pharisees scoffed at this and Jesus told them, "You are those who justify yourselves before men, but God knows your hearts; for what is exalted among men is an abomination in the sight of God" (Lk 16:14-15).

The parable of Lazarus illustrates the radical change which the rich and poor experience at the hands of God. We are told nothing of either man in the story beyond the poverty and sickness of Lazarus and the wealth which allowed the rich man to live a life of comfort. When the two men died, Lazarus went to the bosom of Abraham while the rich man died and went to hell. Across the great chasm separating them a conversation began as the rich man begged for relief only to be reminded by Abraham how he had received good things in life while Lazarus received evil things. The rich man pleaded that his five brothers receive a special messenger from the dead warning them about what lies ahead. His request was denied because if they failed to listen to Moses and the prophets, they would not be convinced by someone rising from the dead (Lk 16:19-31).

The wealthy man found in Mark and Matthew who asks Jesus what must he do to inherit eternal life is a ruler in the Lukan account (Lk 18:18-26). After reciting the commandments, this ruler testified that he had kept them all. He is then told to sell everything he has, give it to the poor and follow Jesus. The man looks very sad when he hears this because he is very rich. Jesus comments that "It is easier for a camel to pass through the eye of a needle than it is for the rich to enter the kingdom of heaven" (Lk 18:25//Mk 10:25//Mt 19:24). This statement is received under protest by his disciples who ask, "Then who can be saved?" They fail to comprehend what Jesus is saying because they do not share his focus. Jesus re-establishes that the point is not what **kind** of people get saved, but **who** does the saving, "What is impossible with men is possible with God." Saving poor people is not impossible to God but wealth creates obstacles equal to the trouble a camel has in passing through the eye of a needle. The speed and ease with which the heart is willing to settle for wealth can never be predicted. Similarly, the degree of wealth which inhibits any further desire for God cannot be known until that point is passed, after which it is a question that no longer has any practical significance.

Zacchaeus was the rich tax collector who spotted Jesus while sitting in a sycamore tree. He was in that position when Jesus looked up and declared that he intended to stay at the house of Zacchaeus that very day. The tax collector came down and received Jesus joyfully as he promised to give half of his goods to the poor, and restore at a rate of fourfold all that he had stolen from others. Jesus' response was that salvation had come to the house of Zacchaeus that day "For the Son of man came to seek and to save the lost" (Lk 19:1-10). Zacchaeus was a rich man whose heart and habits were changed in his encounter with Jesus.

The Lukan account of the poor widow (Lk 21:1-4) who gives far less than the amounts being put in the temple treasury by the rich reminds the reader that God was not interested in partial percentages—no matter how great the amount. She clarifies that the standard amount given to God is everything, the same amount as specified in the great commandment where God is to be loved with one's "whole heart, soul and strength." The second commandment, "to love your neighbor as yourself," governs both how wealth is acquired as well as how it is dispersed. Public opinion is inconsequential compared to the first priority of being attached to the house of God. Since everything flows through that membership, living in a manner that gives evidence of this inclusion within his house is the second priority. If the heart or words or actions disqualify a member, then there is no security to be gained from money or anything else that man has to offer. Anxiety, as the motivating force to accumulate wealth in hopes that it will yield security, is anxiety about the wrong thing, "Seek first the kingdom of heaven and all else will follow."

Hierarchy and separation distort the human image—Social reversals became the order of the day as Jesus moved the focus from acquiring honor through external behavior to the more fundamental area of the heart.

The social world of Jesus' time **did** emphasize the values of interiority, the heart, self-giving, ready forgiveness, unquestioning generosity, propriety and modesty as desirable in **women**. Again Jesus takes that behavior, those values and the expectations, accepts them for himself and teaches that God finds such behavior desirable in **all** members of his household, especially those who are preaching the gospel (Mt 10:5-23). Jesus calls for complete resocialization of all who become attached to him, from the inside out.

Jesus knew that Moses had accepted the condition of hard-heartedness in allowing men to divorce their wives "legally." The Matthean passage accepts the Markan tradition (Mk 10:2-12) and adds a discussion about eunuchs (Mt 19:10-12). As the laws of Israel did not allow women to sue for divorce, neither did Jesus allow men to sue for divorce. Upset over this, the disciples countered that it was better for men not to marry. Jesus agreed that not everyone could receive his saying about no divorce, only those to whom it had been given. "For there are eunuchs who have been so from birth, and there are eunuchs who have been made eunuchs by men, and there are eunuchs who have made themselves eunuchs for the sake of the kingdom of heaven. He who is able to receive this, let him receive it" (Mt 19:12). Jesus' words on not divorcing could not be received by eunuchs because they did not marry.

Wholeness was a prerequisite for presentation before God. This applied to animals that were to be sacrificed as well as to those people who were participating in religious rituals. According to the Torah only those who were unblemished could present themselves before the Lord (Lev 21:16-24; Deut 23:1). Eunuchs were disqualified from ritual participation. Since eunuchs were considered blemished and could not produce children, no father would give his daughter in marriage to such a man. This same man would never have to worry about divorce. Why does the Matthean discussion introduce eunuchs to disciples who cannot accept this teaching of their master?

A number of pious members of the house of Israel had withdrawn from Jerusalem and active participation in the temple around 152 B.C. when Jonathan Maccabee assumed the highpriesthood. Since he was not from the priestly family who was to assume the duties of high priest, these ultra-religious members of Israel withdrew to the wilderness in protest. By the time Jesus proclaimed the gospel of the kingdom of heaven, the adherents of this earlier movement were well known to other members of the house of Israel, particularly those living in Judea. It is not surprising that the Matthean account includes mention of this group since its author is so knowledgeable about all matters and groups pertaining to the house of Israel. No doubt Jesus knew about the community of devout males who saw themselves as the house of perfection and truth in Israel. Initially this group, the Essenes, was believed to have lived exclusively near the Dead Sea by the Wadi Qumran. Since then, scholars tend to believe that this association of pious persons was probably scattered throughout the towns and villages of Judea. Considering themselves as warriors of Israel, a number of these men took vows to remain celibate.

Both Jewish and Hellenistic thinking unanimously agreed that women were obstacles to the higher aspirations of men, including access to God. The Essenes believed themselves to be the pious vanguard who awaited God's deliverance of Israel. They were the expectant army, the true camp of the children of Israel who stood beside the holy angels as they kept themselves in a state of readiness.[15] Josephus writes of his contemporaries, the Essenes,

> The doctrine of the Essenes is this: That all things are best ascribed to God...and when they send what they have dedicated to God into the temple, they do not offer sacrifices, because they have more pure lustrations of their own; on which account **they are excluded from the common court of the temple,** but offer their sacrifices themselves...It also deserves our admiration, how much they exceed all other men that addict themselves to virtue, and this in righteousness; and indeed to such a degree, that as it hath never appeared among any other man, neither Greeks nor barbarians, no, not for a little time, so hath it endured a long while among them. This is demonstrated by that institution of theirs which will not suffer anything to hinder them from having all things in common; so that a rich man enjoys no more of his own wealth than he who hath nothing at all. They are about four thousand men that live in this way, and neither **marry wives,** nor are desirous to keep servants; as thinking the latter tempts men to be unjust, and the former gives the handle to domestic quarrels; but as they live by themselves, they minister one to another.[16]

Jesus credited his disciples with being interested in the true reign of God. Yet, these same disciples could not receive Jesus' teaching on no divorce even though it aimed at restoring the relation between man and woman as God had intended. How does Jesus reconcile the hard-heartedness of his disciples in this area with their desire to see the restoration of God's order? He introduced a group to whom the saying on no divorce did not apply, namely, the Essenes. This group of men made themselves eunuchs by disqualifying themselves both from temple worship as well as from marriage. If Jesus' disciples could not receive his teaching on no divorce, possibly they would "be able to receive" the teachings advocated by the Essenes, who had made themselves eunuchs for the sake of the kingdom of heaven.

This Matthean passage on the question of marriage and divorce (Mt 19:3-9) was followed with the discussion on eunuchs (Mt 19:10-12) and brought back to those whose position in the kingdom is guaranteed,

> Then children were brought to him that he might lay his hands on them and pray. The disciples rebuked the people; but Jesus said, "Let the children come to me, and do not hinder them; for to such belongs the kingdom of heaven." And he laid his hands on them and went away (Mt 19:13-15).

The idea that the kingdom "naturally" belongs to children was easily forgotten by male theologians whose focus was never the domestic domain but the outside, the male arena. Since life in a patriarchy demands hierarchical organization with every element in its proper vertical compartment, male theologians used the passage on eunuchs to limit those who were "eligible" for places of authority in the church to those males who remained celibate. The presupposition was that Jesus considered himself to be a man without a family. Once this presupposition of no family is replaced by a family organized around God as head where men and women become one flesh according to the intentions of God, then the meaning of the passage on eunuchs has to be re-examined. **Both** men and women who follow Jesus live like daughters and wives whose allegiance to the household of God takes precedence over all other relations. Christianity took a fatal turn when it developed into another male activity where women and children were viewed as outsiders.

The next passage is important because it has been used to claim unlimited power for the papacy. The context is a discussion about the identity assigned to Jesus by others and his disciples (Mt 16:13-16; Lk 9:18-20; Mk 8:27-30). The answers include John the Baptist to Elijah to Jeremiah or one of the prophets. When Jesus asked for their opinion, Peter answered, "The Christ, the son of the living God." In Matthew, Jesus' pleasure at the response arises from his recognition of the work of his Father, "...flesh and blood has not revealed this to you, but my Father who is in heaven." Jesus' response was to declare, "You are Peter, and on this rock I will build my church and the powers of death [or gates of hell] shall not prevail against it."

An earlier parable in the sermon on the mount guaranteed that "Everyone who hears these words of mine and does them will be like a wise man who built his house upon rock" (Mt 7:24-27). The evidence of God's activity in Peter inspired Jesus to acknowledge that Peter was just such a rock, strong and dependable enough to be counted on **because** of God's activity in him. The passage continues as Jesus says to Peter, "I will give you the keys of the kingdom of heaven, and whatever you bind on earth shall be bound in heaven, and whatever you loose on earth shall be loosed in heaven."

This passage claims that God's activity flowing through those attached to Jesus enable the leaders of God's household on earth to faithfully reflect the kingdom. Once again, the focus is not Peter, but **God's activity** in Peter. This is a splendid moment for Jesus who had struggled against the concrete, external influences which blinded his disciples to the meanings of his parables. Then Jesus strictly charged them to tell no one that he was the Christ (Mt 16:20).

Immediately following the Matthean passage, Jesus tells his disciples that he must go to Jerusalem and suffer many things from the elders and chief priest and scribes, be killed, and on the third day rise. At this, Peter rebuked or attempted to strip Jesus' words of power by telling him that what he predicted must never happen. This response made it immediately apparent to Jesus that what had been present in Peter in the previous passage was clearly missing now. Struck by the absence of his Father, Jesus calls Peter a stumbling block and Satan, one who is not on the side of God, **but the side of men** (Mt 16:21-23). Peter's conversion to the designs of God was short-lived before he fell back into advocating what was considered appropriate male goals according to cultural norms. Possibly the author of this gospel placed those two passages together to prevent anyone from thinking that either Peter or power was the focus of the previous passage. Instead, apart from God, neither physical descent from Abraham nor the "unbroken succession" from Peter guarantees that the actions done in God's name necessarily reflect God's intentions.

Not only men confuse human goals with the plans of God, so do women. Following the third prediction of Jesus' death in Matthew 20:20 is the request by the mother of the sons of Zebedee that her sons be allowed to sit at the right and left hands of Jesus in the kingdom. This differs from the Markan account (Mk 10:35-45) where the brothers themselves asked for these places. The significance of the Matthean account is the recognition that women accept and foster within their children the values and expectations of society. This is the other side of the coin which we have been examining.

The male role might be designed and created by men for men but it has been supported and sustained by women as well. Accepting the standards of the kingdom is very difficult in families where only some members are oriented around God. Once again, the remaining ten disciples are indignant at the mother's request. But Jesus' position is the same in Matthew as it is in the other three gospels: whoever would be great must be their servant, and the one who is first among them must be slave to all.

Many women and men see themselves as locked out of recognition and success. This limits them to the success they enjoy vicariously in their children's achievements. There is danger in this for the child who is molded to conform to the emptiness, weakness, blindness or failure inherent in their parents. The mother of James and John held out hopes for her sons because **she** had no possibility for a free grant of honor or recognition apart from what her sons received. It is doubtful whether any mother wants to see her child emulate a role based on service and nurture which has traditionally kept **her** in society's last place. The difference is that in the kingdom of heaven, the qualities of service and nurture are valued above all others and considered desirable in both sexes. Contrasting its values with those esteemed by most cultures, the kingdom promises that "the last will be first and the first will be last."

IV.

JOHN: SPIRIT-INFUSED FLESH

THE DEMISE OF THE PATRIARCHAL
PERCEPTION IN JOHN

Vertical boundaries separate God from human beings—As noted in the Introduction, the patriarchal perception of the universe was modeled on the disparity between male and female. Therefore, God was above human beings as man was above woman; God ruled the heavens as man ruled nature. The superiority of the male as well as the unbridgeable distance between male and female was emphasized continuously through these and other replications. The fourth gospel conveys this cosmic disparity in four ways. First, there is the vertical language of descending and ascending between heaven and earth emphasizing vertical boundaries. For example, John the Baptist witnessed the Spirit **descend** as a dove (1:32). Jesus spoke about a time when people would see the heavens open as the angels of God **ascend** and **descend** on the Son of man (1:51). Jesus claims in another passage that "No one has **ascended** into heaven but he who **descended** from heaven, the Son of man" (3:13). Jesus refers to himself as the true bread that has **come down** from heaven (6:33-38). When Jesus knew that his audience had taken offense at his words he asked, "Then what if you were to see the Son of man **ascending** to where he was before?" (6:60-62).

Second, no one is equal to God. What "comes from above" ranks above that which comes from below, the earth. Vertical distance implies disparity. When space is measured horizontally between two points, neither disparity nor inequality is implied. But in a society which is arranged hierarchically, vertical space necessarily implies varying degrees of disparity. High and low, above and beneath embody qualitative value beyond distance or simple direction. The biggest criticism leveled at Jesus by his opponents was that he talked about himself as though he were God's equal (5:17-19; 10:33). This was intolerable language because it was commonly held that "He who comes from above is above all; he who is of the earth belongs to the earth, and of the earth he speaks; he who comes from heaven is above all" (3:31). When Jesus said to his opponents that "You are from below, I am from above; you are of this world, I am not of this world" (8:23), this could only be interpreted as outrageous talk. No self-respecting male would cross the gender role boundaries that separated him from females. Similarly God would not cross the boundaries that separated him from the world of flesh.

Third, the disparity between spirit and flesh is clearly established since they are replications of their unequal worlds, "That which is born of the flesh is flesh and that which is born of the Spirit is spirit" (3:6). Human beings know about earthly things but God is Spirit (4:24) and beyond human experience. The common cultural belief was that nothing could go against its "nature." A thing (or person) is what it is and admits of no real change in its "nature." Therefore God could not become human because it was perceived as being a change in his "nature" which is unchangeable.

Fourth, no human being has ever seen God (1:18). The senses belong to the world of the flesh and are limited to perceiving things from that world. Despite this, Jesus makes reference to the fact that he only does what he sees the Father doing (5:19-20), and he only speaks of what he has seen with his Father (8:38). With complete confidence Jesus declares that those who see him see the one who sent him (12:45): "He who has seen me has seen the Father" (14:9). The boundaries that Jesus crosses in the fourth gospel are the vertical boundaries which separate heaven from earth, the spirit from the flesh, God from human beings.

The gospel of John deliberately breaks with the perception of the cosmos that had been the common property of the peoples of the Middle East before it spread to the western world. Isma'il Al-Faruqi, in *The Cultural Atlas of Islam,*[1] lists five principles which are characteristic of the ancient Mesopotamian religious experience out of which arose Judaism, Christianity and Islam. First, reality is composed of two kinds of being: one that is divine, absolute and everlasting, who is above all and commands all; while the other being is material, human, changing and subject to divine commands. Second, the realm of the divine relates its commands to the human through divination or revelation. Third, human beings are created to serve their creator through obedience and the fulfillment of divine commands. Fourth, since humans are capable of obedience and the divine commands present what ought to be, human beings are held responsible for their actions. Fifth, the divine plan concerns humanity which acts as an organic unity. Thus, society is the primary unit of reality, not the individual. Hence, society "is the object of cosmic action on the part of the deity."[2]

The fourth gospel is organized around God's irreversible departure in the way he related with human beings. That which was 'above all' descended and infused flesh with his Spirit. And while Jesus was a unique union of Spirit and flesh, contrary to Genesis 6:3 ("My spirit shall not abide in man forever because he is flesh...") this union of flesh and spirit was not a "once only" happening. The outrage was to continue, for "Unless one is born of water and the Spirit, he cannot enter the kingdom of God...And I will pray the Father and he will give you another Counselor, to be with you forever, even the Spirit of Truth...you know him, for he dwells with you, and will be in you" (3:5-6; 14:16-17). Because of this radical change in the ordering of the cosmos, divination and revelation were no longer limited to words and language. With Jesus, revelation is conveyed in the flesh. Incarnation is the means of the new revelation. While obedience to divine commands had been the primary human response to God in the past, the "work" of human beings was now to "receive and believe" in Jesus. This new "work" was not submission nor the outcome of threats, but an indication of the Spirit's action within the individual human being. The "group" (e.g. the house of Israel) which had always been viewed as the focus of God and the primary unit of reality was pared down to the individual, society's most inconsequential unit.

Accepting the received tradition that constituted "reality" or the way things are in the world, the gospel of John discarded each plank in the ordering of the patriarchal cosmos. Hierarchy was inverted, disparity was bridged, separation was joined, submission was elevated and flesh bore the weight of the glory of God.

THE THINGS OF EARTH AND THE SPIRIT OF GOD

The Word of God: Language vs. flesh and blood—Of all the phrases that could be used to distinguish the world of nature from the world of God, "flesh and blood" is one of the most commonly used in the Hebrew scriptures. While "flesh and blood" had multiple meanings, one thing that union was **not** was one of spirit. But human beings have resisted the condition that accompanies being "flesh and blood." Most cultures try to "transcend" these givens of natural existence, bending them to cultural purposes. This drive to control nature and the belief that nature should be dominated are present in some form in most cultures. Flesh is a natural symbol that has frequently been the target of cultural intervention.

Pollution is equated with mixture and contamination as well as the unregulated operation of nature, natural energies and processes. Every culture has devised purification rituals which use elements from nature to overcome what is culturally viewed as unacceptable in nature and therefore dangerous to group members. "Thus culture at some level of awareness asserts itself to be not only distinct from but superior to nature, and that sense of distinctiveness and superiority rests precisely on the ability to transform—to 'socialize' and 'culturalize'—nature."[3] Humans create rituals which include parts of nature, words and gestures for the purpose of overcoming other aspects or dimensions of nature. This creation of rituals has led groups/cultures to believe that nature or aspects of nature are dangerous to them. Women have been viewed as more tied to "untamed" or "untransformed" nature. For this reason they have been considered more dangerous to men because of biological processes which are oriented around procreation for most of their adult lives. Male elites have viewed women as inferior to men whom they believed to be more successful in "transcending" nature.

Though the words "body" and "flesh" both express different nuances, they both share the quality of being part of the natural order as opposed to the spiritual order.[4] While used to designate animals as part of the created order, "flesh and blood" can be more narrowly used to mean man or human beings.[5] For those religious systems where God's self-disclosure is strictly limited to revelation in the **language** of the particular group, this action of the Word becoming flesh was the dagger thrust into the heart of patriarchy.[6] Further exacerbating patriarchy's attempt to control God by confining him to texts in one's own language is yet another Johannine passage where Jesus announces that those who do not eat his flesh and drink his blood can have no life in them (6:47-58).

A male so tied to nature and so insistent that his flesh and blood carried the Spirit cost Jesus many followers (6:66). This is not surprising since patriarchies traditionally rank raw nature far below (and often at odds with) their own cultural creations and values. For example, both Judaism and Islam insist that the Hebrew and Arabic languages respectively embody the only worthy and authoritative manifestations of God. Both religions maintain a hierarchical perspective inextricably fused to the social systems in which each religion arose. The patriarchal myth of the origin of the world placed man **"over"** nature as a steward to control and use as he sees fit (Gen 1:28ff; Surahs 2:30, 6:165). Therefore it is not surprising that each religion ranks nature (God's creation) much lower in the hierarchy when compared to language (man's creation). As a man cannot become a woman so God cannot become man. Thus God **would not** have manifested himself in any aspect of his own creation, including a human being. Therefore, God **did not** manifest himself in flesh and blood, in Jesus.

Within Islam, the *Qur'an* is regarded as the most beautiful literary composition the Arabic language has ever known. The evidence for believing that the *Qur'an* is revealed by God rests "on the fact of its sublime beauty."[7] One of the standards that governed which books were accepted into the Hebrew Bible as it exists today is that it must have been written in Hebrew. Through language, the **social group mediates** the relation between its members and God. But within Christianity, the situation is different. Jesus (not the Bible and not the New Testament) is to Christians what the *Qur'an* is to Muslims and the Torah is to Jews. For Christians, Jesus is the Word, the utterance of God. The link between God and Jesus did not begin when Jesus learned to speak; it originated at his conception and was forged in nature, in his flesh. Thus, there has always been some level of realization that God revealed himself in Jesus (flesh and blood/son of man/human being) in the manner which Jews and Muslims believe is **only** possible in the language of a people.

Family relations, natural processes and human needs—God is referred to as Father by Jesus four times in Mark, seventeen times in Luke, forty-four times in Matthew and over a hundred times in John. This term indicates that the setting is domestic where all members participate according to rules different from those that govern behavior among non-family members. It is a private world where the young grow, where concrete physical needs are met, and where the ebb and flow of natural processes is a part of everyday life.

This gospel begins by announcing that those who believed in Jesus would be given power to become children of God. Jesus called his disciples "children" (Jn 13:33; 21:5). At their final meal together he spoke of those generations of believers that would follow his disciples (Jn 17). In the same context when speaking about their sadness at his departure, Jesus compared it to the temporary sorrow of a woman in labor whose great joy at the birth of a child completely eclipses the pain that preceded the birth. In this analogy, the disciples are **like** women in labor because of his absence. "So you have sorrow now, but I will see you again and your hearts will rejoice, and no one will take your joy from you" (16:22). There is no trace of the Genesis interpretation of childbirth which sees it as the primordial punishment for women because of the sin of Eve. Jesus understood something about birth that other men had either failed to notice or discredited out of envy. The pain and "disorder" of childbirth had the possibility of ending in euphoric joy. This made childbirth the best analogy Jesus could find to describe the joy which would characterize his reunion with the disciples.

Food plays a central role in the analogies Jesus used to refer to himself: the bread of God, water that quenches all thirst, flesh and blood as food for eternal life are important elements in John. Jesus spoke to audiences who could relate to analogies about grain that dies to yield fruit; fields that are ripe for harvest; sowers and reapers who have worked in the same fields; vineyards and those who tend vines; shepherds and sheep; fishermen and fish; rooms in the Father's house that are being prepared for them. Jesus frequently spoke about work: that God was working still (contrary to Gen 2:2); that Jesus had much work to do; the importance of working in the light and that belief was the work of his followers. Thus, work was not viewed as punishment because of the sin of Adam. Rather, **God was still working** and Jesus was working as well.

Consistent with the image of God that is found in Mark, Matthew and

Luke, the Johannine God is a Father whose largess and abundance are given indiscriminately to **everyone** in hopes of saving all people from the social/personal experiences that threaten to destroy them. God is not just the "God of Israel" or the "God of history" as nineteenth century biblical concerns would lead us to believe. The God revealed in Jesus is also the God of nature. The miracles are not to be explained away to relieve contemporary embarrassment in the face of "reality" as seen through the limited lens of science. Rather they are an integral part of God's activity in Jesus, the one human being to whom nature is responsive. The Johannine author presents Jesus as the Word that was no longer limited to human language that is controlled by the prevailing social system. Jesus was God's Word-made-flesh, a human being who cultivated a life embedded in God. This unshakable loyalty set Jesus at odds with the house of Israel no less than with the Gentiles. No written word can ever achieve the kind of freedom from its social system which Jesus accomplished.

Eternal Time—Belief in Jesus altered not only the possibility of crossing vertical boundaries but the limitations of how human beings experience time as well. Patriarchy makes time one of the foundations of power. Jesus disrupted the understanding that chronology determines precedence, the degree of power based on who comes first. Conception did not mark the beginning of Jesus' life and death did not end it. The fourth gospel makes reference to a life before birth that Jesus had enjoyed with the Father (1:1–17; 17:5,24). He spoke of patriarchs of Israel who had been dead centuries before his birth, but who knew him (8:57–59). Jesus' ancestors did not enjoy precedence; he was not "possessed" by them because Jesus had existed before them. Only God existed before him, only God enjoyed precedence, only God possessed Jesus.

The fourth gospel exploded the limitations that the human life cycle placed on the perception of time. But there was a cultural predisposition for this perception which does not exist in contemporary Western society. In the world of Jesus, people viewed themselves as living in an "expanded present" where the past and future were simply at different ends of a continuum which was perceived as present time. What is unique to John is the author's interpretation that this sense of a permanent present time was a replication of cosmic time. Cosmic time can be described as endless or eternal: without beginning or end, without boundaries. The author achieved this sense of cosmic or eternal time through the use of repetition.

Repetition and the cosmic cycle—Despite the changing scenes, different characters and numerous analogies that are used throughout this gospel, repetition is one of the central characteristics of John. This repetition is integral to the style of Jesus' discussions, talks and arguments into which the listener (reader) is drawn. Very often it seems that one can listen in at any point in this gospel and eventually hear what was missed. The settings may change, but the main points continue to reappear with a spiraling regularity, seemingly without beginning or end. This is the very quality which elicits an expanded sense of time, a sense of the eternal. In the *Qur'an*, repetition of ideas and patterns of speech are counted as elements of eloquence,[8] an aspect of its perfection which has been designated as its *i'jaz*, or "power to incapacitate" the listener.[9]

Repetition in John creates a rhythm which is like the rhythm of nature. Pulsating at a regular beat is the all-encompassing cycle of the cosmos where creation is ceaselessly initiated by God, human beings are continuously invited by Jesus to become God's children; successive generations produce individuals who accept Jesus' call, signaling the uninterrupted activity of God's Spirit who initiates believers into eternal life. This continuous action of the Spirit empowers believers to become children of God (flesh plus Spirit) as contrasted with the children of men (flesh minus Spirit) who will die. All stages of this cycle might be present in Jesus' talks and discussions but not necessarily in this sequence. Where disbelief interrupts this progression of activity from God leading back to God, a negative break (-) in some stage occurs. The Prologue, 1:1-18, introduces the listener/reader to this pattern: (a) the cycle begins with the **initiative** of God; (b) as Word, Jesus has always been the **means** or agent of creation "spoken" by God; (c) recognizing God's activity in Jesus and **believing** in him is the only adequate response; (d) this response indicates the Spirit's activity and marks the believer as a child of God (flesh plus Spirit) who becomes part of an **eternal** cycle, as contrasted with the children of men (flesh minus Spirit) who will die. Notice this pattern in the following passages.

(b) In the beginning was the Word, (agent) (a) and the Word was with God, and the Word was God. (b) He was in the beginning with God; (the agent and initiator are one)

(b) all things were made through him and without him was not anything made that was made. In him was life, and life was the light of men. (God's agent actively accomplishes his designs)

(b) The light shines in the darkness, and the darkness has not overcome it. (the agent has never been destroyed)

(b) There was a man sent from God, whose name was John. He came for testimony, to bear witness to the light, (John is the means or agent)

(c) that all might believe through him. (appropriate response)

(b) He was not the light, but came to bear witness to the light. (John's witness is the means God uses)

(b) The true light that enlightens every man was coming into the world. (the agent is sent again to the world)

(b) He was in the world and the world was made through him, (the agent is intimately connected with the world from its creation)

(c-) yet the world knew him not. (no belief, inappropriate response)

(b) He came to his own home,

(c-) and his own people received him not.

(c) But to all who received him, who believed in his name

(b) he gave power to become children of God. (the agent authorizes this inclusion in God)

(a) And the Word (of God, the agent of creation)

(b) became flesh and dwelt among us full of grace and truth; (the Word itself became the agent of abundance and fidelity)

(c) we have beheld his glory, glory as of the only Son of the Father (believers see Jesus as the agent of the Father who is beyond human sense experience)

(b) John bore witness to him, and cried, (John was the means)

(c) "This was he of whom I said, 'He who comes after me ranks before me, for he was before me.'"

(d) And from his fullness we have all received, grace upon grace.

(b) For the law was given through Moses (the means); (b) but grace and truth came through Jesus Christ. No one has ever seen God; (a) the only Son who is in the bosom of the Father, (b) he has made him known.

There are many other examples of the repetition of these stages throughout John. John 17:1-26 exemplifies this endless cycle of God's initiative where Jesus is the means of a new creation. This chapter could be called the prayer of generations since it reflects Jesus' belief that his words and actions will bear fruit with no time limits into eternal life. Once again the pattern is: (a) the initiative belongs to God; (b) Jesus is the agent of God's designs who invites people to believe (life); (c) the only adequate response for human beings is belief; (d) belief indicates the work of the Spirit and individual inclusion in eternal life.

(b) Father the hour has come; (for Jesus as agent) (a) glorify thy Son that (b) the Son may glorify thee, (a) since thou hast given him power over all flesh, (d) to give eternal life to all whom (a) thou hast given him. (d) And this is eternal life, (c) that they know thee the only true God, and Jesus Christ whom (a) thou hast sent. (b) I glorified thee on earth, having accomplished the work (a) which thou gavest me to do; and now, (a) glorify thou me in thy own presence with the glory which I had with thee before the world was made (17:1-5).

(b) I have manifested thy name to the men whom (a) thou gavest me out of the world; (a) thine they were, and thou gavest them to me, and (c) they have kept thy word. Now they know that everything thou hast given me is from thee; (b) for I have given them the words (a) which thou gavest me, (c) and they have received them and know in truth (a) that I came from thee; and (c) they have believed (a) that thou didst send me. (b) I am praying for them; I am not praying for the world but those whom (a) thou hast given me, for they are thine; (b) all mine are thine, and (a) thine are mine, and (b) I am glorified in them.

(The signs, +, refers to those dimensions which initially belonged to Jesus alone but are passed on to his disciples.)

(b) And now I am no more in the world, (b+) but they are in the world (the means along with Jesus), and (a) I am coming to thee. Holy Father (a+) keep them in thy name, (a) which thou hast given me, (a+) that they may be one, (a) even as we are one. (b) While I was with them, I kept them in thy name, (a) which thou hast given me; (b) I have guarded them, and (c) none of them is lost (c-) but the son of perdition, that the scripture might be fulfilled. (a) But now I am coming to thee; (b) and these things I speak in the world, that (d) they may have my joy fulfilled in themselves. (b) I have given them thy word; (c-) and the world has hated them (a+) because they are not of the world, (a) even as I am not of the world. (b) I do not pray that thou shouldst take them out of the world, (a+) but that thou shouldst keep them from the evil one. (a+) They are not of the world, (a) even as I am not of the world. (a+) Sanctify them in the truth; (a) thy word is truth. As thou didst sent me into the world, (b+) so I have sent them into the world. (b) And for their sake I consecrate myself, (d) that they also may be consecrated in truth (17:6-19).

In the following verses (20-26), the situation is enhanced for the "grandchildren" (++), those who will believe from the words of his disciples. Jesus asks that succeeding generations share in what he received from the Father and then passed on to his disciples who were the first generation of believers.

b) I do not pray for these only, (c++) but also for those who believe in me (b+) through their word, (a++) that they may all be one; (a) even as thou, Father, art in me, and I in thee, (a++) that they also may be in us, (c++) so that the world may believe (a) that thou hast sent me. (a) The glory which thou hast given me (b++) I have given to them, (a++) that they may one even (a) as we are one, (a++) I in them and thou in me, that they may become perfectly one, (c++) so that the world may know (a) that thou hast sent me (a++) and hast loved them even as thou hast loved me. Father, I desire that they also, whom thou hast given me, may be with me where I am, to behold my glory which (a) thou hast given me in thy love for me before the foundation of the world. O righteous Father, (c-) the world has not known thee, (b) but I have known thee; (c) and these know that thou hast sent me. (b) I made known to them thy name, (b+) and I will make it known, (a) that the love with which thou hast loved me (a+) may be in them, and I in them.

The entire pattern breaks down (as does God's Lordship) when unbelief is present. Additional examples from other passages illustrate this breakdown (-) at various stages in what would otherwise be an eternal pattern:

So Jesus proclaimed as he taught in the temple, (c-) "You know me, and (a-) you know where I came from? But (b) I have not come of my own accord; (a) he who sent me is true, and (c-) him you do not know. (b) I know him, for I came from him and (a) he sent me" (7:28-29).
Jesus then said, (b) "I shall be with you a little longer, (b) and then I go to him who sent me; (c) you will seek me and (c-) you will not find me; (d-) where I am you cannot come" (7:33-34).
b) I am the light of the world;
c) he who follows me (d) will not walk in darkness, but will have the light of life (8:12).
c-) The Pharisees then said to him, "You are bearing witness to yourself; your testimony is not true" (8:13).
b) Jesus answered, "Even if I do bear witness to myself, my testimony is true, for I know (a) whence I have come and whither I am going,
c-) but you do not know whence I come or whither I am going (8:14).
c-) You judge according to the flesh,
b) I judge no one (8:15). Yet even if I do judge, my judgment is

true, for it is not I alone that judge, but (a) I and he who sent me" (8:16).

b) I go away, and you will seek me and (d-) die in your sin; (b) where I am going, (d-) you cannot come (8:21). He said to them, (d-) "You are from below, (a) I am from above; (d-) you are of this world, (a) I am not of this world (8:23). (b) I told you that you (d-) would die in your sin (c) unless you believe that (b) I am he" (8:24).

The Johannine image of Jesus emerges inextricably embedded in God, secure in knowing that those attached to him will share in his relation to the Father. Having crossed the vertical barrier that separated heaven from earth, he was the agent who baptized in the Spirit (1:33). In terms of Israel's religion, this was one description of the end times:

> And it shall come to pass afterward, that I will pour out my spirit on all flesh; your sons and your daughters shall prophesy, your old men shall dream dreams, and your young men shall see visions. Even upon the menservants and maidservants, I will pour out my spirit (Jl 2:28-29).

The repetition of these four stages in John enables the reader to experience something **like** the timelessness[10] and all-inclusiveness of God as Father. Thus, successive generations of believers are initiated into an endless sequence where God is creator/Father/initiator; Jesus is the agent by whom life is given and sustained; while the Spirit is the agent of belief as well as the agent of eternal life.

The Johannine Worlds and Cosmic Time—The locus of Jesus' activity is the world. But the fourth gospel uses the same word to cover several different, and at times conflicting, worlds.

1. In the West, the world of history is the world of the past. The Middle East makes no such sharp distinction as mentioned earlier. The past exists alongside the present and the gospels provide no clue as to the span of time which separates the characters and actions it mentions. Several examples of the past being "folded" into the present in John are: "So he [Jesus] came to a city of Samaria, called Sychar, near the field that Jacob gave to his son Joseph" (4:5). The crowds asked Jesus, "Are you greater than our father Jacob who gave us the well and drank from it himself, and his sons and his cattle?"(4:12). Analogies are made between past and present events as though the audiences had immediate experiences with both. Moses and manna in the desert are referred to as though they were part and parcel of the

experience of Jesus' contemporaries, "If you believed Moses, you would believe me, for he wrote of me"(5:46). Jesus said, "Truly, truly I say to you, it was not Moses who gave you the bread from heaven; my Father gives you the true bread from heaven and gives life to the world" (6:33).

Present as well as past events are subject to diverse and conflicting interpretations. In choosing to use only certain analogies of Israel from its past, the Johannine writer authorized only certain aspects of the Hebrew scriptures as useful in understanding Jesus. Yet, the analogies he chose are open to more than one interpretation. For example, John the Baptist had recognized Jesus as the "lamb of God who takes away the sin of the world" (1:29,36). In using this term, "lamb of God," John was drawing on traditional analogies of shepherds, lambs and sheep which are frequently used throughout the Hebrew scriptures as analogies Israel used for itself as well as for God. John recognized Jesus as the lamb who would take away the sin of the world. Jesus followed the voice of God as the lamb follows a shepherd.

What was the sin that this lamb of God was to remove? The prototypical sin is that of a group which creates its own god to follow. Within the tradition of Israel, the "sin of the world" was epitomized by Israel's creation of the golden calf. Unlike his ancestors, Jesus faithfully projected the image of God in his words and actions even though he was killed. Because of that, he was like the gentle lamb led to the slaughter, "I did not know it was against me they devised schemes, saying 'Let us destroy the tree with its fruit, let us cut him off from the land of the living, that his name be remembered no more'" (Jer 11:19). Thus, when Jesus was called a lamb who takes away the sin of the world, the lamb that provides the analogy is the one who follows the voice of God. This analogy of the lamb is more appropriate in understanding Jesus' death than the first sacrificial lamb who was Isaac (Gen 22:8-13) or the animals which were used in temple ritual. The temple promulgated an image of God which demanded sacrifice as appropriate to God's status as well as to repair his insulted honor at Israel's infidelities (more will be said about this in Chapter V).

Jesus referred to himself as the good shepherd. One of the analogies used for God in the Hebrew Bible was that of the shepherd (Gen 49:24) who fed his flock and gathered "the lambs in his arms, carrying them in his bosom, gently leading those that were with their young" (Is 40:11). God promised to give Israel "shepherds after my own heart, who will feed you with knowledge and understanding" (Jer 3:15). But there was a history of shepherds who were accused of: stupidity and letting the flock scatter (Jer 10:21); trampling God's vineyard (Jer 12:10); feeding themselves while the sheep went unfed and became food for wild beasts (Ez 34:8), etc. Ezekiel had described God's response to those with no shepherd, "For thus says the Lord God, Behold, I, I myself will search for my sheep, and will seek them out" (Ez 34:11). Jesus was the shepherd of lost sheep after the manner and heart of God.

The vineyard is another powerful analogy from the world of Israel's past that figured prominently in Johannine parables. Isaiah 5:1-4 describes the tender care given a vineyard whose vines would yield only wild grapes. Judgment was passed and the decision was made to destroy the vineyard (5:5-6).

> For the vineyard of the Lord of hosts is the house of Israel,
> and the men of Judah are his pleasant planting;
> but behold, bloodshed; for righteousness, behold, a cry! (Is 5:7).

When Jesus declared himself to be the true vine and his Father the vine-dresser, God was imagined as the vinedresser tending Israel. Unlike Israel, Jesus is responsive to the efforts of the vinedresser who prunes away vines that bear nothing. Those who abide in Jesus are the branches that bear fruit (Jn 15:1-17).

These are just a few analogies from the symbols available in the Hebrew epic which this author carefully chose to present a clear and unambiguous interpretation of the designs of God as manifested in Jesus. The world of Jesus' generation was not viewed as significantly different from the generations that preceded it. This popular belief that nothing of significance ever changes in life linked group members of passing generations. It also created a unified perception of group identity as well as the identity of "outsiders." While the people, places and time changed, the "world" remained unchanged in its essentials. This was the all-encompassing world that God had created through his Word (1:10). It was the place that God so loved that he sent his Son (3:16) in an attempt to save it (3:17) precisely because the world had not changed from one generation to the next.

2. The second of John's worlds was the world of Jesus' generation. It was the larger world which housed those who would receive Jesus as well as those who would reject him. The brothers of Jesus realized that he must openly show himself to this world (7:4) as did Jesus (8:26; 18:20). He knew that the Spirit would come into this arena to convince the world of sin, righteousness and judgment (16:8) after Jesus had rejoined the Father (16:28).

3. The third world belonged to those who had received and believed in Jesus. This world was an extension of the kingdom of God. Jesus had declared that those who lived in this world "were not of the world" just as he was not of the world (17:14). This third world knew of no separation or distance from the Father since the vertical boundary separating heaven from earth was now open. For these "not of the world," Jesus' flesh and blood were food and drink for eternal life (6:51). He was their light (9:5); they

would continue to see him after he was gone and they would continue to live because he lived (14:19). These people were his own in the world (13:1) who had been given to Jesus by God (17:6). This was the world for which Jesus prayed (17:9) that the Father would keep them in Jesus' name so that they could be one (17:11) and that his joy might be fulfilled in them (17:13). Jesus gave them his peace and sent them into the (neutral) world as he himself had been sent by God into that same world (17:18). In this world, time was eternal and the space in which they lived belonged to God.

4. The fourth world was populated by those in the present generation who hated Jesus because he declared their works to be evil (7:7). They preferred darkness (3:19), hating his followers (15:19) as they had hated him. This world was made up of those who did not know God (17:25). Their ruler had no power over Jesus (14:30) because he had overcome that world (16:33).

5. The fifth world in John was a unit that was too great for non-believers, e.g. the Pharisees who noted that they could do nothing about Jesus because "the world" had gone after him (12:19), but inadequate for believers, e.g. "the world" was not large enough to contain all the books that might be written about the things Jesus did (21:25).

There were no longer two unequal worlds: the "spiritual" heavens ruled by God, and the earth, an inferior place of flesh and blood inimical to God. The heavens do not enjoy preeminence over the earth as sacred space. The sacred is not restricted in perpetuity for one group and one land only. After Jesus, neither Israel, nor Jerusalem, nor the temple remains as "holy" space. Rather, divine initiative is ceaselessly being taken in the lives of individuals who are invited to call God, "Father." God's presence is signified in the world by individuals whose lives reveal the presence and activity of God's Spirit.

The World of God and the Best That Culture Offers—The world of the Hebrew Bible and the social world in which the author of John and his audience lived provided the analogies which were used to interpret God's activity in Jesus. Not all characters or stories in the Hebrew Bible were appropriate or useful to the author. In the same way, not all the values and customs of society were equally appropriate for use in understanding God's activity in Jesus. The fourth gospel shows a consistent regard in choosing what best highlights the revelation that is Jesus.

First, the use of repetition in John not only elicits a feel of timeless inter-relating but of life totally organized around God as Father, the principal person from whom all good comes. Second, both Jesus' identity as well as his relations flowed from this primary relation with God as Father: "Truly, truly, I say to you, the Son can do nothing of his own accord, but only what he sees the Father doing; for whatever he does, that the Son does likewise. For the Father loves the Son, and shows him all that he himself is doing" (5:19-20). In a patriarchal social system, the father or "patriarch" is the one from whom the offspring (or group member) draws life, identity and a pattern for living. For example, those who disagreed with Jesus claimed to have Abraham as their father. Abraham was the father of the group, the patriarch who bound all the families together. But Jesus declared that their rejection of him indicated that their father was not Abraham but the devil because it was **his** desires that motivated their rejection (8:39-47).

Third, more time is spent "listening in" on the discussions, arguments and the talks of Jesus in this gospel because ongoing conversations and intense discussions are normal features where interpersonal relations take up a good part of one's day. Examples of this include John the Baptist's discussion with his disciples (1:35ff; 3:25ff); the call of Philip and Nathanael (1:43ff); the request of Jesus' mother (2:1ff); Jesus and Nicodemus (3:1ff); Jesus and the woman of Samaria (4:1ff); the woman of Samaria and the townspeople (4:39ff); etc. Discussion constitutes the bulk of John with a smaller ratio being given over to narrative description or to other activities.

Fourth, additional information is included about more people in John so that the listener can "participate" with the same knowledge which is available to an insider. Examples include the woman of Samaria (4:1ff); the man who was healed at Bethzatha (5:1ff); the unbelief of Jesus' brothers (7:1ff); the disbelief of those in authority (7:45ff); the man born blind (9:1ff); etc. Similarly, more is said about Jesus' relation to God and his life before birth than is written in the synoptics. This additional, personal information is also expected where the astute assessment of people is necessary to forge relations that will prove beneficial in meeting the concrete needs of everyday life.

The categories and vocabulary used throughout the fourth gospel compel the reader to look for meaning in the semitic world from which they emerged. In that world the following social premises must be taken into consideration: 1) that the family is the primary social unit which embraces each person and creates the primary sense of identity; 2) that the larger group which claims the family's allegiance creates the secondary identity; 3) that group members can only interact with outsiders, the "Other," through carefully regulated procedures which will not endanger the family or group; 4) that interpersonal relations are the organizing principle of life. With great care, the author of this gospel chose only those values and goals of the social world which personified the cosmic cycle already described.

For instance, when a stranger wants to move from the "outside" of the group to the "inside," the witness and testimony of those insiders who know the stranger in question are indispensable aides before inaugurating a relation. Secondly, determining the kind of power or influence which resides in someone (whether an outsider to the family or to the group) is important before becoming further involved. "Knowing" another is the result of inter-personal experiences over time where truth (reliability and constancy) fosters belief between those involved in personal exchanges. "Receiving" binds the giver and receiver in an ongoing relation of some degree. As these relations endure over time, love comes to be a natural response as people abide in those whose fidelity and care contribute to the maintenance of their lives, those of their families and the welfare of their group. These various dimensions of interpersonal relations can be understood as overlapping clusters of behaviors, values, emotions and expectations. This is what is reflected in the vocabulary and activity in John.

Witness/testimony—Before initiating interpersonal relations with out-siders, someone from within the group must testify on behalf of the stranger. Because Jesus was an insider among human beings he needed no one to bear witness of man because "Jesus knew all men" (2:25). Witness and testimony are required when members of a group have no knowledge of, or experience with, a stranger who comes into their midst. John the Baptist was the man sent from God to "make straight the way of the Lord" as Isaiah had prophe-sied. John bore witness that he had seen the Spirit descend and remain on Jesus, indicating that he was the one who would baptize with the Holy Spirit. Unlike the synoptics in which the voice from the cloud called Jesus "Son," this gospel account includes that designation as part of the testimony of John the Baptist (1:19-34) to show that he is an insider whose testimony is reli-able. The first disciples are those who followed Jesus based on this testimony of John. One of them was Andrew who went to his brother, Simon, announc-ing that they had found the Messiah. Having accepted Simon from the hands of his brother, Jesus bestowed on him the name Peter (1:40-42). Simon was first the recipient of what Andrew knew about Jesus and secondly the recipi-ent of what Jesus knew about him as validated in his name change from Simon to Peter.

The request of Jesus' mother resulted in the first sign where his glory was manifested and his disciples believed in him (2:1-11). The mother showed herself to be an insider and reliable witness unlike her sons whose lack of belief later reveals them to be outsiders (Jn 7:1-9). It is not surprising that this gospel finds Jesus handing over his mother to his beloved disciple (an insider) at the crucifixion **despite** the fact that she had other blood sons who were responsible for her care. New family relations are established around God as Father. Similar to the synoptics, family is redefined and orga-nized around God as Father. Jesus' blood brothers ("whose time was always here and whom the world could not hate"—7:7) were not living with God as Lord; thus, Jesus' mother was given into the care of the beloved disciple.

A woman at Jacob's well (4:1-42) is revealed to be an outsider to Jesus three times over. She is first introduced as an outsider of the local community, further identified as an outsider from the group to which Jesus belongs ("You worship what you do not know, we worship what we know for salvation is from the Jews"—4:22), and a woman (a fact that caused the disciples to be surprised that Jesus spoke with her—4:27). Regardless of these degrees of exclusion, she was the one who received Jesus' teaching. Leaving her water jar behind, the woman went back into the city and told the people about the man who might be the Christ. Believing the woman's testimony (recognizing her as insider among those who followed Jesus), the people came out to the well to listen to Jesus. He stayed among the Samaritans for two days, and by the time he left, many more believed. The woman was told, "It is no longer because of your words that we believe, for we have heard for ourselves, and we know that this is indeed the Savior of the world" (Jn 4:42). When her word is accepted, she is identified as an insider who has provided reliable testimony about Jesus. When the town no longer needs to believe based on her words, they show themselves to be insiders among those who follow Jesus as well. Those who began as outsiders at the beginning of the story had all become insiders with Jesus by the end of the story.

Not only do people bear witness as insiders, but works bear witness to the individual's inclusion in God's family. Doing the work of God was considered by Jesus to be his food (4:34). Food is the general idiom symbolizing bonds and relationships among those on the inside. By using food as the analogy for work, Jesus declares that work also symbolizes the bonds and relationships among those on the inside. These works or signs of Jesus bear witness to the fact that his Father had sent him (5:36; 10:25). The work that Jesus did reflected the tradition that God acted on behalf of his creation and was still at work (5:17). Just as God had expected to be known by his works, so did Jesus expect to be recognized (10:37-38; 14:10-11) by his work as one sent from God. The work to be done by Jesus' audience was to believe in the one whom God had sent (6:29). This belief (not kinship) was the general idiom which symbolized their bonds and relationships.

The death of Jesus was another kind of action that provided testimony. The Johannine passion narrative ends with the side of Jesus being pierced by a lance causing blood and water to flow out. This fulfilled the words from Psalm 34:20 that "Not a bone of him shall be broken." Also recalled are the words from the prophet Zechariah 12:10, "They shall look on him whom they have pierced." Following this, the author writes, "He who saw it has borne witness, his testimony is true, and he knows that he tells the truth— that you also may believe." The gospel of John ends with one final testimony, the last words of the witness,

This is the disciple who is bearing witness to these things, and who has written these things; and we know that his testimony is true. But there are so many things which Jesus did; were every one of them to be written, I suppose that the world itself could not contain the books that would be written (21:24-25).

Power and authority—The basis for God's actions in the world is not patterned after the patriarchal power/submission model. Power and authority as imagined in the fourth gospel perpetuate the cosmic cycle: God initiates and invites; Jesus gives new life to those who receive him and the Spirit's ongoing activity assimilates them into eternal life. In a concrete sense, Jesus was authorized to give life to those whom the Father gave him. Only in this capacity was he empowered by God to act. Jesus repeatedly makes it known in John that he does nothing on his own authority (5:19,30; 8:28), nor does he speak on his own authority (8:28; 12:49; 14:10). Those who desire to do the Father's will know that Jesus is not speaking on his own authority (7:17). Those who speak on their own authority seek their own glory as opposed to those who seek the glory of God. Their word is not true, hence neither reliable nor to be trusted (7:18).

The fourth gospel begins with a new Genesis, the primordial manifestation of God's creative power. The Prologue (1:1-18) establishes the "natural" relation that God initiated between the Word and the world: "all things were made through him, and without him was not anything made that was made" (1:3). Despite this "natural" relation, Jesus was neither recognized nor received by everyone. "But to all who received him, who believed in his name, he gave power to become children of God; who were born not of blood nor of the will of the flesh nor of the will of man, but of God" (1:12-13).[11] This is the new Genesis where generation of God's children was not through family (blood); nor through the desire of human beings (will of the flesh); nor by the decision of human beings (will of man).[12] God's children are brought "into life/belief" by God's choice. This choice, this relation with God, is the root of power.

Power and authority are combined in Jesus **only** to achieve the will of God. Jesus can give life to whomever he wants (5:21) because the Father has "granted the Son also to have life in himself" (5:26). Jesus was given power to judge (5:22), power over his own life, "to lay it down and take it up again" (10:18) as well as power over all flesh, to give eternal life to those whom the Father gave him (17:2). Because of this power, Jesus freely gave himself to each aspect of the life-giving role which had been his from the beginning. He continued adding to it everything that involved nurturing and caring for God's creation. The power and authority which Jesus displayed throughout the gospels is a manifestation and reflection of God's power acting on behalf of his children.

Know/believe and truth—The triad, "know," "believe," and "truth," appears quite frequently in the fourth gospel. Following the account where Jesus arrives in Jerusalem and puts the temple in God's order, Nicodemus, a ruler of the Judeans, came by night to see Jesus while he was in Jerusalem (3:1-21). While he privately expressed his belief that Jesus was a teacher whose works testified that he came from God, Jesus responded by telling him that unless he was born of water and the Spirit, Nicodemus could not enter the kingdom of God, "That which is born of the flesh is flesh, and that which is born of the Spirit is spirit..." When Nicodemus expressed his lack of understanding, Jesus responded, "Are you a teacher of Israel, and yet you do not understand this?" This is more than an isolated question in John; it is both an observation and a reproach that underlies not only this gospel but the synoptics as well.

How is it possible that those who share with Jesus the common background and traditions of Israel do not understand what his works mean nor recognize who sent him? Jesus continues in John, "Truly, truly, I say to you, we speak of what we know and bear witness to what we have seen; yet you do not receive our testimony" (3:11). Like so many others of the house of Israel, Nicodemus showed himself to be an outsider. The Hebrew scriptures are based on the premise that God made himself known to Israel by his words and deeds on their behalf for hundreds of years. Deeds were performed so "that you may know there is no one like the Lord our God" (Ex 8:10); "that you may know that I am the Lord in the midst of the earth" (Ex 8:22); "that you may know that there is none like me in all the earth" (Ex 9:14); "that you may know that the earth is the Lord's" (Ex 9:29). Refrains similar to these are found in nearly every book of the Hebrew Bible where Israel interpreted the hand of God in numerous national events. Jesus had indeed presupposed that their common ground was this "knowledge of God" which was their shared tradition.

As mentioned earlier, the person in the gospels knows with the heart. This kind of knowing involves more than passive perception, it includes active involvement as well. Thus, Jesus "...knew what was in man" (2:25). To know is to experience, and that experience elicits acceptance or desire for possession or rejection. Knowledge is dynamic. To 'know' others is to care for them, to provide, to "acknowledge" them in how one acts. The implication is that **no one can "know"** another **unless s/he wants to know.** Desire for the object is the main motivating force. When Jesus tells the house of Israel that they don't know God, he is not talking about a failure of intellect or some flaw in their judgment. Israel does not know God because they have refused to know. They are no longer motivated by a desire to be involved with God.

Similarly, when Jesus speaks about God knowing him, he implies both God's acceptance and possession of Jesus. Clearly then, both knowledge and love grow together. To "know" God and Jesus secures eternal life because such knowledge presupposes possession where one is actually "in" another.[13] If Jesus' opponents "knew" God, they would "know" Jesus; if they "knew" God they would believe "into" Jesus;[14] if they "knew" God, they would be able to interpret Jesus' signs according to the tradition of God's actions on their behalf. In the book of Ezekiel, the proof-pattern conclusion, so that you/they "will know that I am the Lord," occurs more than sixty times. Psalm 103:7 says, "He made known his ways to Moses, his actions to the people of Israel."

But there was another reality that had been spoken of by Isaiah which described the condition Jesus found: "The ox knows its owner, and the ass its master's crib; but Israel does not know, my people does not understand" (Is 1:3). "Therefore my people go into exile for want of knowledge; their honored men are dying of hunger, and their multitude is parched with thirst" (Is 5:13). It is against this background that Jesus stands and declares his second most important role following that of giving life to the world, "I am the bread of life; he who comes to me shall not hunger, and he who believes in me shall never thirst"(6:35).

In Hebrew, the true "is that to which one can give belief."[15] Such a person or thing must be solid, steadfast, unable to betray the confidence of another, not collapsing under stress or testing. As such, truth presupposes belief and fidelity at the same time. Truth, like knowledge, demands more than intellectual assent, it calls forth personal commitment. A lie is something or someone which is untrustworthy and will ultimately betray the confidence of those foolish enough to trust despite unreliability. Nevertheless, people commit themselves to lies just as readily as others commit themselves to the truth.

The Hebrew word for truth was translated into a Greek word with different nuances within that Hellenistic social system. Insofar as the Greek word also meant something genuine or real, it was like the Hebrew. But for the Greek philosophers, truth was something that was intellectually apprehended while the semitic meaning emphasized truth as something or someone that could be believed and trusted. Fidelity, constancy and reliability are the qualities needed to elicit belief and trust. These are qualities that do not liberate people from ignorance but from improper relations or a lack of righteousness. The integrated model of human beings presumed in the gospels involves concrete interactions between the heart and the external environment mediated by the eyes, mouth/ears and hands/feet. The central values in that world cement relations on all levels, between the earth and humans, among human beings as well as between humans and God.

Human beings create analogies for God which reflect their interpretation of reality and which are based on themselves. Thus, like human beings, God also knows with his eyes and heart. When the temple was built, it was God who "consecrated this house...and put my name there forever; my eyes and my heart will be there for all time"(1 Kgs 9:3//2 Chr 7:16). This insight motivated Jesus to cleanse the temple and then to declare regarding himself, "Destroy this temple, and in three days I will raise it up" (Jn 2:18). As the new temple, Jesus was the place where the eyes and heart of God were located. The work of people was to believe in him. Jesus told the Samaritan woman of an approaching day when God would not be worshiped in any temple or on any mountain, "But the hour is coming and now is, when the true worshipers will worship the Father in spirit and truth, for such the Father seeks to worship him. God is spirit, and those who worship him must worship in spirit and truth" (4:22-23). The presupposition is that in these end times, humans who believe share the same Spirit with God. This allows humans to be constant, faithful and reliable. Thus, worshiping God in Spirit and truth is a real option for believers.

Receive, love, abide—This last cluster to be considered reaches to the heart of interpersonal relations. As previously mentioned, everything is given and received in relations: between the earth and humans, between people as well as between human beings and God. Everyone is bound into a relation according to what one gives and another receives. Those who received insults were bound into a relation of vengeance. Those who received help were bound to do good to those who helped them. Those who received instruction from the Lord were expected to live in a manner showing that they were indeed guided by the "knowledge of God." Those who were wicked were expected to receive according to what others had received from them.

In Mark, Matthew, and Luke, Jesus criticized those whose good deeds were motivated by receiving honor from others in public. Likewise, the fourth gospel mirrors a similar attitude as Jesus says, "I do not receive glory from men" (5:41) and he criticizes those "who receive glory from one another and do not seek the glory that comes from the only God" (5:44). Such motives disqualified actions as binding the actors to God because the intended goal was the honor men gave each other in public (Mt 6:5,16). Such actions bound them only to the audience around them. Those who received the disciples, received Jesus as well as the One who sent him. Ultimately this meant that those who received anyone attached to Jesus were bound in some degree of relation to God who would treat them accordingly (Mt 10:40). The synoptic saying, "for every one who asks receives, and he who seeks finds, and to him who knocks it will be opened" (Lk 11:10; Mt 7:8), describes God's reciprocal response to the needs of those who live in relation with him. The Johannine passage which corresponds to this occurs at the last supper when Jesus says to his disciples, "Hitherto you have asked nothing in my name; ask, and you will receive, that your joy may be full" (16:24).

The synoptics all include accounts about the disciples asking what they, who have left everything and followed Jesus, will receive. The Markan account promises "a hundredfold now in this time, houses and brothers and sisters and mothers and children and lands, with persecution, and in the age to come, eternal life" (Mk 10:30). Matthew promises that they "will receive a hundredfold and inherit eternal life" (Mt 19:29). The Lukan passage promises that there is no one who will not "receive manifold more in this time, and in the age to come eternal life" (Lk 18:30). The promise of eternal life is the fourth stage in the Johannine cycle described at the beginning of this chapter. Eternal life is God's gift to those who believe in Jesus. Nowhere is the relation between receiving, believing and inclusion more clearly stated than in the Prologue (1:12-13), "But to all who received him, who believed in his name, he gave power to become children of God."

Accepting God as Father carries with it some degree of awareness that as God is creator of all, his children are those who are characterized by the understanding of inter-relatedness within creation. This awareness can be externalized in words and actions because attachment to Jesus is the channel through which believers share in his fullness as they receive "grace upon grace" (1:16). The believer is embedded in Jesus as the child is in the mother, and as Jesus is embedded in God. The Johannine perspective includes an understanding that as Word, Jesus has always been an integral part of God's interaction with his creation. As children are not born without mothers, so "were all things made through him, and without him was not anything made that was made. In him was life..." (1:3-4). These analogies are consistent with the image of Jesus and the image of God as Father which are developed in the synoptic gospels. What these images reveal is an image of believer whose total identity arises from receiving Jesus and accepting God's overtures as Father. This carries with it a perspective on the world which is neither compartmentalized nor hierarchically arranged. Radical inter-relatedness is apparent throughout all of creation.

Nature witnesses to just such inter-relatedness. An amoeba, a rose, a hummingbird, a horse, a human being, a juniper and a mountain are each numerically "one" in its own respect despite the diversity and multiplicity of systems contained within each entity. The ocean and land both exist separately. But when viewed from space they constitute one planet, earth. When placed within the context of the universe, earth and all the other planets, stars, etc. existing along with it constitute one gallaxy. This is not a mathematical exercise. Something more profound is being described. God's creation is composed of various systems and levels of complexity, fitting within larger systems of ever increasing complexity.

And how does God exist? As One. The notion of **one** chosen people was the human corollary to the existence of **one** God. When used as a numerical value, "One" reinforces not only exclusivity but separation and disparity as well. For this reason it is an important symbol for patriarchal cultures. Hence, the difference between "one" as a numerical equivalent, and "One" as a description of being, is significant. When scripture says that husband and wife are to become "two in **one** flesh," is that a mathematical exercise or a statement of being? When 1 Samuel 11:7 states, "Then the dread of the Lord fell upon the people, and they came out as **one** man," is that a description of unity or an exercise in subtraction? When Jesus says in John, "I and the Father are one," both Judaism and Islam would correct his response to read, "I and the Father are two." But is Jesus doing simple addition? Each of the last three passages quoted use "one" to mean a description of being which is characterized by unity. Where "one" is used as a description of being, hierarchy, separation and disparity are irrelevant categories. This is the real objection which patriarchy keeps hidden as it purports to defend the Oneness of God. It is not what God loses that is the problem. It is what the elites stand to lose if "One" is accepted by society as a desirable state of being and **not** the confirmation of exclusive status.

Maintaining that Jesus' role is based on that of a wife/mother necessitates rethinking relations and connections among those mentioned in the gospels. Jesus does not take the place of God in any gospel. Jesus lives his total reality as one who is embedded within God and authorized to do everything in God's place. Those who follow Jesus are "like" children who exist in their mother's space and who along with her are embedded in the Father. God's family is not based on accidents of birth. Those who listen to Jesus **choose** belief which is witnessed to by their words and actions. Similarly, Jesus **chose** to live in a relation with God which necessarily included the nurture and care of God's children. Together they all live as one in God. This is the way of nature. The drive toward unity is replicated throughout creation. In relations between God and human beings, this unity is not brought about by accident, coercion or submission but by choice and conviction.

This ordering of the cosmos stands in sharp contrast to that of Israel which arose out of the Mesopotamian ordering of society mentioned at the beginning of this chapter. Following its return to Judea from exile in Babylon, the house of Israel had organized itself around the principle of separation from everything and everyone that compromised the established standards of ritual purity. Maintaining these boundaries guaranteed exclusivity or what was termed holiness. In contrast to this style of life was the perception and life style of Jesus as found in the gospels. The Johannine author first presents Jesus changing the water for ritual purification into wine at a wedding. Second, having demonstrated his zeal in putting the temple in order, Jesus referred to himself as the temple—the new focus of God's eyes and heart. Third, as the previous temple was the focus of all ritual prescriptions and prohibitions, Jesus as the new temple declares the laws regarding ritual purity to be null and void because God will be worshiped in "spirit and truth." Fourth, Jesus declared his own body and blood to be food and drink for eternal life. This radically altered the anti-spirit status of the body and erased the notion that blood is taboo for humans because it belongs to God alone (cf. next chapter). Fifth, despite these radical reversals in standards and behavior, Jesus declared that he had **lost nothing** of what had been entrusted to him by the Father.

In its own way, the Johannine image of Jesus is consistent with that found in the synoptic gospels: Jesus reflects the maternal dimensions of God in relation to the world created through him and sustained by the eternal Father. This is the context in which Jesus talks about believers abiding in him as he abides in the Father where all will abide together in love, as One. Because of the way in which God fathers, reality as interpreted within patriarchies was radically overturned. Time and space no longer existed within the boundaries defined by society. But even more unthinkable and unacceptable, God was not restrained by the boundaries that elites had devised for him.

V.

JESUS: SYMBOL AND FOCUS OF THE HOUSEHOLD

Introduction—John the Baptist played a prominent role in each of the gospels. His life was interpreted as inaugurating the new age and his death signaled the inability of leaders to adapt values that outweighed concerns about honor. Unless the people and their leaders were willing to fully immerse themselves in a new direction, the words and works of Jesus would cultivate envy and rejection instead of belief and inclusion. When Jesus predicted his death, he did not foretell the future. He rather reflected on the past and understood the inevitable clash if behavior and beliefs did not change. His major responsibility was to lose nothing of what the Father had given him. Teaching, healing and feeding those in his care were duties that drew public attention to Jesus. Blinded by their popular image of God, many in his audiences were unable to see in Jesus **God's** activity on behalf of human beings. Despite this inability of eyes to see, ears to hear and hearts to change, Jesus continued to act on behalf of God. As such, Jesus was faithful to his duties, carrying them out according to the heart/mind of God.

Both John the Baptist and Jesus had proclaimed that God's kingdom was at hand and that total immersion in change was the only appropriate response to this advancing kingdom. The activity of the Spirit enabled Jesus to break free of the social hold which disguised itself as the will of God. Jesus and those who followed him began to live in the present as though their liberation from the limitations of social groups was complete and God alone ruled.

The end of the gospels needs to be regarded carefully, for this was the culmination of Jesus' life. The theological explanations or commentaries on the meaning of Jesus' death arose within social systems that were organized around the maintenance of honor. Since honor was the central social value around which all life was organized, it is not surprising that Jesus' death was interpreted as a bloody sacrifice demanded by God to atone for the sins of human beings. Temple sacrifice had been the institution established to maintain the honor of God, and it provided the analogy for understanding Jesus' death. This interpretation failed to take into account the image of God that Jesus revealed. In fact, the image that eclipsed the gospel image of God is

99

that found in the Hebrew scriptures where God demands that Abraham sacri-
fice his son Isaac (Gen 22:1-20). This account as related in the *Qur'an*
(Surah 37:100-113) differs in that the son to be sacrificed is the first born son
Ishma'el. Both scriptures depict Abraham as the social and religious arche-
type of the father who is prepared to sacrifice his children for greater gain
(Gen 22:15-19).

THE SIGNIFICANCE OF PLACE AND TIME

Jerusalem—Since the time of Solomon's temple, Jerusalem had been
considered the center of the kingdom of Israel. There the high priest represented the people to the foreign powers who governed them. He was also the
official who offered the sacrifices in the temple on behalf of the people as
commanded by God. With the division of Solomon's kingdom, the southern
kingdom, Judea, was regarded as a temple state. In the Hellenistic period
Jerusalem was called "Hierosolyma" like other temple cities of Syria and
Asia Minor who termed themselves *hierapolis*.[1] Because the high priest
served in an official capacity in the temple along with being the official representative of his people to civil rulers, the religious, political, economic and
social dimensions were fused together. Boundaries were recognized only
when they were violated, e.g. when the foreign powers wanted to include
their own gods or images in Jerusalem and the people rebelled. Otherwise all
social institutions were welded together and the high priest replicated and
personally embodied that alliance between Israel and secular powers.

Passover—Passover was the time of the year when people were
expected to participate in the full enjoyment of life which included an abundance of food and drink. Whether Passover was celebrated outside Jerusalem
or within the city, people were expected to spend their second tithe on food,
drink and scented oils.[2] This feast was "a memorial and re-enactment of one
of Israel's greatest days, when it passed from the old to the new world of
Israel's blessings and hopes."[3] Passover centered around a meal shared by
families where all members participated. The arrival of the Messiah was
expected at Passover. Male children were taught to ask ritualized questions
"as a recall and a sort of revival of the beginnings of the nation, of the first
taste of liberation and of the profound hope then awakened of final redemption. Family, national and religious feeling reached its acme."[4]

The last supper—The synoptics have set the time period and context
for the last supper as the Passover meal when the ceremonial meal was to be
eaten by families. In addition to this, Jesus' words and actions at this meal
give his insights into the meaning of his death. Each gospel has a slightly different account and the differences are worth noting.

> And as they were eating, he took bread, and blessed, and broke it, and gave it to them and said, "Take, this is my body." Then he took a cup and when he had given thanks he gave it to them and they all drank of it. And he said to them, "This is my blood of the covenant, which is poured out for many. Truly, I say to you, I shall not drink again of the fruit of the vine until that day when I drink it new in the kingdom of God" (Mk 14:22-25).

The bread was blessed. A blessing is an acknowledgment of God's benefi-cence. Blessing bread acknowledges food as part of the cycle of life that originates with God and returns to God. Jesus gave thanks over (blessed) the cup which included not only the wine but the entire passion and death which Jesus refers to in Mark 14:36 as "his cup." After they drink it, he tells them that it is his covenant blood which is "poured out for many." According to the cultural beliefs of Jesus' time, life was in the blood. "For the life of every creature is in the blood of it; therefore, I have said to the people of Israel, You shall not eat the blood of any creature, for the life of every creature is its blood; whoever eats it shall be cut off" (Lev 17:14). Thus, it was forbidden for human consumption because it belonged to God, "for it is the blood that makes atonement, by reason of the life" (Lev 17:11).

Jesus knew that the public religious ritual involving blood and sacrifice was presided over by priests in the temple. They were the only ones who were recognized as offering valid sacrifices. He also knew that blood was not consumed by human beings because blood contained the life which was derived from God. While some of the burnt flesh of the ritual sacrifices might be eaten by the priests and people who participated, the blood belonged to God alone. While Jesus used ritual language when speaking about his blood being "poured out for many," he gave that blood to his fol-lowers, those surrounding him at the last supper. If Jesus had understood his own death to be a sacrifice of atonement for sins, he could not have given his blood to be consumed by his followers. Instead, his words give no indication that he interpreted his pending death as a public sacrifice to appease God's honor. It was precisely **because** Jesus knew that all blood contained life and that all life belongs to God that he gave his blood to be consumed by his fol-lowers. In addition to this, that which was solely and uniquely himself or "his own," namely his body, Jesus gave as well. He gave everything that he had received from God to those whom God had called his children.

Thus, if Jesus did not think about his own death as one of atonement for the sins of mankind, and if he only did and taught what he was authorized to do, then we must conclude that God did not view his death in that light either. His death, which was both brought about by, and officiated over by, anti-God forces, was not **for** God. Jesus was not a stand-in for human beings and killed by the will of God. As the symbol and focus of God's household on earth, Jesus was **God's** stand-in. His death was brought about by leaders who killed him **in place** of God. More will be said about this as the passion account unfolds.

Now the Matthean account of the meal scene:

> Now as they were eating, Jesus took bread, and blessed, and broke it, and gave it to the disciples and said, "Take, eat; this is my body." And he took a cup, and when he had given thanks he gave it to them, saying, "Drink of it, all of you; for this is my blood of the covenant, which is poured out for many for the forgiveness of sins. I tell you I shall not drink again of this fruit of the vine until that day when I drink it new with you in my Father's kingdom" (Mt 26:26-29).

Following the last supper, Peter betrayed Jesus. Eventually he recognized his own complicity: "And he went out and wept bitterly" (Mt 26:75). Judas also recognized his own guilt when he saw that Jesus had been condemned: "I have sinned in betraying innocent blood." His confession changed nothing with the priests and elders. He threw down his pieces of silver in the temple and hanged himself (Mt 27:3-10), a life for a life. Both men had participated in the last upper and shared in the covenant which bound all of them to Jesus. Peter took advantage of that covenant to repent his own betrayal. Judas, on the other hand, did not take advantage of the covenant to repent his complicity in the death of an innocent man, but ended his own life, thus sealing his fate.

The Lukan account of the last supper begins with Jesus telling them that he "will not eat it again until it is fulfilled in the kingdom of God."

> And he took a cup, and when he had given thanks he said, "Take this, and divide it among yourselves; for I tell you that from now on I shall not drink of the fruit of the vine until the kingdom of God comes." And he took bread, and when he had given thanks he broke it and gave it to them, saying, "This is my body, which is given for you. Do this in remembrance of me." And likewise the cup after supper, saying, "This cup which is poured out for you is the new covenant in my blood" (Lk 22:17-21).

This is the only gospel account that contains the command to "do this in remembrance of me," and that command only follows Jesus' words, "This is my body which is given for you—do this in remembrance of me." It is not clear whether Jesus means for people to give themselves for others in memory of him (not their deaths as these words do not follow his blood being poured out), or whether this refers to the entire ritual as such.

The account that stands out in the minds of many Christians comes from Paul's first letter to the Corinthians (11:23-26):

> For I received from the Lord what I also delivered to you, that the Lord Jesus on the night when he was betrayed took bread, and when he had given thanks, he broke it, and said, "This is my body which is for you. Do this in remembrance of me." In the same way also the cup, after supper, saying, "This cup is the new covenant in my blood. Do this, as often as you drink it, in remembrance of me." For as often as you eat this bread and drink the cup, you proclaim the Lord's death until he comes.

The tradition Paul hands on intimates an understanding of the meaning behind the death of Jesus quite different from that found in the gospels. The question remains why that tradition superseded the traditions found in the gospels. But more will be said about Paul's theology in Chapter VI.

The Lukan last supper narrative also voices the disciples' concern over who is the greatest among them, the issue with which Jesus began the last supper in John. Jesus' response is consistent throughout all four of the gospels: the oldest becomes the youngest and the leader serves everyone. The journey motif, followed by their reunion in the kingdom of God (or house in which there are many rooms—Jn 14:2), is common to all the gospels. Peter's denial is predicted at the Lukan last supper by Jesus, while both Matthew and Mark wait until Gethsemane before including it. Finally, the Lukan account narrates a change in the ground rules for missionary activity. Such activity was now to take on the characteristics of a much longer journey (compared to shorter distances where they were commissioned to spread the gospel).

In summary, Jesus asked to be remembered in the context of a family meal where everyone participated to celebrate their liberation from bondage to serve God. Jesus' blood replaced that of the Passover lamb; the demands of the kingdom eclipsed the obsession with land. His followers would be saved from assimilation into the kingdoms of men and would one day experience fully the kingdom of God when Jesus would drink wine again with them. The original exodus set out from a foreign country to a land of their own. Jesus' personal journey began in this "promised land," a land which was no more ruled by God than Egypt had been. Jesus' death and his cross became the symbol of how far both Israel and the Gentiles were from ruling according to the heart/mind of God.

The gospel of John: The last supper (13:1–17:26)—John does not include an account about bread and wine within the context of the last supper. Instead there is an earlier discourse which takes place near the Passover time of his second year of public life. Jesus had escaped the crowds who had been impressed enough by his feeding of the five thousand to want to make him king. This was the occasion which prompted him to talk about his flesh and blood as food and drink for eternal life (Jn 6:22-71). John uses the word which means "flesh" as opposed to the word used in the synoptics which means "body." What both terms share in common is their antithesis to the spirit. In the synoptics when Jesus makes his body and blood the essential ingredients in the new covenant meal, he is giving his followers his body (which in and of itself has no life) joined with his blood (which contains his life). Since Jesus was raised from the dead and lives at the right hand of God (Acts 2:33-34), believers who eat his body and drink his blood share in his eternal life. But the synoptics do not labor over the meaning or implications of what Jesus does—perhaps not to create significant obstacles for the uninitiated.

The last supper in the gospel of John takes a different approach from that found in the synoptics,

> Now before the feast of the Passover, when Jesus knew that his hour had come to depart out of this world to the Father, having loved his own who were in the world, he loved them to the end (13:1).

The third passover, in John's chronology, is **just approaching** when Jesus eats his last meal with his disciples. He is aware that "the Father had given all things into his hands, and that he had come from God and was going to God." At that point, he girded himself in a towel and began to wash their feet. The sequence for Jesus' action is significant: he was at a point of maximum power since the Father had given all things into his hands and he was returning to God. The departure theme was a central theme in the fourth gospel as well as in the synoptics. But what did he hope to accomplish in washing the feet of his disciples? His answer first came in response to Peter's protest that Jesus should not wash his feet, "If I do not wash you, you have no part in me" (13:8). When he finished, he took his place and asked if they understood what he had done.

Jesus' final action was charged with meaning on several levels. First and most obvious, he inverted the hierarchy upon which the social order was built and maintained. Regardless of what was the custom in the houses of men, within God's household, it was considered appropriate behavior for those with greater power to serve those with less or no power. Most houses did not have slaves, so Jesus' followers were expected to act **like** those who acted like servants, e.g. women, girls, children. Second, washing feet was the transition ceremony in which dirt from the **outside** was washed off so that one might be adequately prepared to go **inside**. As teacher and leader, Jesus took personal responsibility for the inclusion of others in God's household, the same task that fell to women in charge of their children who needed to be washed before coming inside. Jesus expected his disciples to continue this activity in his absence so that no one would be excluded. Merely knowing this was inadequate; they were blessed only if they **acted** on what they knew (13:17).

Status and integrity vs. self-expenditure—Status is "normally and actively protective of itself, does not allow of being mistaken for what is lower, insists on being acknowledged for what it is and makes vigorous and vigilant assertion of itself. How is it that God's Messiah shared a greater affinity with those whose forms of status consist in giving themselves away, in cherishing the other at its own expense?"[5] Jesus' status as Son of man and Son of God was fulfilled not in self-reservation, that is in the maintenance of his own integrity (wholeness) or the integrity of his group, but in self-expenditure on behalf of others.

Patriarchal cultures in the ancient world (as well as today) took for granted that the male was superior to the female. It was believed that males alone possessed integrity or completeness, the fullness of human expression. The emphasis placed on loyalty and friendship among males affirmed the position they shared as social equals. That is, they were subjects in relations while women were the objects or means by which males satisfied their sexual desires, produced children and had the domestic domain supervised.[6] As master or teacher of his disciples, Jesus' role was that of subject, the one in charge who judges, acts and makes decisions on behalf of his group. In this capacity, according to the rules which applied to male groups, his failure to deal with Judas before his treachery could undermine the integrity of the entire group is a striking breach of male values.

Jesus' failure to act according to the expectations of male leaders is consistent with his entire public life. It is clear that he regards both the disciples and his followers as being more like children, those family members whose age and inexperience do not require the same behavior as that expected of adults. Even in families, there is a greater tolerance of human weakness and error among members than is shown among non-related, adult males in public where choosing reliable males for intimate companions is an area related to honor. Jesus' request in Luke that giving his body be repeated in memory of him, and his insistence in John 6:35-59 that his body and blood continue to be consumed for eternal life signified that this loss of his bodily integrity was positively valued by him. In patriarchal cultures, "bodily integrity" belonged only to males who were thought to have "the perfectly formed, complete and therefore normative body."[7] The maintenance of rigid gender roles was to protect the male from any activity that would threaten this completeness and integrity by acting like a female.

The Passion and Death Accounts—Every gospel testifies to the betrayal of Judas, the flight of Jesus' disciples when he is arrested and Peter's denial (another kind of betrayal). Both Mark 14:26 and Matthew 26:30 begin their accounts in Gethsemane when Peter's denial is predicted. He protests vehemently along with all the disciples that they will never deny him. Next Jesus advises Peter, James and John to watch and pray with him but they fail to do either. In each of the synoptics, Jesus asks the Father that his cup might be removed or passed from him. But each time (three times in Matthew and Mark, once in Luke) he makes that request, he concludes it by saying, "yet, not what I will, but what thou wilt" or, as in Luke, "nevertheless, not my will but thine be done."

This concluding prayer is alien to rabbinic Judaism where the hope of the request being granted is a necessary component. Prayer exists to be heard and answered by God. Ending prayer with the words "Not my will but thine be done" undercuts the premise on which Jewish prayer is based, namely that God should hear and do as he is asked.[8] This kind of prayer which presumes God should do as he is asked was antithetical to Jesus' belief that the world of man was to be organized around God, not God around the world of man.

Arrest and trial (Mk 14:43–15:20//Mt 26:47–27:31//Lk 22:47–23:31//Jn 18:2–19:16)—The arrest scenes in the synoptics all have Jesus commenting that those who have come after him look as though they have come to arrest a robber. As the events unfold, Jesus was first taken to the high priest, the public representative of Israel. There, Jesus was accused of blasphemy; by speaking of himself as God's equal he was stealing prominence that belonged to God alone. When taken to the Roman authorities, the crowds called for the death sentence to keep him from stealing power that belonged to Caesar alone. Both Judean and Roman accusations cast him in the role of a brigand (social bandit) at very high, symbolic levels.

As previously noted, envy is an emotion directed against someone that "stems from the desire to acquire something possessed by another person, while jealousy is rooted in the fear of losing something already possessed."[9] Since everything in life was limited, the popularity of Jesus was viewed as taking away the authority and prominence as well as the followers to which other leaders laid claim. If those leaders could strip Jesus of his following, he would no longer be a contender, and life would reassume its proper balance. But because the admission of envy is the admission of inferiority, human beings cloak envy in a variety of rationales and symbolic actions. There is ample evidence in all the gospel texts that envy was the root of escalating hostility as well as the driving force which set in motion those who desired Jesus' downfall. His popularity had exceeded what was appropriate for his status. Evidence of envy is present in the following words and actions:

1) in a line of questioning by authorities who wanted to determine if Jesus saw himself as the equal of God and/or Caesar;

2) in Pilate's explicit realization that the Judeans handed Jesus over out of envy in Mark 15:10 and Matthew 27:18;

3) in the taunts of the soldiers and bystanders in all the gospels aimed at humiliating or reducing Jesus from the status they felt he had falsely assumed, e.g. that he should prophesy blindfolded concerning who is hitting him; the derisive use of the epithet "King of the Judeans"; the taunts at the cross that Jesus could build the temple in three days and/or save others, but could not save himself;

4) in the physical treatment meant to humiliate and shame Jesus in his own eyes as well as in the eyes of his followers;

5) in the choice the crowd made to free Barabbas who certainly aroused no envy in anyone (according to Mark 15:7 and Luke 23:19, he had committed murder during an insurrection; in Matthew 27:16, Barabbas was "a notorious prisoner"; and John 18:40 states that he was a brigand);

6) in dividing Jesus' clothing among soldiers to deprive him quite concretely of his personal belongings;

7) in death by crucifixion which casts Jesus outside the house of Israel, stripped of his inheritance, his people and his God,

> And if a man has committed a crime punishable by death and he is put to death, and you hang him on a tree, his body shall not remain all night upon the tree, but you shall bury him the same day, for **a hanged man is accursed by God;** you shall not defile your land which the Lord your God gives you for an inheritance (Deut 21:22-23).

In all accounts Jesus is charged with being "King of the Judeans." In the Matthean arrest in the garden, Jesus told his followers that his Father could send twelve legions of angels if he asked (Mt 26:53). In Matthew 26:64, Jesus talks about the Son of man sitting at the right hand of the Power (Lk 22:69) and coming on the clouds of heaven. In the Johannine account, Jesus tells Pilate that his kingship is neither of this world nor from the world (Jn 18:36). Then Pilate asks him if he is a king, and Jesus answered, "You say that I am a king. For this I was born, and for this I have come into the world, to bear witness to the truth. Everyone who is of the truth hears my voice" (Jn 18:37). The Markan answer to Pilate's question was merely, "You have said so" (Mk 15:2). In no account does Jesus back down from the role that the Son of man enjoys in the kingdom. The power and authority with which he speaks, the power with which he heals, casts out spirits, etc. is an extension of his position in the kingdom of God.

The crowds—Since power is something to fear, one common way of seeking relief from the tension that fear creates is to make a grotesque figuration or to make the person grotesque in order to elicit comic relief.[10] "Horror is kept at bay by its debasement to ridicule."[11] Jesus' scourging, crowning with thorns and the mockery to which he was subjected reduced him to a grotesque figure that elicited humor in the crowds that had already gathered when Pilate allowed them to choose between Jesus and Barabbas. In the act of becoming grotesque, "male bodies take on precisely the characteristics regularly attributed to female bodies; they lose form and integrity, become penetrable... Like women's bodies, the grotesque male body is no longer clearly differentiated from the world, but transferred, merged, and fused with it."[12]

Abuse, deformity, torture and derision were conditions that elicited humor in people long before the middle ages and continue to do so among many people today. For those who find themselves on the bottom of society's hierarchical ladder, others who fall victim to public censure and abuse provide the temporary setting for an anonymous public to find its voice and enjoy momentary power over someone who is beneath them. The greater the fall in status for the group-designated victim, the greater the enjoyment and enhanced feeling of security and power the crowd feels.

Death and burial (Mk 15:22-47//Mt 27:33-66//Lk 23:33-56//Jn 19:17-42)—There are no additional words, symbols or explanations in the synoptics beyond those at the last supper where Jesus talks about his blood of the covenant which is poured out for many. "His blood be on us and on our children" (Mt 27:25) was the explicit statement made by the Judean crowd in the Matthean scene when the death sentence was pronounced. At the death of Jesus, the Lukan crowd was visibly repentant. "And all the multitude who assembled to see the sight, when they saw what had taken place, returned home beating their breasts" (Lk 23:48). Since everyone is "covered" by the new covenant in Jesus' blood, there is time until the person's death to repent and accept God's saving action. The Johannine account recalls the words from the prophet Zechariah 12:10, "And I will pour out on the house of David and the inhabitants of Jerusalem a spirit of compassion and supplication, so that when **they look on him whom they have pierced,** they shall mourn for him, as one mourns for an only child, and weep bitterly over him, as one weeps over a first-born." (The highlighted words are those quoted in John 19:37.)

Apparently the Gentiles in the Markan community were not concerned about Judean complicity or their repentance. Instead, the Markan Jesus utters words from Psalm 22, "My God, my God, why hast thou abandoned me?" (Mk 15:34). These are not spiritual words about a faith crisis. The context is the concrete circumstances where Jesus has been left in charge of what belongs to God. Had God been there taking care of his own affairs, none of this would be happening to Jesus. But the world of human beings is governed by man and the kingdom of heaven is ruled by God. Those two worlds came together in Jesus. But men do not rule according to the designs of God. And while rulers have considerably less power than God, they hold the power of death in their own world.

Passover was the appropriate time for this new covenant-in-blood. As Son of man, Jesus followed the Father's voice and designs at the cost of his own life. He held fast to what God expected of him even after John's death when he knew that such relentless activity on his part would result in his own death as well. However, Jesus' death would have yielded nothing had it not been for God's initiative to raise Jesus from the dead and transform him.

THE RESURRECTION: GOD RESTORES JESUS' HONOR

Gospel accounts (Mk 16:1–20//Mt 28:1–20//Lk 24:1-53//Jn 20:1–21:14)—All gospel accounts write that the resurrection of Jesus was discovered on the first day of the week by Mary Magdalene. All but Matthew go on to say that the stone had already been rolled away and Jesus was gone. Each account includes variations in time (whether it was still dark, dawn or the sun had risen); in who goes to the tomb, e.g. Mary Magdalene is alone in John and accompanied by one or more women in the synoptic accounts; in what happens at the tomb: Mark speaks of one young man seated inside; Luke speaks of two men who stood in dazzling apparel; John speaks of no one until Mary returns with Peter and the beloved disciple—they then see two angels in white inside the tomb. But Matthew does something more in keeping with the role of Moses which Jesus was steadily superseding.

Matthew presents a scene at the site of Jesus' tomb following his resurrection that recalls the appearance of Yahweh on the third day to Moses and the assembled crowds:

> Now at daybreak on the third day there were peals of thunder on the mountain and lightning flashes, a dense cloud and a loud trumpet blast, and inside the camp all the people trembled (Ex 19:16).

Compare this with the account in Matthew:

> Now after the sabbath, toward the dawn of the first day of the week,

> Mary Magdalene and the other Mary went to see the sepulchre. And
> behold, there was a great earthquake; for an angel of the Lord descend-
> ed from heaven and came and rolled back the stone, and sat upon it. His
> appearance was like lightining and his raiment was white as snow. And
> for fear of him the guards trembled and became like dead men (28:1-4).

There are two more comparisons to be made between the activity of God
through Moses and the activity of God as witnessed in Jesus:

> Yahweh said to Moses, "Go down and warn the people not to pass
> beyond the bounds to come and look on Yahweh, or many of them will
> lose their lives" (Ex 19:21).

> And behold, Jesus met them and said, "Hail!"And they came and took
> hold of his feet and worshiped him. Then Jesus said to them, "Do not
> be afraid; go and tell my bretheren to go to Galilee, and there they will
> see me" (Mt 28:9-10).

The activity of God-in-Jesus allows for closeness unlike the God-encounters
in the Hebrew scriptures, including the encounters with Moses.

Matthew closes with the eleven disciples on the mountain in Galilee
where ". . . they worshiped him; **but some doubted**" (28:17). The condition
which Jesus labored to change was there until the very end. Those were the
best that the house of Israel had to offer, his hand-picked disciples, the ones
who had watched him, followed him and frequently misunderstood him.
Matthew ends with an edict:

> And Jesus came and said to them, "All authority in heaven and on
> earth has been given to me. Go therefore and make disciples of all
> nations, baptizing them in the name of the Father and of the Son and of
> the Holy Spirit, teaching them to observe all that I have commanded
> you; and lo, I am with you always, to the close of the age" (28:18-20).

As for Mark, some ancient manuscripts of this account have nothing
beyond 16:8. The man at the tomb who was dressed in white had told the
women that Jesus had risen and gone before them to Galilee. The women are
to tell the disciples to meet him there. "And they went out and fled from the
tomb; for trembling and astonishment had come upon them; and they said
nothing to anyone, for they were afraid" (16:8). Some manuscripts added,
"But they reported briefly to Peter and those with him all that they had been
told. And after this, Jesus himself sent out by means of them, from east to
west, the sacred and imperishable proclamation of eternal salvation."[13]

The longer ending that follows 16:8 includes an appearance to Mary Magdalene the same morning that Jesus was raised from the dead. Following this, she told the others that he was alive, but they would not believe her. Later, he appeared to two of them as they were walking in the country. When they reported to the other disciples, these witnesses were not believed either. Following that, Jesus appeared to the eleven as they were eating, "and he upbraided them for their unbelief and hardness of heart because they had not believed those who saw him after he had risen" (Mk 16:14). Despite this, he goes on to empower them to spread the gospel,

> Go into all the world and preach the gospel to the whole creation. He who believes and is baptized will be saved; but he who does not believe will be condemned. And these signs will accompany those who believe: in my name they will cast out demons; they will speak in new tongues; they will pick up serpents, and if they drink any deadly thing, it will not hurt them; they will lay hands on the sick and they will recover.
>
> So then the Lord Jesus, after he had spoken to them, was taken up into heaven, and sat down at the right hand of God. And they went forth and preached everywhere, while the Lord worked with them and confirmed the message by the signs that attended it. Amen (Mk 16:15-20).

As Jesus had continued the work of proclamation and baptism begun by John the Baptist, the disciples of Jesus were expected to continue the same activity. The signs which showed the activity of God in Jesus were expected to be seen by his disciples as well.

The gospel of Luke includes an account that takes place on the road to Emmaus. It involves an appearance of Jesus to two followers. One is named Cleopas and the other remains unknown. The two men returned to "the eleven gathered together and those who were with them" (Lk 24:33b) to describe their encounter with Jesus on the road to Emmaus. While recounting their experience Jesus appeared in the midst of his gathered followers. But even when they all saw Jesus, they could neither believe their own eyes nor understand what his resurrection meant. Finally he took a piece of broiled fish and ate it so they could see that he was no spirit from the dead. As he explained many things to the two on the road to Emmaus, he did so again to the gathered disciples,

> Thus it is written, that the Christ should suffer and on the third day rise from the dead, and that repentance and forgiveness of sins should be preached in his name to all nations, beginning

from Jerusalem. You are witnesses of these things. And behold, I
send the promise of my Father upon you; but stay in the city,
until you are clothed with power from on high. Then he led them
out as far as Bethany, and lifting up his hands he blessed them.
While he blessed them, he parted from them, and was carried up
into heaven. And they returned to Jerusalem with great joy, and
were continually in the temple blessing God (Lk 24:45-53).

In this Lukan account Jesus leaves his followers in Bethany. The shorter
Markan ending tells the women that everyone is to meet Jesus in Galilee. The
longer ending seems to infer that he appeared to his disciples in Jerusalem and
left from there. Matthew clearly states that Jesus led them to a mountain in
Galilee where he disappeared from their sight. The fourth gospel has its own
way of recounting the basic message that Jesus was raised and transformed
from the dead; those attached to him were to be cared for by his disciples as
proof of their love for him and the proclamation of the kingdom was to continue.

John states that Jesus appeared to Mary Magdalene in the garden where
the tomb was located. Finally recognizing him, she addressed him as
Teacher. He tells her, "Do not hold me, for I have not yet ascended to the
Father; but go to my brethren and say to them, I am ascending to my Father
and your Father, to my God and your God" (20:17). Mary told the others, and
on the evening of that same day, Jesus appeared before them even though the
doors had been locked out of fear of the Jews. He showed them his wounds
so that they would believe it was he. He then gave them the Holy Spirit along
with power to forgive sins. Despite the witness of everyone present, Thomas,
who had been absent, did not believe that Jesus has been raised. When finally
confronted by Jesus, Thomas believed, but Jesus said to him, "Have you
believed because you have seen me? Blessed are those who have not seen and
yet believe" (20:29).

By the next scene, everyone has returned to the Sea of Tiberias
(Galilee) where they are fishing. The miraculous catch of fish (a parallel
found in Luke 5:4-11 immediately before Jesus calls Peter) is the result of
Jesus' command to cast the net on the right side of the boat. They did this
without recognizing him until after they saw the size of their catch. The
beloved disciple told Peter that he recognized the man on the shore as Jesus.
Described as his third appearance, he cooked breakfast for them on the shore
(21:9-14). Following this, Jesus asked Peter three times if Peter loved him.
Each time after Peter said "yes," Jesus told him to tend and/or feed his sheep.
After that, he told Peter to follow him. The beloved disciple is mentioned
again as starting out to follow them when Peter asks, "Lord, what about this
man?" Jesus tells him that the beloved disciple is to remain until Jesus

comes. This started a rumor that the beloved disciple was not to die. The gospel ends:

> This is the disciple who is bearing witness to these things, and who had written these things; and we know that his testimony is true. But there are also many other things which Jesus did; were every one of them to be written, I suppose that the world itself could not contain the books that would be written (21:24-25).

The one aspect which all resurrection accounts make no effort to hide is the disbelief that greeted any announcement that Jesus was alive. His resurrection was no easier for his disciples to accept and interpret than his parables or the actions of his life had been. His disciples were no more heroic at the news of his resurrection than they had been at the scene of his death. They were no quicker in accepting this new reality than they had been in accepting other aspects of Jesus' life and teaching. Nonetheless, he empowered his followers to carry on what he had taught them. Despite the fear which prompted Peter to deny Jesus and all of them to abandon him, there was no recrimination or rejection from Jesus.

The Resurrection: God's Validation of Jesus as Focus and Symbol of the Household—From the onset of the gospels, Jesus' total immersion in the changes initiated through his baptism underscored the belief that he did not exist apart from God and the establishment of God's household.[14] The tests that followed revealed that Jesus was so totally embedded in God that no competing security, power or promise exerted any control over him. This total dependence on God enabled Jesus to establish a household on earth that reflected the standards of the kingdom of heaven. Jesus was both functionally and symbolically associated with God's household. That is, his actions and identity were intimately linked with it. His most important achievements were those that led to the creation and maintenance of believers who became children of God. This was the activity that most clearly validated his identity in God. Jesus was authorized to act and speak on God's behalf in the interest of his household.

Jesus mirrored the Father in heaven to his family on earth. Thus, Jesus' activity with his disciples can be interpreted as accomplishing the task of social reproduction according to the standards of the kingdom: 1) by fostering an environment where the 'young' or new members were allowed to grow and mature; 2) by commissioning those he chose and socialized to continue his activity; 3) by contributing to the renewal and regeneration of older members. His teaching as well as his example of suffering communicated to his disciples how to struggle well, how to cope with the need to work hard in a hard world and how to resist the personal erosion that comes from this work.

As mediator between the privacy of the household and the public, Jesus acted as sentry guarding the boundaries of the domestic domain from the unwanted intrusion of outside influences. It was his responsibility to establish and maintain control of what polluted or defiled (not blood, sickness or death, but what comes from the heart). Words and actions were to mirror the intentions and actions of God on behalf of his creation. Thus, Jesus was given power over various aspects and manifestations of: 1) nature as reflected in human biology, e.g. healing the sick, reviving the dead; 2) human nature as created in social groups, e.g. overturning what had previously been the customs, beliefs and values; 3) nature as environment, e.g. stilling the storm, multiplying bread for the crowds.

The move from the outside of the house to the inside totally changed the quality of social relationships as the Fatherhood of God recast all believers in a different network of relations. The self-image of each member reflected this primary source of identity as children of God. Food was the general idiom in which this new set of relationships within the household was expressed, e.g. feeding of the multitudes; eating with sinners; the abandonment of purity regulations; bread and wine as body and blood; and a meal celebration of a new covenant that linked the members of the household on earth to Jesus.

He personally symbolized the relationship between the house of God and the houses of men. Jesus was personally the target for criticism which was leveled against him, e.g. his teachings as well as his disciples' behavior. Nonetheless, Jesus' words and example moved "outside" in search of believers who would be included in God's household. These new members carried inside the alien customs, values and beliefs which they held. It was Jesus' responsibility to overcome by word and example these contradictions that existed between what his household members individually reflected and what the Father wanted.

In the passion and death of Jesus, the social isolation of God's house was symbolized by Jesus as a social figure. This isolation was communicated by him as a social participant and it was re-created by Jesus as a social actor. His death was the direct result of his attachment to and total embeddedness in God. It also reflected that within this household, Jesus made every effort to ensure that God was in control, even when it resulted in his own death. Jesus' subordination to God in all things made him the weaker one and God the stronger. Jesus' obedience muffled the limits which the world outside the household placed on God's efforts on behalf of his creation. Jesus turned God's public impotence into his own private impotence, obscuring the Father's rejection by the kingdoms of men with his own death.

Not limited by the social rules that normally circumscribe the legitimate use of power, Jesus criticized Jewish leaders who took advantage of the poor and powerless. While Jesus himself had no legitimate power to change anything, he subverted and disrupted normal social relationships. If power is most often seen in what men control, then Jesus was powerful over various manifestations of nature and demons. But he was totally dependent on the persuasive powers of his words and actions to influence human beings on behalf of God. The fact that Jesus was arrested, tortured and killed despite his innocence and goodness indicates that being a moral symbol endowed him with no real power as defined in the world of men.

The body of Jesus both represented and replicated his house (that is, those attached to Jesus who called God Father) within the social world. Authorized and empowered to act in God's place, Jesus symbolized the isolation of the house of God and its utter alienation from the kingdoms of men. While foxes had holes and the birds of the air had nests provided for them by nature, the Son of man had nowhere to lay his head (Mt 8:20//Lk 9:58). Turned into a grotesque mockery of the power that was alternately feared and envied in him, Jesus was tortured, stripped and killed by crucifixion because of what he had done in God's name. It is clear from the last supper accounts that Jesus did not consider himself to be either priest or sacrifice, he was not dying to atone for sins. He was killed because those who "officially" represented God and interpreted his will had established a social system at odds with the designs of God as revealed in Jesus. He was a stand-in, but not for man whom God wanted to punish; he was a stand-in for God whose overtures human beings rejected.

Jesus died as a "ransom" because he freed God's children from the total control of the kingdoms of men. His life was the ransom paid to the houses of Israel and the Gentiles so that the children of God might be free of culture's social/religious hold which went against the designs of God. His death gave resounding witness to just how far society was from the heart/mind of God. The traditional analogy which interprets the death of Jesus as a necessary sacrifice demanded by God for the sins of mankind was created out of that same patriarchal religious perspective that had first failed to see God's activity in Jesus. It is not surprising that traditional theology continued to use the patriarchal public perspective for interpreting the death of Jesus as an act of sacrifice to God in place of sinful human beings.

Jesus' death as a revelation of God—It is ironic that the God of Abraham eclipsed the God of Jesus in the minds of Christians. Earlier in Genesis Abraham had been willing to sacrifice Sarah for the personal gain he received from this arrangement with the Egyptian pharaoh (Gen 12:10-20) and again with the king of Gerar (Gen 20). Abraham became a wealthy man through these deceptions, and not surprisingly his son Isaac followed his example with his own wife, Rebekah (Gen 26). The "God" who **tested** Abraham had earlier been threatened by the tower of Babel because "they are one people, and they have all one language; and this is only the beginning of what they will do; and nothing that they propose to do will now be impossible for them. Come, let us go down and there confuse their language that they may not understand one another's speech" (Gen 11:1-10). This God bears a striking resemblance to the God in the garden who expelled Adam and Eve from there "because the man has become like one of us, knowing good and evil; and now, lest he put forth his hand and take also of the tree of life, and eat, and live forever" (Gen 3:22). What these accounts have in common is not a revelation of God but the replication of a patriarchal potentate who will do anything to remain securely in control. Abraham himself is a good example of just such a man.

The God who was revealed by Jesus is creator of the universe and Lord of the worlds. BUT he does not violate the boundaries of those who are less powerful either to meet "his needs" or to achieve his ends—no matter how beneficial his designs would be for all involved. What Jesus tried in numerous ways to tell people about God was validated in the **kind of death** that Jesus died. God did not intervene and seize power from those who arrested, tried and killed Jesus. Nor did he abstain from seizing power because Jesus was meant to die as a sacrifice of atonement. God did not intervene because he has given autonomy to human beings. The autonomous response of Israel's elites and the Gentile leaders was to reject Jesus and to kill him. God's response was to raise and to transform Jesus, validating him as **the** standard for human beings who desire to know God.

The gospels teach that God does not use other human beings to punish those on whom he allows the sun to shine and the rain to fall. While untold numbers of warriors throughout history have personally believed that God helped their side win, the death of Jesus testifies to the fact that God does not "take sides." If the individual human heart accepts the values and goals of the kingdom, then human actions on earth reflect God's intentions. Whether this is the situation or not, life on earth is the time for people to live and continue changing until they reflect God's love or until they die. Jesus' parables of the final judgment (Mt 25:31ff), the great catch of fish (Mt 13:47-50) and the final harvest (Mt 13:36-43) make it clear that no one in this life is to destroy or harm those who are evil. Healing and change are not brought about by threats, beatings, punishment, imprisonment or killing. These activities do not reveal God's will for the sinner.

Jesus as Savior—The evils from which human beings need to be delivered and the sin from which they need to be saved arise within social systems which are created and maintained at odds with the intentions of God. While the masculine side of patriarchy is organized around power and honor, the feminine side was to be integrated with nature and nurture. God's power and honor have been the source of countless theological debates within Judaism, Islam and Christianity: how is an all-powerful God understood in the face of evil? He must either create evil or condone evil. When bad things happen to human beings, God must either be punishing them or using them as a sacrifice. Only Jesus consistently revealed how utterly misleading are these analogies for God based on power, honor, revenge, sacrifice, etc. that arise from the male's public side.

Culture and society do not offer adequate analogies to understand the revelation of God. In the world of nature made by God, all that comes into being is to achieve the fullness for which it was created. This process finds the categories of power, honor and obedience to have very limited benefits. Where autonomy is required for growth and maturation, obedience and control are usually harmful. Wherever honor is the central value around which society is organized, growth, autonomy and maturation are necessarily thwarted. Where punishment and revenge are employed, healing and restoration are impossible—as amply demonstrated by penal systems and prisons.

The words and example of Jesus were organized around the healing and restoration of human beings. What diminishes or endangers human growth was declared as antithetical to the designs of God. Since every culture embraces a person's complete reality, there is no way out of that "social bondage" without Jesus. His dual roles as Son of man in charge of the household, as well as Son of God in the kingdom, put him in the unique place of offering an option to everyone. Each family can be organized around the values and standards of the cultures that surround it, or each family can accept God as Father and reflect the care he shows all of his creation. Through this process, human beings are saved as they immerse themselves in the changes necessary for them to become members of God's household. The resurrection is God's validation of what Jesus said, of how he lived and the promises he made. Because of the resurrection, Jesus **continues** in his previous role as symbol and focus of the household as he nourishes and sustains those given to him by God according to the standards of the kingdom.

Theologians have come from patriarchal social systems where the political/public group has been consistently male. By interpreting Jesus' death as the revenge exacted against man to assuage God's anger and insulted honor, Jesus became the ultimate example for males who have always been expected to sacrifice themselves willingly for their family, religion or civil powers. While the analogy makes apparent Jesus' heroism in his decision to step forward on behalf of others, it underscores the ambiguity of an image of God that required the torture and death of an innocent man whom he called Son to reinstate humans in his favor. This image of God does not inspire belief because such a "God" is not trustworthy, not someone in whom anyone can "believe." Jesus' death was interpreted according to patriarchal values which glorify the human sacrifice of men, women and children who are used as objects by "parent" figures and elites to maintain, regain or enhance their own honor.

The feminine or the domestic aspects of Jesus' image found in the gospels have been suppressed by selective inattentiveness in theology because they made Jesus an unacceptable model for male emulation according to dominant gender expectations. While experiences and insights from the male world have provided the cultural model or framework in which Jesus has been publicly interpreted, there is no denying the existence of subordinate groups whose cultural models, while influenced by the dominant group, do more than merely replicate the values, insights and identity of elites. "Such models are 'muted' in the face of dominant ideology and may be only vaguely articulated by the members of the subordinate group themselves."[15]

The interpretation of Jesus described in this book has arisen from the muted model of the domestic world of women and children as lived in patriarchal cultures. For this reason it is not accurate to say that Jesus "transcended" his culture or that he was "counter-cultural." He found the idealized social role of women to be more amenable to the designs of God than the public, jural role created for men. This does not imply that all or most women have lived or acted as the idealized woman envisioned by the group. Nor does this statement suggest that the cultural limitations placed on women were supported by Jesus. Rather, nurture, healing and restoration to wholeness were the central values of Jesus' life in relation to both men and women.

In the role of focus and symbol of the household, Jesus accepts the feminine role and designates its concern with nurture and nature to be essentially appropriate for males in the kingdom of God. Thus, those values and goals which support and enhance the domestic sphere are the very ones around which **the public** is to be organized and not the other way around. Quite unlike either Islam or Judaism, the focus of Jesus was not on the political order nor on social control through government. Totally at odds with other males who are portrayed in the Hebrew scriptures and in the *Qur'an*, Jesus focused solely on the development of qualities which have nothing to do with honor or displays of power as esteemed by society. Because the kingdom of God was the larger group into which Jesus socialized those who followed him, he showed no desire to create a political order where someone would act "in God's name." In the radically personal approach of Jesus, it is **the individual who comes to know God through Jesus**, not through religious or social leaders. Jesus remains the focus and symbol of God's household on earth, and believers who continue to be socialized according to God's kingdom will be in society what light is to darkness and what leaven is to flour. This is a radically different relation between the individual and society than that which is envisioned within either Islam or Judaism.

VI.

THE GOSPEL IMAGE
SUPPRESSED BY
PAULINE ANALOGIES

INTRODUCTION

Paul as hero—The Acts of the Apostles is the sequel to Luke and witnesses to the spread of the gospel beyond Palestine. When the author chose
Paul to dominate the second half of Acts, he portrayed a hero who was very
different from Jesus, the hero of Luke. Though called the apostle to the
Gentiles, Paul most frequently spoke in synagogues where he addressed Jews
and others who displayed an interest in the God of Israel. There are significant differences between the style as well as the content distinguishing Jesus
from Paul:

1) When preaching the gospel, Jesus never presented credentials
except his actions (works), while Paul relies on the "special merits" of his
own autobiography and the epic of the Hebrew people.

2) While the transfiguration was at least as dramatic a vision as Paul's
conversion, Jesus did not use it to establish his own credibility nor did he
allow the disciples (witnesses) to mention it before his resurrection.

3) Jesus' main mode of teaching was through parables that highlighted
the values and goals of the kingdom of God as opposed to those of group
consensus. Paul more typically argued from Hebrew scriptures, accepting as
normative the social values, customs and expectations of his social world.

4) While Jesus and his disciples were supported by women of means, it
was a source of pride for Paul that he continued to support himself, relying
on no one most of the time.

5) Jesus taught that suffering was a natural part of being attached to the
household of God when surrounded by social forces that reject God's rule.
Displaying little understanding of social customs that were at odds with the
kingdom of heaven, Paul interpreted his own suffering as unique and extraor-
dinary, strengthening his credentials and bolstering his personal authority.

6) Whereas Jesus accepted his fate at the hands of Judean authorities

120

knowing he was innocent, Paul refused to accept similar judgment and made his appeal as a Roman citizen to avoid the fate that Jesus suffered.

The author of Luke and the Acts of the Apostles portrayed two members of the house of Israel who related to others in vastly different ways. Paul conducted himself according to the standards set for men in public places while Jesus conducted himself according to the norms and expectations laid down for women who created and maintained households.

Paul: In Defense of Honor—Paul continued to be an apostle both to Jews who considered him to be deviant as well as to Gentiles (other nations) who knew that he belonged to the house of Israel. Since each person was totally embedded in the group, receiving his/her identity, security and self-worth from affiliation within it,[1] Paul's opinion of Gentiles (the outgroup) had been completely formed according to the beliefs of his own group. Similarly, from the Gentile perspective, Paul was not an individual, but a member of the house of Israel, an outgroup to them. Gentile-Christians further realized that the official position of the house of Israel was rejection of Jesus and persecution of his Jewish followers. Despite the widespread disbelief of his own group, Paul was unable to disassociate himself from them,

> I am speaking the truth in Christ, I am not lying; my conscience bears me witness in the Holy Spirit that I have great sorrow and unceasing anguish in my heart. For I could wish that I myself were accursed and cut off from Christ for the sake of my brethren, my kinsmen, my race. They are Israelites, and to them belong the sonship, the glory, the covenants, the giving of the law, the worship, and the promises; to them belong the patriarchs, and of their race, according to the flesh, is the Christ, God who is over all be blessed forever (Rom 9:1-5).

A shameless condition—Paul knew that the law had never accomplished its goal as he understood it: submission to God so that everyone could live in the unbroken order that obedience guarantees. He also knew that the house of Israel referred to itself as stubborn, rebellious, stiff-necked and hard-hearted. It represented itself as having broken covenant promises as well as having spurned the advances God made through his prophets. While Jesus was considered by some Judaeo-Christians (Paul included) to be the greatest overture God made to his people, Israel had managed to bring about Jesus' death in collusion with the Gentiles. But God had raised and transformed Jesus, deliberately and speedily restoring his honor as a sign of divine approval of his life. Israel's response to the news of Jesus' resurrection was continued disbelief followed by expulsion, repudiation and persecution of fellow Jews who believed in him.

Individual shameful actions do not constitute a shameless condition. Paul knew that his culture judged a shameless person to be one who **repeatedly** failed to observe the boundaries, duties, values and responsibilities to which he (or his group) had previously agreed.[2] With their rejection of Jesus, Paul believed that the house of Israel was giving up all desire for, as well as the hope of regaining, honor, accepting shame resulting from the death of Jesus as a permanent condition. He realized that this lack of serious, consistent desire to regain honor by repenting and remaining faithful to God, coupled with their traditional inability to live in a covenant, testified to a shameless condition which Paul had already experienced in himself (Rom 7:14ff).

Depending on one's gender, there are several responses that can be taken to a shameless person in that social world. Women might be killed by male relatives to regain the honor of their families. Men, on the other hand, would more often be publicly expelled and cut off from their families as a public acknowledgement of the shameful behavior of the offending member. Within that social system, it was not possible for good people to have ongoing relations with a shameless person and maintain their own honor (e.g. Jesus was criticized for keeping company with sinners and tax collectors whose shameless behavior called his own honor into question).

If Paul saw rejection of Jesus as the most recent action of a shameless people, what can be said about a God who remained faithful to such a faithless people? He might be judged by onlookers to be: 1) also shameless and no more trustworthy than the house of Israel; or 2) a fool; or 3) increasingly vindictive in retaliation for shameless behavior; or 4) severed from those who are shameless; or 5) utterly independent and beyond the contamination of anyone's shame, including that of a covenant partner.

Paul's response to shame—In the light of Israel's rejection of Jesus and the contempt with which Paul's social world viewed shameless people, his unflagging attachment to his group created four major problems which lead us into the main body of this chapter. For Paul's orientation is clearly toward public opinion where honor is the pivotal value. First, how does Paul "save face"[3] for the house of Israel when their recurring faithlessness makes them a shameless people according to their own traditions (i.e. the Torah, prophets and psalms) and social criteria (i.e. what constitutes honorable behavior)? Second, how does Paul convince the Gentiles that disbelieving Israel continues to be God's chosen people **without dishonoring God**? Third, how does Paul try to get Israel to accept Jesus? Fourth, despite what Christian Gentiles believe to be the shameless behavior of the house of Israel, how does Paul maintain his own honor **apart from** his group's reputation?

Obviously there are aspects of Paul's thinking which do not fall under any of these questions. These are features which did not arise from his problems with honor. This chapter focuses only on those strategies which Paul used to save, regain or increase honor for himself and/or Israel that have come to be regarded as theology. In order to appreciate the magnitude of the problems that arose with his acceptance of social religious values which stand at odds to those of the gospel's kingdom of heaven, historical examples of the distortions that subsequently arose from living-out Paul's "theology" are included as they fit within the scope of these four areas.

HOW DOES PAUL SAVE FACE FOR ISRAEL IN FRONT OF THE GENTILES?

Paul's approach—He assured the Gentiles ("the nations") that:

1) Israel had only stumbled, not fallen. But BECAUSE they had stumbled, salvation is now open to the Gentiles (Rom 11:11);

2) God had a relation with Israel which Paul characterized as "natural" while the Gentiles were told, "...you have been cut from what is by nature a wild olive tree, and grafted, **contrary to nature**, into a cultivated olive tree..." (Rom 11:17-24);

3) the Gentiles should not forget that earlier they had been separated from Christ, alienated from the commonwealth of Israel, and strangers to the covenants of promise, having no hope and without God in the world. But now, in Christ Jesus, you who once were far off have been brought near in the blood of Christ (Eph 2:11-13).

4) The real person to blame for this alienated situation was Adam (and Eve).

> Therefore as sin came into the world through one man and death through sin, and so death spread to all men because all men sinned—sin indeed was in the world before the law was given, but sin is not counted where there is no law. Yet death reigned from Adam to Moses, even over those whose sins were not like the transgression of Adam, who was a type of the one who was to come (Rom 5:12-14).

According to this passage, the sin of the Gentiles must not have counted because they were not held under the law. Paul goes on to say that the law given by God had not been effective because the flesh had already been weakened. For Paul, God's back-up plan was to send his Son.

> For God has done what the law, weakened by flesh, could not
> do: sending his Son in the likeness of sinful flesh and for sin, he
> condemned sin in the flesh, in order that the just requirement of
> the law might be fulfilled in us who walk not according to the
> flesh but according to the Spirit (Rom 8:3-4).

Thus, Paul saves the face of Israel by presumably convincing his audience that sin entered the world through Adam and created a situation which only God could rectify. While Israel had stumbled, its "trespass" benefited the Gentiles who had nothing until Israel's rejection of Jesus and his death. Both of these components were necessary before God gratuitously grafted the Gentiles (contrary to nature) onto his chosen people.

Questioning Paul's presuppositions—Even if all members had received Jesus, why does Paul doubt that God would have included the Gentiles? If the Gentiles didn't have to become Jews to become children of God, why should they "be grafted into" Israel at all? If Israel's own tradition cites its shameless behavior, why would the Gentiles want to be "grafted in"? Since Jesus was available to anyone who believed in his God and acted on their beliefs, what did the Gentiles gain by this "grafting in" except an inheritance of shame for broken covenants to which they were never partners? The social contagion of shame was a reality for both Jews and Gentiles. The seeds of anti-Jewish sentiment were sown into Christianity by Paul who takes for granted the inferiority of the Gentiles in his attempts to save face for Israel despite its rejection of Jesus.

The fissure in Paul's model of human being—First, he proposed the Hellenistic model of man where the mind is alienated from the flesh: "So then, I of myself serve the law of God with my mind, but with my flesh I serve the law of sin" (Rom 7:25b). This is totally at odds with the gospel model where man is seen as three zones of interconnected activity: eyes/heart as emotion-fused judgment; mouth/ears which communicate the thoughts of the heart; hands/feet as the zone of activity which carries out the desires of the heart (cf. Chapter II). Paul accepts the Hellenistic "split-person," the inferiority of the body as well as the cultural analogy that female is to male what nature is to culture. In this analogy, culture is equated with the idea of human consciousness both in terms of systems of thought as well as technology. As human beings have sought control over nature, so males see their role as necessarily dominating their own bodies and those of women who are seen as closer to nature.[4] "The body was as different from the soul, and as intractable, as were women, slaves... The soul must learn to exercise gentle violence on the body, much as the husband groomed his young bride..."[5]

Bad mother/good mother—The problems in this model of human being are compounded by Paul's (uncritical) acceptance of the Adam and Eve account in Genesis where the woman is introduced as the one who was seduced by the snake that caused the fall of Adam (2 Cor 11:3). Subsequent centuries validated this myth as reality by repeatedly using it to understand male/female relations: men must fear the influence of women.[6] The Christian male received another theological blow: not only was he, as a Gentile, inferior to the Jew; but as a male he was also weaker than the female who could destroy him. Christian tradition treats this perspective with its usual level of ambiguity, placing it side by side with declarations about the weakness and inferiority of Jews and women. While theologically characterized as alien creatures, both Jews and women share more similarities with Gentile males than differences.

In the centuries that followed Paul, Eve as the 'bad mother' was compensated for by Mary, who was taken from near obscurity in the gospels and molded to assume central position as the "good mother." Second and third century writings which were never accepted into the New Testament (the New Testament Apocrypha) contain numerous stories which give additional 'information' about Mary, i.e. *The Proto-Gospel of James* and the *Gospel According to the Pseudo-Matthew.*[7] By the fourth century when Christianity had become a political religion, there was a liturgy of the Virgin composed in Syria.[8]

The patriarchal culture provided the perfect conditions for Mary's creation as the counterfoil of its earlier creation, Eve. Without Eve, the social role of women would not be interpreted as necessarily resulting from sin. Mary's perpetual virginity, unaltered by motherhood, would be meaningless. Thus, the symbolism of Mary remains dependent on accepting the Genesis account of Eve as the historical origins of women. However, the revelation of Jesus reversed the Genesis interpretation that nature, nurture and the suffering they involve are evidence of sin and punishment. By word and example, Jesus declared the suffering involved with nature and nurture to be inevitable for members within his household; appropriate for himself and other males as the reflection of **God's** designs. However, the popular role created for Mary eclipsed that of Jesus as focus and symbol of the household. For this reason, her popularity deserves further analysis from several perspectives. For example,

1) Mary is to Jesus what Muhammad is to the *Qur'an*—Gospel texts unanimously agree that Jesus was not an only child though the number of siblings vary. If four brothers are named and sisters are referred to in Mark and Matthew, Mary had at least seven living children: five sons and at least two daughters (Mk 3:31, 6:3; Mt 12:46, 13:55–56; Jn 2:12, 7:3ff; Lk 2:7, 8:19; Acts 1:14.). Yet, the post-Constantinian church is compelled to insist that Mary remained a virgin before, during and **after** giving birth.

Why? Some understanding can be gained from looking within Islam where there is a similar determination to maintain that Muhammad was utterly illiterate and unable to write before the *Qur'an* was revealed. He was as uncontaminated by words as Mary was uncontaminated by sexual relations. Muhammad's illiteracy parallels Mary's virginity.

a) Just as Mary was a virgin who had not known man when Jesus was conceived, so was Muhammad utterly illiterate when his revelations began.

b) Just as Mary was declared free of original sin so as not to contaminate her son, so did Muhammad's freedom from literacy preserve God's revelation from contamination.

c) Just as Mary was declared to remain a virgin who did not give birth to Jesus in the natural manner so as not to destroy her virginal status, so was Muhammad free of human limitations in the transmission of the *Qur'an* to his companions.

d) Just as Mary was to remain a virgin throughout her life even after the birth of Jesus, so did Muhammad's revelations continue uncontaminated by literacy for the duration of his life.

e) Just as Mary's body was assumed into heaven after her death so as not to experience physical deterioration and corruption which is the result of sin, so also has Muhammad's message and character been protected from corruption throughout these hundreds of years.

f) Both Muhammad and Mary uphold within their own traditions the belief that learning and sex respectively, which are not carefully controlled and supervised, necessarily diminish God's power and contaminate his word as it is understood in each religion.

2) Cultural ideal: virgin/mother and first-born son—Another reason for the rise in the Virgin/Mother cult is to be found within the Mediterranean culture which created a role for Mary based on the **status** that was popularly accorded her son. According to cultural expectations, if Jesus was the Son of God as well as Mary's, **then** his mother must have been a young virgin who knew nothing about sex but came to be pregnant without ever finding out about men or the pains of childbirth. By special dispensation, she never had to worry about the stranger who would take her sexually and "dominate" her. There were never other siblings to compete with the first born son for her attention. Just as no man stood between this mother and her son, no wife would compete with this mother and diminish her influence.

Since paternity is attributed to God alone, both she and her son benefit in this culturally created story line: a) she will never get pregnant again with the discomfort and work this holds; b) her son has special status and powers because of his paternity; c) those who are loyal to him will be measured according to the standards she sets; and d) she will rule over her son's "family." In the next life, that same mother will become the spouse of her son, ruling as queen next to her son who sits at God's right hand.

3) The son: maternal access to power—Because females in a patriarchy are considered by male elites to be worthless until they give birth to a son, a) as mothers, they exercise real power over their infants and children as well as gaining status through their sons; no other power relation is as totally asymmetrical as that which exists between a mother and her fetus and/or infant and child; b) sons (and daughters) can be overwhelmed by their own weakness and inadequacy as children when coupled with the needs of mothers whose social worthlessness makes them dependent on the birth of male children for social value and personal power; c) the determination with which patriarchies keep women socially powerless, convinced of feminine weakness and separated from men, continues to be upheld by adult males whose lives began as little boys with mothers whose needs and unlimited power left these male children feeling permanently inadequate and hostile to women.[9]

Arising out of this social deprivation is a mythical all-powerful mother who meets every human need. Inflated with power and goodness far beyond her minor role and modest image in the gospels, Mary is the super Virgin/Mother in a religious pantheon organized around meeting the needs of "her children." The first presupposition is that God himself is neither interested nor capable of taking care of his children. The second presupposition is that Jesus never existed except to give his mother power. In the name of motherhood, Mary replicates the patriarchal belief that the world is a place "to be used and manipulated." This role and its script is meant to compensate those whose basic needs went unmet in childhood.[10]

The cult of Mary is organized around the perfect woman as envisioned, created and maintained by patriarchies where fathers are not expected to take an interest in the concrete needs of their own children. Her virginity intact, the "Mother of **God**" (of **Jesus**!) rules eternally attached to her only son. As such, this cultural creation symbolically embodies the very deviations which make adult women dependent on their sons in a way that is more appropriate in relations between husbands and wives. Perpetual virginity of a mother keeps men safe from the sexual needs of women in general, as well as protected against the incest violations of mothers and "family" women. Secondly, the Virgin/Mother cult is meant to conceal the deprivations which children feel when their parents are inadequately prepared to meet the primal needs of their children. In terms of God's household, there was nothing lacking in Jesus' care and nurturing of the Father's children. The absent element appeared only later in the tradition which reflected the patriarchal insistence that nature and nurture were the primary work of women alone. The Virgin/Mother cult arose to keep the male role unchanged.

HOW DOES PAUL CONVINCE THE GENTILES THAT THE JEWS CONTINUE TO BE GOD'S CHOSEN PEOPLE DESPITE THEIR SHAMELESS BEHAVIOR, WITHOUT DISHONORING GOD?

Broken branches vs. mercy to all—First, Paul teaches that God "broke off" the non-believing members of Israel, thus saving himself from the contagion of their shameless behavior. If God would do this "to the natural branches," then the Gentiles should not become proud but continue in God's kindness lest they also taste his severity (Rom 11:19ff). Several lines later, in the same epistle, Paul tells the Gentiles that Israel is an enemy of God only regarding the gospel, and that is for **their** (the Gentiles') sake! But Israel is beloved because of their ancestors, and furthermore God's gift and call are irrevocable (Rom 11:28ff).

> Just as you were once disobedient to God but now have received mercy because of their disobedience, so they have now been disobedient in order that by the mercy shown to you they also may receive mercy. For God has consigned all men to disobedience, that he may have mercy on all (11:30-32).

Ambiguity cancels out Paul's solutions—The ambiguity in Paul's thinking causes each solution given above to cancel out the other. Paul says that God causes hard-heartedness (Rom 11:8-10) and then rejects those who are disobedient, while at the same time maintaining that God causes disobedience so that he can have mercy on all (11:30-32). Both statements presuppose an all-powerful God who must certainly **control** everything and everyone, including human choice. The first statement insists that only the elect received what the law failed to give and the rest were lost. God's honor is saved by casting off those with a hardened heart. The second statement finds God's mercy to be beyond any limitation which human behavior might place on him. How can God be both forced to defend his honor according to the demands of society, while at the same time extending mercy to all?

Disciples of the Pauline tradition projected onto the Gentiles the expectations and failures that belonged to the house of Israel because of its covenant status,

> Now this I affirm and testify in the Lord, that you must no longer live as the Gentiles do, in the futility of their minds; they are darkened in their understanding, **alienated from the life of God because of the ignorance that is in them, due to their hardness of heart; they become callous** and have given themselves

up to licentiousness, greedy to practice every kind of uncleanness. You did not so learn Christ—assuming that you have heard
about him and were taught in him, as the truth is in Jesus. Put off
your old nature which belongs to your former manner of life and
is corrupt through deceitful lusts, and be renewed in the spirit of
your minds, and put on the new nature created after the likeness
of God in true righteousness and holiness (Eph 4:17-24).

This theology spreads on sin with a trowel, keeping Gentile-Christians from
assuming that they are better than Jewish-Christians whose group members
were described as hard-hearted, callous and the like in their rejection of
God's overtures. But while the sins of Israel enabled God to do what he
could not have otherwise accomplished, that is to include the Gentiles, the
sins of the Gentiles have no similar redeeming merit. It is necessary to
remember that Jewish-Christians assimilated their "knowledge" of and feelings for the Gentiles as members of the house of Israel long before their conversions to Jesus. Of course there is no evidence that their opinions of
Gentiles changed with baptism. Pauline theology, which preaches Jewish
superiority over Gentiles even in sin, produced another plank in the early
Christian foundation of anti-Jewish sentiment.

HOW DOES PAUL TRY TO GET ISRAEL TO
ACCEPT JESUS?

Shaming—"Making someone jealous" is a common shaming pattern[11]
which seeks to diminish the target in his/her own eyes by pointing to another
who (unlike the shamed person) is adequate, worthy and fully valid as a
human being. This pattern also inspires jealousy or fear of losing what is
already possessed or promised. The outcome is individuals who are conflict
prone and mistrustful of others on their own level as well as those "above"
and "below" them.[12]

So I ask, have they stumbled so as to fall? By no means! But
through their trespass salvation has come to the Gentiles, **so as to
make Israel jealous**. Now if their trespass means riches for the
world, and if their failure means riches for the Gentiles, how
much more will their full inclusion mean!
Now I am speaking to you Gentiles. **Inasmuch then as I
am an apostle to the Gentiles, I magnify my ministry in order
to make my fellow Jews jealous**, and thus save some of them.
For if their rejection means the reconciliation of the world, what

will their acceptance mean but life from the dead? (Rom 11:11-15).

Another technique of shaming is to reassign what had previously belonged to one to someone else. This also fosters jealousy as the targeted offender is made to fear that s/he will lose what has already been gained. Paul states that Christ is the offspring of Abraham (Gal 3:16) and that those who belong to Christ are also "Abraham's offspring, heirs according to the promise" (Gal 3:29).

> For not all who are descended from Israel belong to Israel, and not all are children of Abraham because they are his descendants; but "through Isaac shall your descendants be named." This means that it is not the children of the flesh who are the children of God, but the children of the promise are reckoned as descendants (Rom 9:6-8).

The children of the flesh are those who count their membership by circumcision while the children of the promise are those whose membership is guaranteed because of belief in Jesus. Paul attempts to delegitimize what he claims in another passage is eternally Israel's by virtue of God's irrevocable covenant. The outcome is another layer of ambiguity as Christians (both Jewish and Gentile) are told that they are now heirs of the promises made to Abraham through their belief in Christ, while the Jews (children of the flesh) are no longer heirs of the promises made to Abraham.

Paul's standpoint reveals the difficulties Jewish-Christians had in accepting Gentile-Christians. This was the same problem faced by the authors of Matthew and Luke. However, they did not resort to the tactics of Paul who takes Israel as the standard. Rather they proceeded on the understanding that the kingdom sets the standards and that those standards were not those of society as mirrored in Israel. Thus the gospels have no need to include the Gentiles as heirs of Abraham because those who follow Jesus show themselves to be the children of God. This is the primary link which makes all other group memberships superfluous. Thus, no other aspect of Israel's customs or laws had to be accepted by Gentiles along with baptism (though in fact numerous customs regarding purity and women were passed along). While the gospels introduce the larger category of the Fatherhood of God which makes inclusion within Israel unnecessary, Paul's approach is to rewrite membership in Israel and then adapt Gentile-Christians to fit **within** his group.

Christian appropriations—What originated as Paul's desire to shame Israel into accepting Jesus escalated into a theological tradition where

Gentile-Christians appropriated: 1) the Hebrew scriptures giving them (at least on the popular level) equal weight with Jesus as the word of God; 2) the titles by which the Jewish people referred to themselves as the chosen people, priestly people, people set apart, the elect, etc.; 3) the Hebrew myth of chosen people, promised land and manifest destiny (to be the light to the nations); 4) the belief that suffering confirms special status in God's eyes. These appropriations were first made by Jews who were also Christians. When accepted by Christians who were Gentiles and who formed the majority culture, identity enmeshment was established as a theological position which originated from Paul's shaming his fellow members. At the heart of centuries of identity confusion where Christianity is enmeshed with Israel's national identity and values are multiple levels of boundary violations. History is replete with examples which testify to the disasters that arose from these "Israel-enmeshed Christian" values, goals, aspirations and actions.

1) The Christians appropriated the Hebrew scriptures, giving them equal weight with the gospels as the entire Bible is considered to be the Word of God. The Hebrew scriptures entered the church with the first Jewish-Christians and remained in central position until the mid-second century. By the close of that century, the gospels and Pauline letters were also being used "as scripture."[13] The process through which certain books were accepted as inspired and declared authoritative covers many centuries and is not the central issue here. The problem is one of influence where the Christian writings and Hebrew scriptures have eclipsed, blurred, altered or diminished the authority of Jesus as the Word of God for Christians.

Where God or the actions of God in the Hebrew Bible are not compatible with the revelation of God in Jesus' words and actions (as presented in the gospels), the Christian finds not the Word of God, but the Hebrew epic.[14] The house of Israel, intrinsically embedded in a patriarchal social system, can more accurately be described as Jesus' springboard, **not** his drawing board. Similarly, the same standard may be applied to the *Qur'an*: wherever God is perceived as merely the extension and patron of a patriarchal social system, the writing is Arabic epic and not revelation from the Christian perspective.

Likewise, ALL writings that have come to be included in the Christian tradition must be evaluated in the light of the gospels. Those that oppose the reversals and changes mandated in the gospels may have value as historical documents but they are not authoritative regarding normative Christian behavior or belief according to the standards of the kingdom. Maintaining that the Hebrew scriptures and all New Testament writings are uniformly the Word of God when their images of God and standards for behavior are antithetical to those found in the gospels has institutionalized ambiguity, frequently and effectively canceling out what Jesus said and did. The attraction of the Hebrew Bible and the other New Testament writings has consistently been their compatibility with the patriarchal cultures where Christianity has taken root.

2) Analogies by which the Hebrew scriptures refer to the house of Israel as the chosen people, priestly people, people set apart, the elect, etc. have been usurped by Christians carrying with them much that was reversed by Jesus' words and examples in the gospels.

a) Chosen people—Titles, as well as the analogies and symbols they embody, elicit emotion and inspire behavior that reflect the past and interpret the present according to the analogies adopted. One example of the power of analogy to determine behavior can be seen in the middle ages when Christendom reintroduced Hebrew warrior figures as Christian models for crusaders who claimed the holy land as their "inheritance" through Christ, the true heir of Abraham. This analogy reincorporated rights to land based on group membership as central symbols within Christianity because they were all part of the original Hebrew story from which the analogies had been drawn. The armies that first left Europe for Palestine began by practicing on the "enemy" that lived among them: the Jews. They were subjected to the same crusader violence which was eventually directed against all who were not "chosen": Islam, Greek Orthodox Christians, and ultimately the "heretic" Christians in Europe.

Bernard of Clairvaux, a celebrated Cistercian monk, was able to baptize the warrior role, wed it to monasticism and introduce warrior monks in the twelfth century. He found no incongruity between following the example of Jesus and fighting as professional warriors.[15] The title of Bernard's warrior monks, the Knights of the Temple of Solomon (Knights Templar), shows the part of the Bible out of which they had been carved. While killing did not endanger their souls, they were warned about very real dangers from another area:

> The company of women is a perilous thing, for through them the ancient demon denied us the right to live in Paradise; and therefore women may not be received as sisters into the Order...and we believe it is dangerous for any religious man to look too much at women's faces. And so none of you should presume to kiss a woman, neither widow, nor maiden, nor mother, nor sister, nor aunt, nor any other woman; therefore the knights of Christ must always flee from women's kisses.[16]

This reflects the belief that war can be invested with "holiness" while women cannot. When Paul created theology using analogies based on athletes and warriors, he reduced Christian behavior to another male activity. The metaphor traditionally used for women in the early church who aspired to live uncompromising Christian faith was that they had "become male."[17] Uncritical acceptance of the Hebrew Bible by Christian theologians perpetuated society's interpretation of women and war as the "revelation" of God. As such, the feminine undermines not only the essence of masculinity, but sanctity as well.

The Latin kingdom lasted within changing boundaries for two hundred years fighting like Joshua, Saul, David or the Maccabees. Like an arrow being painstakingly removed from the body of the Middle East, the Western Christian invaders (three terms that are still synonymous in the Middle East today) were expelled. Western attitudes that denigrate Islam are rooted in these encounters and have not been subsequently re-evaluated. Middle Eastern attitudes toward the Christian West has had little opportunity to improve as the crusaders were replaced by subsequent centuries of varying forms of European colonialism, including the most recent, Zionism (which was authorized and empowered by the Christian West).

b) Priestly people—The analogy of priestly people carries with it altar, blood, sacrifice, priest, atonement and an image of God where His followers are ranked hierarchically around sacrifices and the appeasement of his honor. The gospels talked about mercy rather than sacrifice, a table and not an altar, body and blood as (covenant) food (for eternal life); Jesus as the symbolic focus and servant (not priest) in whom generations of believers would be joined. This was the new covenant which necessitated that followers immerse themselves in change so that their behavior would be appropriate to the household of God. The New Testament tract, Hebrews, carries analogies of priesthood and sacrifice into the heart of Christian theology where it inspires standards for child raising which are quite abusive. Abraham and Isaac retain their mythic importance where religion and society necessitate and glamorize human sacrifice to benefit those in power.

c) Companion categories and treatment of the non-elect—The difficulty with chosen people is the companion category, unchosen or non-chosen people; the problem with the elect as a category is its corollary, the non-elect. None of these analogies are adequate for the third millennium of Christianity where the planet is comprised of various and diverse groups struggling to realize their potential as people. The image Christians have of themselves should be based on the image they saw mirrored in Jesus. How they treat outsiders, "the enemy," the weak and powerless would likewise be derived from how they understand the activity of God-in-Jesus toward the poor, the powerless and the enemy. Adapting titles that the house of Israel reserves for itself has sent Christianity down the wrong path in its own self-understanding, in its relations to non-Christians as well as to other Christians.

3) The Hebrew myth of chosen people, promised land and manifest destiny has been "relived" to the detriment of all involved. While it has been claimed that "the Book of Exodus has become one of the parables of mankind...a light to the Western peoples in their long and weary warfare for liberty,"[18] those subjugated people who were not chosen, not elect and not Western see a very different reality.

a) The Protestant reformation: Hebrew revival—Medieval Christendom which marked the warrior with a cross and blessed him on his way veered farther and farther away from Jesus as the standard for Christian actions. Obsessed with the desire for uniformity and conformity, the inquisition rose and fell over several centuries as the Roman Church, allied with civil powers, used torture and death to arrive at obedience and truth. Reacting against this authoritarian structure and the control it demanded in all aspects of life, many European Christians chose personal inspiration from the Bible as their sole authority.

The Protestant reformation of the sixteenth century has been called a "Hebraizing" or "Judaizing" revival. The themes of a chosen people, a promised land and a unique, historical role galvanized those Christians reorganizing themselves apart from Rome and Catholicism. The language, tradition and values of Israel of old gained a place of pre-eminence among the Puritans in England as well as in the Protestant Netherlands.[19] The contemporary Jewish community was not influential in this Hebraizing revival among Protestants. The Hebrews they sought to emulate, the ones who fired their imaginations, were those they found in the Old Testament.

The United States—The Puritans of seventeenth century England were the most radical heirs of Calvinism. Persecuted by the Church of England, the Puritans resonated with the sufferings of the Hebrew people. They saw themselves as the chosen people who fled from Egypt (England) for the promised land (America) and a destiny that promised greatness. As Sydney Ahlstrom writes,

> If the Puritan's Bible reading led him to Amos and Saint Paul, it
> also led him to Moses. The Law was dear to his heart, and
> through the centuries he and his Reformed kindred have dwelt
> unremittingly on the value of the Law as teacher and moral guide
> for the Christian. Detesting those who were "at ease in Zion,"
> determined to have a church whose holiness was visible, the
> Puritan turned to Holy Scriptures, where he found a witness to
> the Creator that inspired him to be a fruitful part of God's order

as a citizen and in his vocation. He recognized that governments, constitutions, and laws were instituted to restrain man's sin and hence were truly of God. So long as conscience allowed, therefore, he was law-abiding and loyal. He also found much specific guidance in the Scriptures, very often in the Old Testament, for the ordering of personal life, the regulation of society, and the structuring of the Church.[20]

The Hebrew Bible was used as the source book for group identity. The fact that it could also be used for naming children as well as towns further replicates how closely the Puritans identified with Israel of old. America was settled amid fervent messianic and millenarian expectations of the Jews being restored to their own land as part and parcel of Christian American thinking. The natural Israel was made up of Jews while the spiritual Israel was populated by Christians. How clearly Paul can be heard making the distinction between Israel of the flesh (Jews) and Israel of the spirit (Christians).[21]

The outcome of this combination of religious and civil elements was separation of church and state, **not** separation between the Hebrew epic and the American mythic identity. Thus, America sees itself and the rest of the world through a patriarchal religious lens very similar to that of present day Israel which is based on the same folk epic. The founding fathers of the United States, Benjamin Franklin, Thomas Jefferson and John Adams, suggested that the Continental Congress adopt as the seal of their country a picture of the Israelites and Moses standing on the shore, while Pharaoh and his army drowned in the Red Sea, surrounded by the motto, "Rebellion to Tyrants is Obedience to God."[22] This is certainly not at odds with the beliefs of either Judaism or Islam, but it does not reflect the sermon on the mount.

South Africa/Israel—Members of the Dutch Reformed Church leaving Holland for South Africa and North America also saw themselves as the chosen people. What has come to be called the "Apartheid Bible"[23] was a fairly recent creation, though the passages about Ham and Canaan were read to prove or disprove slavery much earlier. The Exodus narrative came into focus in the period of the Voortrekkers ("pioneers," Afrikaners who left the Cape Colony in the 1830s with a deep sense of grievances against the government). "Pharaoh" was replaced by "Britain"; "Israel" was replaced by "Voortrekkers"; and the "Canaanites" were replaced by the "blacks."[24]

As mentioned earlier, "chosen people" carries with it the complementary category of non-chosen people. As expected, there are many similarities between the development of apartheid in South Africa and segregation as practiced by Israel toward Palestinians in Israel (as well as those in captured territories living under military occupation). Afrikaners took extreme racial measures in 1948 to ensure that British imperialists who had subjected them to a "century of wrong,"[25] which had included the first concentration camps, would never gain power over them again. The state of Israel was likewise founded in 1948 following Hitler's Third Reich which was responsible for the massive destruction of Slavs, Gypsies, Jews and others deemed undesirable and consequently interred in concentration camps.

There is a notable quote by South Africa's General Hertzog (whose government in 1924 began the Afrikaner era) that "nationalism is but the 'I' of politics, similar to the 'I' of the person. Nationalism is only a bad thing if the 'I' is over accentuated, but what would become of us if we did away with the 'I'?"[26] Great emphasis was placed on developing their respective native languages (Afrikaans and Hebrew) as an important component of the national "I." Both Afrikaners and Israelis created forms of religious nationalism arising out of their "chosen" status by God and interpreted the roles of surrounding peoples according to the original elements of the ancient Hebrew epic.

While the Afrikaners are described as possessing a "laager mentality" (laager is the Dutch word for dykes; also the fort in Cape Town which symbolized self-protection against powers from the outside), the Israelis are frequently cited for their mind set as victim. What Thomas Friedman wrote about Begin is applicable to Israel as a group, that what made him "even more dangerous was that his fantasies about power were combined with a self-perception of being a victim. Someone who sees himself as a victim will almost never morally evaluate himself or put limits on his own actions. Why should he? He is the victim."[27] The siege mentality of the Afrikaners is another variant of the victim mentality of the Israelis. The outcome for "the natives" of both countries has been very similar.

Israelis would agree with Afrikaners that religion and history became the anchors which saved them from extinction. Both share a unique sense of calling (or, as in the case of Israel, recalling) to a special land. This idea originated in the Old Testament idea of Israel's election. "The more the Dutch colonist became isolated in the interior of the country, the more literally they applied the Old Testament instructions to themselves. The ministers of the Voortrekkers practically all chose Old Testament texts for their sermons, while the pet theme, especially during people's festivals, was the Exodus of Israel to Canaan."[28] The Voortrekkers have been described by Afrikaners as the "Fathers of Israel" who left behind place names which recalled the Exodus tradition.

"Back to the Word" was first the motto of the reformation and subsequently chosen by the General Synod of the Dutch Reformed Church that favored open membership for all races in South Africa as recently as 1987.[29] Many African Christians grew more and more uncomfortable with apartheid because it was clearly antithetical to the gospels. And while American

Christians demand one standard of morality in South Africa, they support a totally different standard of morality in Israel. This inconsistency arises from Protestant theology blended with American history, experience and political expediency:

1) America's national myth is the Hebrew myth of "promised land, chosen people, manifest destiny"; 2) Protestantism gave rise to Zionism three hundred years before Jewish Zionism, and fundamentalist Christians support the return of the Jews to Israel as a pre-requisite for Jewish conversion to Christianity and the arrival of the "end times"; 3) boundary confusion between Christians and Jews creates a moral blind spot in Christian ethics as Jewish agendas are empowered by ancient Hebrew myths and subsequently adopted by Christians; 4) while the United States has theoretically progressed beyond a medieval mentality with regards to the equality of human beings, it still clings to Arab and Islamic stereotypes that originated in the middle ages; 5) public allegations of antisemitism and financial contributions are potent political forces in determining American foreign policy.

The United States found apartheid to be morally insufferable and established peaceful policies to force the dismantling of it. But for the Israeli government who created and embodied the original script, "chosen people, promised land, manifest destiny," the United States has thus far manifested complete and unquestioning encouragement for its segregation policies.[30] Despite the protests of Amnesty International, documented evidence and live film coverage, the American government refuses to recognize Israeli abuse of Palestinians as violations of their human and civil rights. In fact, it is Israel who sees **itself** as being "picked on," while other countries "get away with far worse." But even this Zionist interpretation flows from an understanding of suffering with roots in the Hebrew scriptures and subsequent Jewish theology. It too was appropriated and adapted by Paul for Christians.

4) Christians have adopted the belief that suffering confirms special status in God's eyes—According to the Hebrew scriptures, God attempted to curb the rebelliousness of Israel by allowing the Gentiles more power, e.g. "The wind shall shepherd all your shepherds, and your lovers shall go into captivity; then you will be ashamed and confounded because of all your wickedness" (Jer 22:22); "From the days of our fathers to this day we have been in great guilt; and for our iniquities we, our kings, and our priests have been given into the hand of the kings of the lands, to the sword, to captivity, to plundering, and to utter shame, as at this day" (Ezr 9:7); "Because the land is full of bloody crimes and the city full of violence, I will bring the worst of the nations to take possession of their houses; I will put an end to their proud might and their holy places shall be profaned" (Ezr 7:23-

24), etc. Thus, the disasters that befell Israel were interpreted as God "shaming" Israel into better behavior by allowing the foreigner more power.

Judaism believes that suffering testifies to Israel's status, and that punishment testifies to God's "love" for Israel. The following pattern emerges from these presuppositions: 1) pain and suffering are primary expressions of God's love; 2) love is inseparable from shame and/or guilt (the feeling that arises when not acting according to norms set by "the group"); 3) whether Assyrians, Babylonians, Greeks, Romans, Europeans or Arabs, all non-Jewish neighbors are forever cast into the role of potential enemy who could be used by God either to punish Israel, or to offer it as a sacrifice to God. While punishment "corrects" shameful behavior, sacrifice can be demanded because of Israel's chosen status and exemplary obedience judged according to the standard set by Abraham and Isaac.[31] Originating in ancient Mesopotamian civilization, the concept of punishment from God in this life continues to be a pivotal belief in Judaism, Islam and Christianity today. The official use of the term "holocaust" (burnt sacrificial offering) used by Jews to designate only Jews who were killed under Hitler continues to reflect a God who demands human sacrifice. Introduced into Christianity as part of its Jewish roots, Christians uncritically accept the image of a punitive God who causes suffering in this life either because of sin or because of exemplary obedience (e.g. the death of Jesus). In either case, this is not the God revealed by Jesus in the gospels.

Paul kept this basic story line with adjustments regarding who was considered the "outsider," the potential enemy: 1) pain and suffering are the primary expressions of God's love ("He did not spare his own Son but gave him up for us..."—Rom 8:32); 2) "crucifixion of the flesh" is a necessary component to end shame and guilt; 3) the flesh will destroy men. Unless the flesh is crucified, women, as the ever present force of "outsiders," wait to destroy believers. While non-Jews of all races and social locations were accepted into Christian communities without benefit of circumcision or any other Jewish practice, woman remained the "outsider," viewed as unchanged and held under the law (1 Cor 14:34-35), even though baptism presumably initiated both sexes into full membership.

The gospels, on the other hand, present suffering as a normal aspect of Jesus' role in much the same way that suffering was the common experience for girls who married, got pregnant, experienced labor and childbirth with the unending duties which followed. Suffering was part of interpersonal relations that grew out of nurture and caring for others. This is very different from Paul's emphasis on self-control and perfection which necessitates "crucifying" the flesh as the ultimate weapon in the war against the body.

DESPITE THE BEHAVIOR OF THE JEWS, HOW DOES PAUL MAINTAIN HIS OWN HONOR IN FRONT OF THE GENTILES?

Paul demonstrates that: first, he accepts and supports the wider social system as directly linked to God; second, he reinterprets Christianity according to socially approved male goals in the public arena; third, he interprets himself and his struggle against the flesh according to public expectations and male analogies; fourth, he reorganizes those in the Christian hierarchy from the lowliest believer all the way to God in order to eliminate any uncertainty about Jesus as a heroic male figure.

Paul supports the social system as directly linked to God—Civil powers need not be concerned that Christianity will question civil authority or undermine the existing order because it is linked directly to God

> Let every person be subject to the governing authorities. For there is no authority except from God, and those that exist have been instituted by God. Therefore he who resists the authorities resists what God has appointed, and those who resist will incur judgment. For rulers are not a terror to good conduct, but to bad. Would you have no fear of him who is in authority? Then do what is good, and you will receive his approval, for he is God's servant for your good. But if you do wrong, be afraid, for he does not bear the sword in vain; **he is the servant of God to execute his wrath on the wrongdoer**. Therefore one must be subject, not only to avoid God's wrath but also for the sake of conscience (Rom 13:1-5).

Among the New Testament epistles that similarly reflect this attitude are 1 Peter 2:13ff, 1 Timothy 6, and Titus 2. Many themes in the epistles reflect the adoption of social values, customs and expectations that became "Christianized," e.g. how one should speak and conduct himself with outsiders, avoidance of any activity which might upset others, perpetuation of previously defined roles for men, women, children, leaders, slaves and those in the public eye.

While the gospels substitute the standards of the kingdom for the standards of the larger social group in Israel, the epistles support the existing social order of the nations and fuse it with their image of God, making the social group coterminous with as well as inseparable from God. The feminine is accepted as inferior to the masculine, and the private sphere of the house (the proper domain of the woman) is judged inferior to the public sphere (the proper domain of men). The gospels have not only been commonly interpreted in the light of Paul, but in the light of the other epistles and the Hebrew scriptures to conform to the patriarchal viewpoint of society.

Paul reinterprets Christianity according to socially approved male goals in the public arena—Paul established certain goals that had been introduced as virtues much earlier among the Greek warrior aristocracy of the archaic (ca. 750-500 BC) period. "Virtue" was something that originally and properly belonged to the warrior aristocracy and could only be found in the nobility. "The principle meaning of *arete* (virtue) was strength, skill and valor in war; it was manifest in heroic deeds, such as victory in battle, and was rewarded with honor and praise. It was victory which secured imperishable fame. Here we see that *arete* is indissolubly linked with gender and social class."[32]

> For he will render to every man according to his works: to those who by patience in well-doing **seek for glory and honor and immortality**, he will give eternal life; but for those who are factious and do not obey the truth, but obey wickedness, there will be wrath and fury (Rom 2:6-8)

The goals for which Paul strives are "glory, honor and immortality," key values attainable by free men within the Gentile social system. No male need worry about becoming a Christian and giving up what the culture has promised him as goals. Conversely, no woman need think that she will either become or receive more within Christianity than either the culture or Israel allowed her in public. The harsh words directed against the factious and disobedient are consistent with the value placed on obedience and control in patriarchal cultures.

Paul elicits support for this struggle in analogies from the public/political sphere which was the proper domain of men. Two major areas were athletic competitions and war:

> Do you not know that in a race all the runners compete, but only one receives the prize? So run that you may obtain it. **Every athlete exercises self-control in all things.** They do it to receive a perishable wreath, but we an imperishable. Well, I do not run aimlessly, I do not box as one beating the air; **but I pommel my body and subdue it,** lest after preaching to others I myself should be disqualified (1 Cor 9:24).

Competition, self-control and winning is the triad that looms large behind these solitary analogies which arise from the world of sports. While Pauline writings often use slave, e.g. slaves of sin, slaves of God, etc., the focus is just as frequently on power rather than weakness, winning rather than losing, on individual competition as opposed to mutual assistance.

> Finally, be strong in the Lord and in the strength of his might. Put on the whole armor of God, that you may be able to stand against the wiles of the devil. For we are not contending against flesh and blood, but against the principalities, against the powers, against the world rulers of this present darkness, against the spiritual hosts of wickedness in the heavenly places. Therefore take the whole **armor of God**, that you may be able to withstand in the evil day, and, having done all, to stand. Stand therefore, having girded your loins with truth, having put on the breastplate of righteousness, and having shod your feet with the equipment of the gospel of peace; besides all these, taking the shield of faith, with which you can quench all the flaming darts of the evil one. And take the helmet of salvation, and the sword of the Spirit, which is the word of God (Eph 6:10-17).

In choosing analogies from the public domain, Pauline theology is "male talk" about a male "God." The audiences of Jesus might also have been made up predominantly of men but there is a radical difference in the approaches of both men. Whereas Paul reduced Christian behavior to another male activity, Jesus took the idealized role expected of women and declared it as appropriate for both genders **in their relations to God and responsibilities toward others**. The household centered around God as Father was quite different from Pauline goals of honor, glory and immortality for men. The kingdom as the main social influence for the household of God was in opposition to the cultural matrix which Paul accepted and incorporated into Christian theology.

Paul's interpretation of his struggles against the flesh replicates public, male opinion—Numerous passages describe the struggle where Paul's flesh/sin is at war with his mind/spirit. In the growth and development of human beings, the earliest strata of memory is lodged in the body.[33] Whereas emotions can be suppressed, denied, projected, isolated, reversed and sublimated, the senses cannot be reprogrammed or controlled. While the mind can "forget," rewrite memories, rationalize, human skin is a memory unto itself, a memory that will not forget. Flesh embodies painful memories of weakness, physical and sexual abuse, the invasion of personal boundaries. When parents and the group stand above reproach and outside criticism (protected by the fourth commandment in the Bible and various surahs in the *Qur'an*, e.g. "Show gratitude to Me [God] and to thy parents" (Surah 31:14), the child bears in his flesh the shame which he is forbidden to remember and/or reveal. Without access to one's personal past and the feelings that occurred, healing is not possible. The personality is contorted around personal clusters that both reveal and conceal shameful experiences.

> We know that the law is spiritual; but I am carnal, sold under sin. For I do not do what I want, but do the very thing I hate. Now if I do what I do not want, I agree that the law is good. So then it is no longer I that do it, but sin which dwells within me. **For I know that nothing good dwells within me, that is, in my flesh**. For I do not do the good I want, but the evil I do not want is what I do (Rom 7:14-19).

> **...but I see in my members another law at war with the law of my mind** and making me captive to the law of sin which dwells in my members. Wretched man that I am! Who will deliver me from this body of death?...I of myself serve the law of God with my mind, but with my flesh I serve the law of sin (Rom 7:23-25).

The magnitude of this enemy can only be gauged by the weapon that is needed to destroy it, crucifixion. That weapon is placed within Paul's heroic masculine panorama in an attempt to resocialize his peers whose response is one of revulsion to crucifixion as the ultimate act of shame and degradation. Since "the best defense is a good offense," Paul acknowledges that the cross is the major stumbling block and proceeds to cover it in glory because it alone can control the flesh.

> For the word of the cross is folly to those who are perishing, but to us who are being saved it is the power of God.... For since, in the wisdom of God, the world did not know God through wisdom, it pleased through the folly of what we preach to save those who believe. For Jews demand signs and Greeks seek wisdom, but we preach Christ crucified, a stumbling block to Jews and folly to Gentiles, but to those who are called, both Jews and Greeks, Christ the power of God and the wisdom of God (1 Cor 1:18-24).

Paul leaves no doubt that without Jesus, the "body of sin" would win the battles waged against the law, the mind and the spirit. It is in light of this personal realization that Paul sees the necessity for each Christian to replicate Jesus' crucifixion: "... those who belong to Christ Jesus **have crucified the flesh with its passions and desires**" (Gal 5:24). Hence, Paul's under-

standing of Jesus' giving his body and blood at the last supper is quite different from what can be understood from the gospel texts themselves. Since
crucifixion of the body is the central solution for a weakness in the flesh
which the law could not remedy, all Christians must participate in order to
crucify their own passions and desires. Thus, the symbolism of crucifixion
provides the criteria against which Paul measures himself. His honor is saved
despite his group's rejection of Jesus because Paul imitates Christ (1 Cor
11:1) and because "I have been crucified with Christ; it is no longer I who
live but Christ who lives in me; and the life I now live in the flesh I live by
faith in the Son of God who loved me and gave himself for me" (Gal 2:20).
He calls upon others to follow his example and experience a similar crucifixion against which true discipleship is measured.

Thus far, Paul has established his credentials and maintained his honor
because his individual battle is never waged against the values of the group;
the flesh carries the full burden for all that is evil. Paul fights the flesh like an
athlete in training or a man going to war to win glory, honor and immortality.
The cross has been elevated because it alone can win the decisive victory
over flesh which frustrates the spirit and the mind. But there is one more
maneuver he uses to enhance his honor.

**Pauline theology reorganizes those in the Christian hierarchy from
the lowliest believer all the way to God**—There are three parts to this final
step where Pauline traditions gain, save or augment honor among the
Gentiles. While Paul's instinctive need to remasculinize Jesus has not been
mentioned specifically thus far, it has been visible in Paul's choice of exclusively male analogies which arise from the public domain. Added to that, he
has consistently maintained that he would like everyone to be unattached like
himself (1 Cor 7:1-7) and that marriage is for those who cannot exercise self-
control (1 Cor 7:9). Paul completely disregards women and children who
have no legal status apart from husbands or male relatives. But there is an
unexpected turn in other letters that presume Pauline authority.

Ephesians 5:22 begins with encouragement for wives to be subject to
their husbands **out of reverence for Christ,**

> For the husband is the head of the wife as Christ is the head of
> the church, his body, and is himself its Savior. As the church is
> subject to Christ, so let wives also be subject in everything to
> their husbands. Husbands, love your wives, as Christ loved the
> church and gave himself up for her, having cleansed her by the
> washing of water with the word, **that he might present the
> church to himself in splendor**, without spot or wrinkle or any
> such thing, that she might be holy and without blemish (Eph
> 5:23-27).

This letter accepts culture's belief that women are in need of being saved by a man. God is left out of the analogy completely. Jesus is given the place assigned to God and the church is given the role previously occupied by Jesus. By casting the church in the role of wife, the author is able to accomplish several things at once: 1) to confirm that women in the new order are expected to submit to their husbands; 2) to reaffirm the social belief that only men can save women from the fate assigned to them at birth; 3) to enforce this analogy as a pattern to be imitated by Christians with Pauline teaching as the sole authority over all Christians who are expected to act like the submissive wife.

> Even so husbands should love their wives **as their own bodies.** He who loves his wife loves himself. For **no man ever hates his own flesh,** but nourishes and cherishes it, as Christ does the church, because we are members of his body (Eph 5:28-30).

These words provide another example of ambiguity when set against other phrases previously encountered: "nothing good dwells within me, that is, in my flesh"; "with my flesh I serve the law of sin"; "the mind that is set on the flesh is hostile to God"; "make no provision for the flesh to gratify its desires"; "I pummel my body and subdue it"; "all those who belong to Christ Jesus have crucified the flesh with its passions and desires." Given the consistent disdain with which Pauline theology has regarded the flesh, coupled with no mention of God in this new analogy, who gained from this standpoint?

The answer is clearly articulated in 2 Corinthians though it has been alluded to whenever Paul or those who wrote using his name feel someone undermining Paul's authority and Pauline traditions,

> **I feel a divine jealousy for you, for I betrothed you to Christ** to present you as a pure bride to her one husband. **But I am afraid that as the serpent deceived Eve by his cunning, your thoughts will be lead astray** from a sincere and pure devotion to Christ (2 Cor 11:2).

This passage and Ephesians 5:21ff represent one major effort at relocating Christ within a world more recognizable and acceptable to Mediterranean males. Christ is placed as the head, the location of both personal and group honor.[34] In the gospels, Jesus made it clear that God was to grant and to defend the honor of those attached to him. It was not necessary for Jesus to cut Judas out of the group before his betrayal brought shame on Jesus as the focus of God's household. Jesus' willingness to be arrested with no defense and to die without protest testified to his willingness to leave his honor in God's hands. Pauline theology not only must defend Paul's honor but clarify the status assigned to Jesus as well. By portraying himself as the matchmaker, Paul cast the church in the image of Eve as the primary danger to men. As Eve was fooled, so might this bride (the church) be deceived by listening to others. Mandatory public silence imposed on women is the safeguard Pauline theology wants to keep in place and see replicated in the church as a whole. Conflict would be eliminated as a single, authoritative male voice reigns in the midst of unbroken silence and submission.

> As in all the churches of the saints, the women should keep silence in the churches. For they are not permitted to speak, but should be subordinate, **as even the law says.** If there is anything they desire to know let them ask their husbands at home. For **it is shameful[35] for a woman to speak in church**. What! Did the Word of God originate with you, or are you the only ones it reached? If anyone thinks that he is a prophet, or spiritual, he should acknowledge that what I am writing to you is a command of the Lord. **If anyone does not recognize this, he is not recognized.** So, my brethren, earnestly desire to prophesy, and do not forbid speaking in tongues; **but all things should be done decently and in order** (1 Cor 14:33b-40).

Thus, Paul is able to: 1) confirm the hierarchial social order with men in charge; 2) remasculinize Jesus by locating honor in him as head while leaving God out of the equation (thus eliminating those aspects of the feminine or domestic domain which were characteristic of Jesus' relation to God); 3) maintain control of, and separation from, women by keeping them bound by the Torah (1 Cor 14:33-40); and 4) cast the church as wife of Christ permanently indebted to Paul, the "matchmaker." As the woman should be kept silent and not argue, so as not to shame the male in whom she is embedded, so should the church remain obedient and aware of its debt to Paul. This relation will protect it from becoming another Eve who was led astray by the cunning of the serpent (2 Cor 11:3).

Finally, the tradition that began with Paul evolves to a point where Jesus is elevated and crowned with status that exceeds the limitations of being human,

> For **in him all the fullness of God was pleased to dwell**, and through him to reconcile to himself all things, whether on earth or in heaven, making peace by the blood of his cross (Col 1:15-20).

> **For in him the whole fullness of deity dwells bodily**, and you
> have come to fullness of life in him, who is the head of all rule
> and authority (Col 2:9-10).

While Jesus is the image of the invisible God, the fullness of God cannot
reside in a human being. God was in Jesus like music in a symphony,[36] wind
in sails, fire in coal, art in sculpture and poetry in a piece of writing. One
concrete manifestation cannot exhaust everything that is contained within art
or music. Likewise, what can be said about God was not exhausted in Jesus.
The title Son of God does not exhaust the possibilities of God. While it is a
statement about paternity, it also reveals possession, just like other terms, i.e.
God's word, God's works, God's initiative, God's Son, etc.[37] As previously
mentioned, the patriarchal perception is that children receive everything from
their father. In all four gospels, Jesus constantly points to the fact that the
Father is greater and that, as Son, **everything** Jesus has comes from the
Father. Thus it can be said that Jesus was totally possessed by God. For this
reason, the title "Son of God" best describes Jesus as the complete and utter
recipient of God.

Pauline traditions gave Jesus glory according to the titles and status
which would appeal to males in his social world. Additional roles which people found meaningful were those of a son offering his life out of obedience to
his father and that of a man heroically accepting death at the hands of his
own people. While both of these images bolstered the values of patriarchy,
they did so at the expense of God's image, the one area Jesus had been determined to change. Unable to leave his honor in God's hands as Jesus had
done, Paul fashioned his theology to fit the curve of his shame as a member
of the group who rejected God's initiative in Jesus. Paul retained the shame-
bound social system into which he had been born. By not adopting the standards of the kingdom as the norms used by Jesus, Paul continued to accept
the standards that prevailed in the social world around him. This unquestioning acceptance of values that Jesus had rejected accounts for the Pauline perception and theology which are so different from those of the man to whom
Paul was so passionately attached.

VII.

TURN AND BECOME
LIKE CHILDREN

Religious Dimensions of Patriarchies—There were several primary differences that set Jesus apart from Paul. The first was Jesus' allegiance to the kingdom of God which eclipsed his allegiance to any other group. The second was his exclusive use of the title, "Son of man" (male human being), when referring to himself. This title was devoid of either ethnic or religious identification and implied no status over other human beings. The third factor was Jesus' unique manner of speaking in parables which gave him the independence to use the content of Israel's religion as he saw fit. The fourth factor was the role Jesus forged for himself which was based on that of women who created and maintained households. This allowed Jesus freedom **from** the social values embodied in the male role, hence freedom to pursue the kingdom. Jesus introduced God as Father in a domestic setting which was not dependent on Israel's public ritual nor tied to Israel's traditional, highly ambiguous images of God.

All four of these factors must be taken into consideration to discern how those attached to Jesus discover their own identity as children of God. In addition to this, there are several adjacent problems which must be acknowledged and resolved. The first problem is that Pauline theology has interwoven the Christian's identity with the epic of the house of Israel. There are very few Jewish-Christians today, and it is misleading in the extreme to continue talking about Jesus as though contemporary audiences were still composed primarily of Jews. This perspective uselessly burdens the Christian with a tradition that was highly problematic to and for Jesus in many respects.

The second problem for Christian identity arises because there has been no distinction made between the general social system and the religion embedded in it in the first century. This lack of boundaries has "sanctified'" a social system and created social identities which are antithetical to the values, standards and goals of the kingdom of God in many respects. This gives no support to contemporary Christians as they try to determine whether or not the social systems in which they live are compatible with the kingdom of God as proclaimed in the gospels.

147

The third problem that retards the contemporary formation of Christian identity is the acquisition and promulgation of the Hebrew Bible and New Testament letters as uniformly the Word of God. Jesus, as he emerges in the gospels, is the Word of God. Jesus is the standard by which all "revelation" is evaluated. Yet in Christian rituals, sections are read from all parts of the Bible with little concern about the ambiguity, the images of God or the conflicts that arise between those writings and the gospels. Instead the speakers worry about how these diverse writings thematically "fit together" without questioning whether or not certain writings should be excluded from Christian celebrations altogether.

A closer look at the religious expressions of patriarchy—Judaism, Islam and Christianity are all rooted in Middle Eastern and Mediterranean patriarchal social systems. While Jesus was as semitic as both Moses and Muhammad, his revelation of God was quite different from that of either Israel or, subsequently, that of Islam. The differences between Israel's God and the God of Jesus have been overlooked or explained away because the Hebrew scriptures have been uncritically accepted as relevant to Christians. The link between religion and culture has been lost as the entire content has been accepted as the Word of God. It might be easier for Christians to see the link between culture and religion in Islam. The *Qur'an* can be read without so many built-in "blind spots." The difficulty in studying Islam lies in the West's anti-Arab/anti-Islamic bias that stems from the middle ages. This traditionally cultivated attitude makes an understanding of and appreciation for Islam very difficult for Christians to achieve. This is rather tragic for contemporary Christianity since familiarity with Muhammad and the *Qur'an* might be the easiest way to gain a perspective on Jesus that Christian enmeshment with Israel's religion has made impossible. The advantage of this procedure is the clear way in which one can highlight the differences between patriarchal perceptions and standards, and those advocated in the gospels. Judged according to the patriarchal standards of idealized male behavior, Jesus remains an anomaly.

In order to reduce the "foreignness" of Islam, it might be best to begin with a consideration of Islam alongside the more familiar aspects of Judaism. Both religions:

1) claim divinely revealed scriptures which are retained in their original semitic languages (extending some element of the sacred to both Hebrew and Arabic);

2) maintain oral traditions as important additions to scripture, the oral Torah of Moses (the Mishna and Talmud) and the *Sunna* (Hadith) of Muhammad;

3) uphold the Oneness of God as a numerical equivalent (answering

the question, "How many?" and not the ontological question, "How does God exist?" As One);

4) prohibit the making of visual images of God;

5) place Moses and Muhammad as receivers of the Torah and *Qur'an* respectively, in unique roles within their traditions;

6) claim descendence from Abraham (the Jews through Isaac and the Muslims through Ishma'el, Abraham's first born son by Hagar);

7) see themselves as a legal religion in which the Jewish Halakha and Muslim Shari'a share much in common;

8) have no ordained clergy or priests but rely primarily on men of religious learning (the ulama in Islam and the rabbis in Judaism);

9) see themselves as a people who must remain separate from outsiders to preserve their special character and status with God;

10) reflect and support a patriarchal social system within their laws;

11) claim as integral religious symbols: the land, the group and religious self-rule;

12) ethically maintain non-members as second-class citizens within boundaries governed by religious rule;

13) regard the heroes and wars that expanded their lands as religious activities;

14) follow kosher rules which include prohibition of pork as well as rules to be followed in the slaughter of animals;

15) set aside times of the day for ritual prayer (three times for the Jew, five times for the Muslim) which require the fulfillment of ritual purity laws;

16) strictly separate women from men during religious rituals (with the exception of recent western forms of Judaism);

17) severely restrict the use of musical instruments in ritual services among the Orthodox believers of both groups;

18) place the group above the individual whose identity and self-worth is largely constituted by membership in the group;

19) divide the world in two parts: the house of Islam (Ummah) and outsiders (the house of war); the house (people) of Israel and the goyim ("the nations");

20) prepare for the future by striving to relive the past, e.g. Jewish fundamentalism is expressed in: a) claim to land lost two millennia ago, b) the desire to build another temple, and c) orthodox control of all facets of national life; similarly, Islamic fundamentalism seeks to recapture the time of Muhammad through a return to strict orthodoxy which is interpreted as necessarily antithetical to Western influences.

Both religions reflect what Al-Faruqi lists as the five principal characteristics of the ancient Mesopotamian religious experience introduced in Chapter IV. First, reality is composed of two kinds of beings: one that is divine, absolute and everlasting who is above all and commands all, while the other being is material, human, changing and subject to divine commands. This particular dimension is the very soul of Islam around which its entire religious expression is organized. Second, the realm of the divine relates its commands to the human through divination or revelation. This gives the prophets in either religion the highest position that human beings can occupy in relation to God. Third, human beings are created to serve their creator through obedience and the fulfillment of divine commands. Both religions are "legal" religions because religious law and the fulfillment of that law are the central responsibility of human beings. Fourth, since humans are capable of obedience and the divine commands present what ought to be, human beings are held responsible for their actions. While the group is the focus of God, the individual must fulfill his or her responsibilities as a group member. Fifth, the divine plan concerns humanity which acts as an organic unity. Thus, society is the primary unit of reality, not the individual. Hence, society "is the object of cosmic action on the part of the deity." This explains why the sense of a "people set apart" from the other nations is a central principle in both Islam and Judaism.

Both religions maintain that the order of the cosmos is necessarily hierarchical and gender based. Because of this order, disparity exists between the various levels in the hierarchy and will be replicated throughout the social system (between God and man, between man and woman, between adult and child, between human and animal, etc.). Separation is important for proper boundary maintenance in systems where diversity necessarily means inequality. Muslims states and the Jewish state organize social life according to this perspective of the universe.

Muhammad in the context of other semitic heroes—Another important dimension of Islam that needs to be re-examined by Westerners is the prophet Muhammad (570-632). For centuries, he has been recognized as the semitic hero without peer by those who live in the Middle East. He is loved and revered by Muslims with a loyalty and passion few people have inspired during the course of world history. There is nothing too small or too insignificant in this man's life not to warrant attention among vast numbers of Muslims. Never believed to be more than a human being, Muhammad is revered as the perfect man, the beautiful model and the second after God.[1] In receiving the *Qur'an*, Muhammad is the Islamic equivalent of Moses who received the Torah. He was relentless in his proclamation of the One God. His success in turning hearts to God exceeded that of any Hebrew prophet. Without a doubt, he was at least David's equal in his passion for God, government, battle, poetry and wives. Muhammad conquered lands more vast than the lands conquered by Joshua or David or subsequently by the

Maccabees. He personally embodied every element which the perfect male in patriarchal societies aspires to achieve.

A decade after his death, his followers had conquered Iraq and Syria. By the end of the second decade, Egypt and most of Persia were counted within the house of Islam. By the end of the seventh century the North African coast was added as well as Spain before the first quarter of the eighth century.[2] His followers continued to push out in all directions long after Muhammad's death. The world of Islam covers territory in northern Africa stretching throughout the Middle East, through southern Asia and India all the way to Indonesia, the last named comprising the largest Muslim population. This rapid gain in territory is not to be confused with forced conversions to Islam. First embodied in the example of Muhammad, clearly written in the *Qur'an* (2:256) and further stipulated in Muslim law, the freedom of religious belief remains an Islamic ideal. While there were individual leaders who acted against this basic Muslim principle, the expansion of Islam and its tolerance of other religions (Judaism, Christianity, Zoroastrianism, Buddhism and Hinduism) was an ideal quite different from what was experienced by others living under Christian rule at that time.

Muhammad is the **type** of hero that inspires admiration not only in the Middle East but in the West as well. He came from an insignificant background, enjoyed no benefits due to family or social connections, inspired tremendous affection and loyalty among those who knew him, successfully integrated religion with politics and was acknowledged in his own life as a great leader. His personal reputation was based on his generosity, modesty, trust, forgiveness and passion for all that pertained to God. It is no wonder that Muslims are so offended at derogatory Western stereotypes of their prophet. The tragedy of these stereotypes is that Christians remain ignorant in areas where an understanding of and respect for Muhammad could inspire new insights into Jesus.

While Muhammad basically accepted the social order, there were changes he sought to bring about. For example, the custom of killing unwanted female children at birth was vigorously opposed by the prophet. He tried to restore unity whenever divisions resulted among the different families and tribes. An heir to the ancient laws of Hammurabi which specified "an eye for an eye, a tooth for a tooth," Muhammad too sought to keep revenge in check and urged forgiveness whenever possible. Nevertheless Muhammad believed that fighting was necessary to keep evil from spreading. Were Jesus and his life to become the object of admiration and interest to Christians as the life of Muhammad is to Muslims, Christianity would be a very different religion. As it is, interest in Jesus has been eclipsed by numerous saints and the cult of the Virgin/Mother in the Catholic tradition. In the

Protestant tradition, Paul and Old Testament figures have eased out Jesus from the central position.

Jesus: From the patriarchal perspective of Islam—Jesus is mentioned a number of times in the *Qur'an*. While the *Qur'an* agrees with the Hebrew scriptures that Israel killed its prophets (Surah 2:61//3:21,112,181// 4:155//5:70), this is not accepted about Jesus. It is not clear within the *Qur'an* why the crucifixion of Jesus is rejected. Perhaps some understanding for this denial can be found in the social perception of reality. The basic cultural presupposition is that powerful patrons who abandon their clients act in a dishonorable manner. Jesus was the last prophet before Muhammad and therefore God's special client. It is impossible for Muslims to believe that God abandoned Jesus to the torture and death which Christians believe ended his life. Since God is all-powerful and the patron of prophets, Jesus did not die by crucifixion because such abandonment would reflect dishonorable behavior that is not possible with God.

> However, they did not slay him, and neither did they crucify him, but it only seemed to them so; and verily, those who hold conflicting views thereon are indeed confused, having no knowledge thereof, and following mere conjecture. For, of a certainty, they did not slay him: nay, God exalted him unto Himself—and God is indeed almighty, wise (Surah 4, 157,158).

The commentator, Muhammad Asad, goes on to point out in the footnote that relates to this passage, "Thus, the *Qur'an* categorically denies the story of the crucifixion of Jesus."[3] This understanding of how God works clearly reflects the Muslim reflection on how God cared for their own prophet. It also reflects the limitations which social perception place on the possibility of belief in Jesus. First, God must be all-powerful. Second, God must use his power to control human actions. Both premises reflect a God who acts like human beings who have power, e.g. the ruler over those below him, the parent over the small child, the school master over the students. Third, what constitutes honorable behavior in Middle Eastern society must necessarily indicate what constitutes honorable behavior with God. Fourth, the relation between God and Jesus must be like that of patron to client. Thus, social roles and values do shape perception. They also limit and block out other perspectives.

The *Qur'an* goes on to address Christians,

> O followers of the Gospel! Do not overstep the bounds in your religious beliefs, and do not say of God anything but the truth. The Christ Jesus, son of Mary, was but God's Apostle—the fulfillment of His promise which He had conveyed unto Mary—and

a soul created by Him. Believe, then, in God and His apostles,
and do not say, "God is a trinity." Desist from this assertion for
your own good. God is but One God; utterly remote is He, in His
glory, from having a son; unto Him belongs all that is in the
heavens and all that is on earth; and none is worthy of trust as
God (Surah 4, 171).

While not commenting on this surah as such, Asad writes that "the Qur'an
states that God is utterly remote from every imperfection...complete in
Himself, and therefore free from the incompleteness inherent in the concept
of 'progeny' as an extension of one's own being."[4] The presupposition here
is that human beings have children because they are limited or incomplete.
Utterly at odds with this is the revelation of Jesus that God's children are
born out of his unlimited abundance and urge to relate. Each child evolves
his/her own destiny within a relation to God as Father whose abundance can
offset the limitations inherent in that traditional, patriarchal perspective
where the offspring remains an object carved out of incompleteness. The
child is but the extension (if male) of the man who will die.[5]

The essence of Islam is *tawhid*, the act of affirming that "there is no
God but God." Reality consists of two orders, creator and creature: the first
order has but one member, God, and he is utterly unique, eternal and tran-
scendent with nothing like him; the second order belongs to space-time,
experience and the total order of creation including earth, heaven, humans,
animals, etc.

The two orders of Creator and creation are utterly and absolutely
disparate as far as their being, or ontology, as well as their existence and careers are concerned. It is forever impossible that the
one be united with, fused, con-fused or diffused into the other.
Neither can the Creator be ontologically transformed so as to
become the creature, nor can the creature transcend and transfig-
ure itself so as to become in any way or sense the Creator.[6]

God is so unlike his creation, so totally other than human and different from
nature that he cannot be comprehended, let alone described or in any way
represented. Islam claims that it is this absolute separation between God and
nature which allows man to be respected as a creature without on one hand
making him into a god, or on the other hand claiming that he is less than
human.

And thus have We willed you to be a community of the middle
way, so that you might bear witness to the truth before all

mankind, and that the Apostle might bear witness to it before
you (Surah 2, 143).

Heir to the social perception of the Middle East, Islam considered God to be
"totally other." At the same time however, God is expected to think and act
like an all-powerful ruler who achieves what he wants by force and control.
When this fails, punishment is required to stimulate compliance and obedience.

Reflecting on past Christian history and the contemporary political
choices of Western Christians, it is difficult to understand the animosity and
hostility that are directed at the memory of the prophet. For while the life of
Jesus has been widely extolled, it is the example of Muhammad that Western
Christian men have chosen to emulate. The sermon on the mount is not
reflected in Christian history, but this passage from the *Qur'an* mirrors
Christian actions very closely:

> Fight in pursuit of the way of God those who fight against you
> but do not provoke hostility. God has no love for those who
> embark on aggression. Slay them wherever you encounter them
> and drive them out from places whence they have driven you.
> Subversion is a worse thing than slaughter. Do not do battle with
> them, however, in the vicinity of the sacred mosque unless they
> are warring with you there. If they fight you, slay them: such are
> the deserts of those who deny the faith. But if they desist, God is
> certainly forgiving and merciful.
>
> Fight them until there is no more subversion and religion is
> wholly God's. If they desist, hostility is at an end save for those
> who commit evil. Things sacrosanct allow of retaliation, so if in
> the sacred month let it be in the sacred month. Who-ever makes
> aggression against you, take up hostilities in the same measure
> against them, fearing God. Know that God is with those who fear
> Him.
>
> In the path of God, be ready for what it will take and do
> not, by the work of your hands, contrive your own destruction,
> but accomplish what is good. For God loves those who do so.
> (Surah 2:190-195).[7]

Christian tradition is in agreement with the *Qur'an* (and the Hebrew Bible)
that external force is "the arm of God." "It was not you who slew the enemy,
but it was God who slew them" (Surah 8:17//2 Chr 29:15). So while
Christians hold up Jesus as superior to Muhammad, Jesus has inspired little
imitation.

Western charges of the "cruelty" inherent in Muhammad and Islam can only surface because Western Christians apply different standards to the identical behavior of their own religious and national heroes. For they speak with equanimity and pride of the historical periods where powerful Western Christian nations conquered and ruled others. Charges of cruelty are rare even among the religious prototypes such as Joshua who methodically and deliberately destroyed large numbers of Canaanites whose sophisticated civilization equaled that of the Phoenicians, or the deeds of David who "brought back their [Philistine] foreskins and counted them out before the king so that he could be the king's son-in-law" (1 Sam 18:27). Those for whom the term *jihad* (holy war) elicits moral condemnation are usually unaware that Muslim rules for *jihad* share more similarities with Christian rules for just war than differences.[8] Similarly contemporary Judaism supports war and invasion to secure and extend the boundaries of modern day Israel which subjects everyone within its borders to rule based on Jewish assumptions and beliefs.

Jesus: from the patriarchal perspective of Jewish/Christian tradition—One of the greatest sources of pleasure and the central art form in the Middle East for hundreds of years has been poetry. The audiences who first listened to the *Qur'an* were so inspired by its beauty that they could only attribute such a work to God. Both the *Qur'an* and Muhammad epitomize the reciprocal relation which can exist between culture and religion. When linked together, both religion and culture enhance, fortify and extend the other. In some areas, e.g. literature, architecture, music, clothing, customs, etc., it is nearly impossible to judge whether religion or culture has the greater influence. Boundaries tend to disappear when religion and culture are so interwoven. This realization makes it possible to understand that Israel's rejection of Jesus was based on far more than "religious" differences. At the same time, the vital importance of God's household being located within and influenced by the kingdom of God can be more easily understood and appreciated.

Given the standards, values and goals against which males are judged and found worthy of esteem, Jesus does not contain the stuff of which heroes are made. Jesus' revelation of God as Father is not shared by either Judaism or Islam because it defies the boundary maintenance which separation and disparity require. Similarly what Jesus envisioned as proper interpersonal relations is nearly incomprehensible because male honor is not taken into account. Furthermore, power displayed as service finds little appeal among those for whom "status is normally and actively protective of itself, does not allow of being mistaken for what is lower, insists on being acknowledged for what it is and makes vigorous and vigilant assertion of itself."[9] Jesus' parables are insignificant from the standpoint of aesthetics and too vague to be made into laws. His miracles just as frequently inspire disbelief as they inspire belief.

Jesus' eligibility for emulation by others was a problem from the very beginning. In Islam, it is necessary to negate the shameful death of Jesus in order to protect the honor of God and the prophetic role which Islam attributes to Jesus. According to popular Jewish belief, the only thing that sets Jesus apart from other deceased Jews is the determination of his followers to make something more out of him. Paul's solution to this problem was to establish Jesus as the primary archetype of sacrifice. This solution was largely accepted in the West because it validated the parents' (or state's) right to use, abuse or ultimately to kill their own children and those of the enemy, to secure what the parents want. This analogy confirmed that the role of elites was based on the example of God who demanded the death of his innocent Son to restore his honor and to re-establish relations with those who had disobeyed him. Implicit in this story line is the corresponding prerogative to train children and to treat human beings according to whatever method secures the obedience that facilitates implementing those parental (state, church, etc.) rights.

Perception, Authorized Images and Tradition—No group has ever proven itself to be trustworthy in replicating the standards of the kingdom of God. The spread of the gospel depends on individual conversion and the healing of one heart at a time. Yet, how does the individual get beyond the perspective of his or her own personal past, family and group? Perhaps the first step lies in understanding how perception, images and traditions are formed. This awareness might enable individuals to evaluate their own personal and social "realities."

The creation and control of perception by social groups—The first premise is that social groups (e.g. whether ethnic, racial, religious, gender or kinship based, etc.) interpret and assign meaning to every aspect of life. The second premise is that each person comes to know "reality" through the social "lens" of the groups to which the individual belongs. The standpoint of the group forms a part of the "social lens" through which every group member interprets reality. There is no "neutral" or "objective" reality which can be perceived without first filtering it through some standpoint. Interpretation depends on a standpoint to organize raw data (e.g. actions, values, people, experiences, etc.) so that they can be understood by group members. Because "reality" must be interpreted in order to be understood, and because standpoints are needed to organize material, all "reality" is standpoint-dependent. Nothing can be known apart from a standpoint. The standpoint which is used is that of the group.[10]

This brings us to the third premise, that "reality has come to us through the eyes and ears, hearts and minds, images and perceptions, in short, the life experience of the male. Our reality is standpoint-dependent, and it's the standing point of the male."[11] The males referred to have been the elites whose interpretation of reality has been accepted by the entire group. Very few men in any given culture at any given time belonged to those elites who have interpreted and authorized "reality" for all members. Since each person's particular identity, sense of belonging, comfort, meaning and support come from the group(s) to which the person belongs, most people accept "reality' as interpreted (or created) by their elites.

While the first three premises deal with perception, the fourth premise concerns the mechanism by which certain perceptions are filtered out before they enter awareness. Daniel Goleman introduces the concept of socio/personal schemas which make the "mind aware of the meaning of an event **before** that event and its significance enter awareness. In schema terms, this preawareness means that schemas which are activated but are out of awareness, **organize experience and filter it out before it gets into awareness.** Once the most relevant schemas are activated, they 'pop into awareness.'" Goleman goes on to say that while schemas guide awareness, they remain outside of awareness. We know of their existence only by their effects.[12] These schemas render people unconsciously deaf, dumb and blind to both options and inconsistencies that exist in the "reality" promulgated by their elites.

Thus, a standpoint is a social/personal construction which allows group members to interpret or to "see" reality while at the same time filtering out of conscious awareness anything which causes dissonance among certain core symbols. These symbols can be defined as signs filled with social meaning, value and emotion around which personal identity is developed and organized. When conflicts arise which cannot be filtered out of consciousness, a crisis is precipitated which demands the evaluation, reformulation and reorganization of core symbols to reduce anxiety or chaos and regain personal/social equilibrium.

"Reality" is socially interpreted according to the standpoint of its social system. The social system of Jesus' society and those which subsequently interpreted the meaning of Jesus were patriarchal. "Patriarchy has a view of the human as normatively male: the illusion that when you've seen life from a male point of view you have seen life from the human point of view."[13] Thus, the functions, positions and roles assigned to God, nature, men, women, children, animals, insiders, outsiders, emotions, thinking, etc., are interpreted and assigned value from a male perspective or, more accurately, the standpoint of male elites.

Authorized images and history—Understanding how individuals or groups are described or represented to the public enables a person to discover and evaluate the adequacy of the authorized images that portray individuals based on group membership. As Margaret Miles asks, "By what 'system of power' are certain representations authorized while others are blocked, prohibited, invalidated or ignored?"[14] For various reasons, the images that are publicized in any social system may not represent the collective perception of the subordinate groups which are being described. The following examples depict situations where the publicized "image" of a group is either inadequate or totally misleading.

First, there may be little or no unanimity among subordinate group members as to the validity of the collective image being authorized by the dominant group. For example, women have been considered a subordinate group in patriarchies. As such, there is a collectively held image of woman which appears in the popular imagination as well as in legal, religious, historical and philosophical texts. Despite the longevity of this "traditional" image, it has been impossible to achieve unanimity among **women** as to what constitutes an adequate image because there is no single image or type of woman with which all women identify. Hence, while the "received" image of woman was not accepted by all women, it remained unchallenged by them for a long time.

Second, the collective sense of identity of the subordinate group might remain unknown or unarticulated among subordinate group members themselves. For example, children fall into this category of a subordinate group whose lack of cognitive development makes them unable to represent themselves in abstract categories. As such, children's behavior has been variously interpreted by adults. One significant contributor to the "received" Western image of children is Sigmund Freud. He took the desires and behaviors which he knew were present in the adults who abused children and claimed that they existed not in the abuser but in the victim. Thus, Freud created theories of child development that suppressed the extent to which he knew children were sexually, physically and emotionally abused by the adults in their families, and other adults to whom they had been entrusted for care. His allocation of adult motives and behavior to children enabled Freud to regain the support of his peers which he had lost after publicizing his original findings regarding the abusive treatment of children and its long term effects.[15]

Third, the image of the subordinate group authorized by the dominant group might never be challenged, either to insiders or to outsiders. For example, Western stereotypes of Arabs and Islam[16] are given so little weight among Arabs who live in the Middle East that most Arabs living in the West as a subordinate group do not feel compelled to protest derogatory stereotypes.

In light of the limitations which exist in creating an adequate image of any subordinate group, it would serve each of us well to live with the ongoing suspicion that certain representations may reveal more about the dominant power that created and authorized them than they reveal about the group being represented. By asking **who gains** from the image that is publicized, Edward Said discusses this problem of image-making as it affects Arabs and

Muslims in general, and Palestinians in particular.[17] If the researcher knows who publicizes and authorizes certain representations of the subordinate group, then she or he also knows who benefits from the image projected. Usually the dominant group, the audience for whom the author writes, is the one who benefits from the images it approves and publicizes about subordinate groups. Certainly Freud is a good example of someone who sacrificed children (the subordinate group) to benefit his own career by regaining the support of his colleagues (the dominant group).

Writing history is another example of how the dominant group solidifies its claims not only by interpreting what happened according to its own viewpoint, but also by creating history as it must have happened or as it should have happened. The dominant group that recorded history in America was composed of white, Anglo-Saxon, Protestant males who portrayed all other ethnic, religious and gender groups according to the accepted WASP, male standpoint. Thus, American history is another example of the social interpretation of reality according to the social/personal standpoint of historians, who either omitted "outsiders" or portrayed them in their narratives according to the expectations of the dominant group. Since "authorized versions" play such a crucial role in maintaining the dominant group in power, the relation between knowledge and power cannot be taken for granted.

"Knowledge" plays a crucial role in giving one group power over another. Edward Said makes a suggestion for cross-cultural studies which is equally valid for any group that views non-members as outsiders to be studied for purposes of control. Said proposes that the category "interpretation" is preferable to the category of "knowledge" when discussing non-members or outsiders. The category of "interpretation" is a far more flexible category which is amenable to changing insights, while the category of "knowledge" implies something fixed or permanent that is subsequently recorded, mastered and passed on for posterity with little possibility of change. "Interpretation" implies an awareness of human limitations in understanding the unknown, while "knowledge" tends to generate certainty with little need to re-evaluate. "Interpretation" does not presume control, while "knowledge" is the outcome of a process which begins with gathering "information" for the purpose of gaining control over some field, area or group.[18] In this sequence, "information" produces "facts" that contribute to "knowledge" which aids in gaining control of an "outgroup" or "subgroup." Various dominant groups have authorized and publicized their "knowledge" about the previously cited subordinate groups to the detriment of both subordinate group members and "outgroup" members as well.[19]

The relation between social perception and personal identity—The social system in which the individual matures constructs the categories in which both males and females understand themselves and the world. While pure patriarchy is declining wherever the legal rights of women and children are being recognized and the male role is changing, residual effects are seen in every area of life. Originally this bias against the flesh and sexual inequality were institutionalized in traditional patriarchal systems where women were excluded from legal identity, social status, economic and political power. While this situation is slowly changing in many social institutions (though not many religious ones), the attitudes which continue to foster these prejudices against nature and those closely associated with it can be categorized under "patrism" (like its equivalent, racism). Patrism is characterized by discriminatory, prejudicial and paternalistic beliefs about the inferiority of females, the domestic domain, children and nature as well as the values, needs and services which maintain them.[20]

Socialization involves a process where personal subjectivity, each person's sense of "I," is "created and informed by relationships and by the symbolic provisions of culture."[21] Thus, each social system contributes to the "I" each person uses as uniquely his or her own. Where strongly cohesive groups fuse individual boundaries, the group has nearly total control of the personal content of each "I" in the group. Group power is used to shape individual identity through its history, traditions, customs and laws. Christian tradition continues to promulgate as authoritative a wide range of writings (and scriptures) that debase and denigrate women. And while it was the gender role socially created and assigned to the **male**[22] that required significant changes to bring it in line with the gospels, today it is the **female role** which is more often being recast in the image of the male role.

Becoming Like Children and the Child Within—The gospel images of God as Father and of believers as his children require interpretation from the domestic perspective. Jesus' life and teachings reveal a God whose fathering is not impaired by deprivation, emptiness, caprice, cruelty or revenge. God acts out of such utter abundance as to defy human imagination which is always tempered by human experiences of privation. Furthermore, Jesus' role in the household of God demonstrates that he also acted from a position of abundance, not deprivation. Those who have been deprived of what they needed in childhood organize their adult lives around "filling their empty places." Such deprivation has a profound impact on human growth, perception and subsequent parenting.

The gospel axiom, "Truly, I say to you, unless you turn and become like children, you will never enter the kingdom of heaven" (Mt 18:3//Mk 9:37//Lk 9:48), gives children a place unprecedented in either Judaism or Islam. Both religions share an interpretation of nature rooted in a patriarchal perception that human beings tend toward evil (Gen 6:5ff, Surah 10:23).[23] Jesus' words and actions are at odds with that interpretation of nature. The gospels testify that the roots of human innocence and goodness are found in childhood (contrary to Genesis 8:21, ". . . the imagination of man's heart is evil from his youth"). Placing the child as a core symbol, Jesus set himself against everything which threatened to erode the innocence and goodness which is the human condition at birth. A good part of Jesus' efforts and energies were expended in the task of helping to restore these gifts of childhood once they were lost. This task of restoration and healing continues today among those who seek to uncover where the "Child Within" was abused, lost or abandoned. This process facilitates the healing and restoration of human beings who are called to full growth and happiness as children of God.

Human nature: What all human beings share—Nature has come to be known through the same process of social perception already described. There are multiple perspectives as to what constitutes optimal human behavior. The gospels do not accept patriarchy's authorized images of children which require punishment as a necessary part of "training" or "child rearing." While Jesus' understanding of human development is implied in his words and actions, it was never articulated. What remains for believers is to discover and promulgate an understanding of human nature, growth and needs which are in harmony with the expectations of the kingdom of God. The works of Alice Miller and J. Konrad Stettbacher[24] are used here because their understanding of human growth, primal needs and the child are compatible with the image of goodness and innocence that Jesus presumes when he declares that the kingdom of God belongs to children.

Everyone comes into the world as an infant. The senses are an integral part of the physical body. Sense perceptions and a person's reactions to these perceptions form the earliest strata of human development. Physical sensing gives rise to the second level of perception which is feelings. Together these two most basic functions determine that what gives pleasure is good while that which causes pain is bad. Written into the earliest strata of human memory are experiences which serve as premonitions about what is bad and what is good. These premonitions form the foundation for the choices each person will make. The cognitive level (thinking) will take longer to evolve than either the physical or emotional levels which are operative at birth.

This lack of cognitive development in these early stages makes it impossible for the infant (and child) either to interpret what is happening or to understand it. It is the responsibility of those who care for the child to meet a wide range of physical and emotional needs which will enable the child to establish and maintain a positive, healthy, confident and vital relation with the self and the environment. If the child's primal needs are not met, a growing sense of uncertainty will elicit fear and pain. When there is either no response, a harmful or an inadequate response to the child's cries and other signs of distress, the child's ability to form relationships will become increasingly impaired. Along with this is a growing fear of his or her own needs coupled with feelings of inadequacy or failure. Experience leads the child to expect pain when it senses and feels a need. When the need becomes stronger than the fear and pain it initially triggered, the child will be willing to accept whatever the environment makes available as a substitute for the real needs which continue to go unsatisfied.

All injuries to the primal integrity of the infant arise from the negation of his or her needs. Unfulfilled needs impair a person's ability to form relationships. This impairment or disturbance in one's ability to form relationships is caused by others who are themselves disturbed. One manifestation of an impaired ability to relate is the inability to perceive human needs, to respect them and to satisfy them. Other manifestations include defective reactions toward the self and/or others that confuse, inhibit, endanger or damage either the self or the other(s). The evolving capacity to think, to reflect and to understand will reflect the disturbances that already exist in the individual's primal integrity.[25]

If the primal needs are satisfied, the child within (also known as the real self) can be described as follows:

> Our Real Self is spontaneous, expansive, loving, giving and communicating. Our True Self accepts ourselves and others. It feels, whether the feelings may be joyful or painful. And it expresses those feelings. Our Real Self accepts our feelings without judgment and fear, and allows them to exist as a valid way of assessing and appreciating life's events.
>
> Our Child Within is expressive, assertive, and creative. It can be childlike in the highest, most mature, and evolved sense of that word. It needs to play and to have fun. And yet it is vulnerable, perhaps because it is so open and trusting. It surrenders to itself, to others and ultimately to the universe. And yet it is powerful in the true sense of power. It is healthily self-indulgent, taking pleasure in receiving and in being nurtured. It is open to that vast and mysterious part of us that we call our unconscious. It pays attention to the messages that we receive daily from the unconscious, such as dreams, struggles and illness.
>
> Our false self is a cover-up. It is inhibited, contracting and fearful...It is envious, critical, idealized, blaming, shaming and perfectionistic...it is over-conforming...covers up, hides or denies feelings.[26]

Personal, social and generational boundaries—The creation and maintenance of personal boundaries are primal needs. Boundaries are important because they are lines that mark limits. Each person has a right to physical, emotional, intellectual and spiritual boundaries of his/her own. Violation of any of those boundaries creates a sense of shame. Most adults have experienced some blurring or violation of boundaries in several areas before they reach adulthood.

1. The most personal boundary is the ego boundary which "guards an individual's inner space, the very means he or she employs for screening and interpreting the outside world and for modulating and regulating his or her interactions with that world." A person with clear boundaries can mature and develop into a complete and competent self. Without clearly defined boundaries, one cannot establish an identity.[27] Separation from the mother for **both** males and females is the beginning of this process. Distinguishing the self from other things around leads each person to distinguishing between external things.

Boundary formation continues as cognitive abilities evolve. As the child first discovered that he or she was separate from the mother, so must the individual be able to perceive himself or herself as separate from the larger groups which create reality and control perception. Eye-heart formation continues throughout this evolution of identity which depends on the creation and maintenance of personal boundaries.

2. Another important category of boundaries exists between generations: the family boundaries between generations as well as those areas outside the family which replicate the parent/child imbalance of power and experience. First, generational boundaries must be set by adults to protect those young members whose lack of experience, autonomy and power places him/her at high risk in adult/child relations (or teacher/pupil, doctor/patient, employer/employee). Second, well-maintained boundaries protect the growing identity of the child/novice from incorporating the blame for the failings of parents and authority figures. Adults who fail to establish and maintain this boundary are responsible for the sense of shame or personal diminishment which inappropriately becomes a part of the beginner's "I." Third, inter-generational boundaries keep the failures of previous generations from necessarily perpetuating themselves among members of the new generation who had no choice or influence over what their parents or forefathers did but who can make their own decision.

Where boundaries among internal members are fused,[28] those who are in positions of power and influence (whether physical or symbolic) can readily violate the physical, sexual, emotional and spiritual boundaries of those who are weaker or less experienced or who are isolated. Thus **any member** in the system whose personal boundaries have been violated experiences a pervasive sense of shame on several levels, feeling that s/he is "fundamentally bad, inadequate, defective, unworthy, or not fully valid as a human being."[29]

Healing the child within—Boundary violations, whether emotional, physical, sexual, psychological, spiritual or intellectual, impair the process of creating/discovering one's own personal identity. Since individual roots are grounded in childhood out of which the adult emerges, growth is profoundly affected by early violations. Yet, the human drive toward health and integration is not halted even in the face of overwhelming shame. Communication (mouth/ears) and actions (hands/feet), which appear to be at odds with what the heart/mind desires at the **present time**, nevertheless reveal an **earlier** strata when abusive experience(s) impaired the eye/heart zone because they were never acknowledged as personal violations. Innocence and goodness can only be restored by helping blocked memories expose shameful experiences along with the feelings which were forbidden in the original situation. This process allows for the restoration of innate abilities which have come to be lost to human beings as the result of childhood abuse.

The first boundary violations often take place in the family of birth, the arena in which the child learns to become "deaf, dumb and blind." The parents are the child's first experience of a "God" figure and can retain that aura even after children have become adults. Family roles and behavior are not random or open ended. There is a script or an organizing principle which may not be initially conscious or obvious. The family functions as a system where the individual is but one component who is needed to continue performing in the manner in which s/he was raised. Systems are self-perpetuating and depend on all the components working together. Each member might play several roles from which his or her identity evolved and remained, largely unchanged, into adulthood. Family systems that are organized around secrecy and abuse will fight those members who threaten "to expose" the family secret even to its own members who have been trained to minimize, to rationalize or to deny it.

Family members who become adults intent on healing from abusive past experiences may not find straightforward support or encouragement from the family unit. No other human relation comes close to the totally asymmetrical power relation that exists between parent and child. Even when the child grows to adulthood, varying degrees of the original power relation still remain. Because of this, insistence that victims forgive abusers can halt the victims' recovery. Where abuse and power were never experienced as separate but necessarily fused together, "forgiveness" is interpreted as restoring the abuser to power by "divine" decree. If the abuser is "reinstated" by forgiveness, then victimhood appears to be permanent and all hope for healing and autonomy is lost. Under these circumstances, forgiveness is not only disruptive to recovery but making forgiveness either the goal or standard of health can make recovery impossible altogether. The goal is complete healing and restoration of the individual's full potential.[30]

Often enough, healing is not possible within the family structure, though relations between individual members might continue. Nevertheless, total change is mandated as an appropriate response to the Gospel. Personal changes necessarily affect, alter and sometimes upset the maintenance of interpersonal relations (including family ones) which are both detrimental to healing as well as impediments in organizing one's life around healthier goals and standards.

There are adults whose identity was the result of "committee work" where parents, siblings, teachers and other significant people "created" a lifetime identity for children who were to benefit someone else's needs, weaknesses or blindness. This kind of formation necessarily violates boundaries, creates a false self and perpetuates a shame-bound social system characterized by control, perfectionism, rigidity, blame and denial. Children who were raised to devalue feelings and physical pain will have to reincorporate the use of their senses, rediscover and learn to value their feelings. The boy or girl whose body has been violated by physical or sexual abuse will need to reintegrate the physical dimensions with a new sense of self. Neither detachment from feelings nor crucifying the flesh leads to restoration and wholeness. The body is **not** an object but an integral part of identity and interaction with the world. For those who were prohibited from learning by either neglect, hunger, chaos, abuse or poor pedagogy in their childhood, learning and thinking skills will have to be incorporated. Those children who lost their "NO" ability, their autonomy, their decision-making abilities or their perseverance, will have to forge piece by piece the ability to choose, to act and to carry through to completion.

Ignoring primal needs frustrates human nature—Primal needs are part of human nature. How these needs are perceived is determined by the group. How well these needs should be satisfied in individual children reflects the group's interpretation combined with the personal experiences of those who deal directly with children. The relation between childhood experiences and adult behavior is also a matter of group perception. This relation is subject to diverse and conflicting interpretations. The following passage by Alice Miller[31] describes the process that begins when primal human needs are discounted or frustrated. When the satisfaction of needs is replaced by their frustration, human beings adapt to that frustration in various ways.

1. All children are born to grow, to develop, to live, to love, and to articulate their needs and feelings for self-protection.

2. For their development children need the respect and protection of adults who take them seriously, love them, and honestly help them to become oriented in the world.

3. When these vital needs are frustrated and children are

instead abused for the sake of adults' needs by being exploited, beaten, punished, taken advantage of, manipulated, neglected, or deceived without the intervention of any witness, then their integrity will be lastingly impaired.

4. The normal reactions to such injury should be anger and pain; since children in this hurtful kind of environment, however, are forbidden to express their anger and since it would be unbearable to experience their pain all alone, they are compelled to suppress their feelings, repress all memory of the trauma, and idealize those guilty of the abuse. Later **they will have no memory of what was done to them**.

5. Disassociated from the original cause, their feelings of anger, helplessness, despair, longing, anxiety, and pain will find expression in destructive acts against others (criminal behavior, mass murder) or against themselves (drug addiction, alcoholism, prostitution, psychic disorders, suicide).

6. If these people become parents, they will then often direct acts of revenge for their mistreatment in childhood against their own children, whom they use as scapegoats. Child abuse is still sanctioned—indeed, held in high regard—in our society as long as it is defined as childrearing. It is a tragic fact that parents beat their children in order to escape the emotions stemming from how they were treated by their own parents.

7. If mistreated children are not to become criminals or mentally ill, it is essential that at least once in their life they come in contact with a person who knows without any doubt that the environment, not the helpless, battered child, is at fault. In this regard, knowledge or ignorance on the part of society can be instrumental in either saving or destroying life. Here lies the great opportunity for relatives, social workers, therapists, teachers, doctors, psychiatrists, officials, and nurses to **support the child and to believe her or him.**

8. Till now, society has protected the adult and blamed the victim. It has been abetted in its blindness by theories, still in keeping with the pedagogical principles of our great-grandparents, according to which children are viewed as crafty creatures, dominated by wicked drives, who invent stories and attack their innocent parents or desire them sexually. In reality, children tend to blame themselves for their parents' cruelty and to absolve the parents, whom they invariably love, of all responsibility.

9. For some years now, it has been possible to prove, thanks to the use of new therapeutic methods, that repressed trau-

matic experiences in childhood are stored up in the body and, although remaining unconscious, exert their influence even in adulthood. In addition, electronic testing of the fetus has revealed a fact previously unknown to most adults: **a child responds to and learns both tenderness and cruelty from the very beginning**.

10. In the light of this new knowledge, even the most absurd behavior reveals its formerly hidden logic once the traumatic experiences of childhood no longer must remain shrouded in darkness.

11. Our sensitization to the cruelty with which children are treated, until now commonly denied, and to the consequences of such treatment will as a matter of course bring to an end the perpetuation of violence from generation to generation.

12. People whose integrity has not been damaged in childhood, who were protected, respected, and treated with honesty by their parents, will be—both in their youth and adulthood—intelligent, responsive, empathic, and highly sensitive. They will take pleasure in life and will not feel any need to kill or even hurt others or themselves. They will use their power to defend themselves but not to attack others. They will not be able to do otherwise than to respect and protect those weaker than themselves, including their children, because this is what they have learned from their own experience and because it is **this** knowledge (and not the experience of cruelty) that has been stored up inside them from the beginning. Such people will be incapable of understanding why earlier generations had to build up a gigantic war industry in order to feel at ease and safe in this world. Since it will not have to be their unconscious life-task to ward off intimidation experienced at a very early age, they will be able to deal with attempts at intimidation in their adult life more rationally and more creatively.

Human nature contains within it the raw material that enables human beings to become children of God. This potential can be impaired or destroyed at the social level in several ways. The social perception, first, controls how nature, the growth process and children are viewed; second, decides what human needs are and how they should be met; and third, shapes the identity of its members in the images it creates and publicizes about insiders as well as outsiders. Individual experiences on the personal level often replicate the social perception which devalues those who are powerless, vulnerable and in need of care.

Jesus: For "The Nations"—The gospels remain as the most trustworthy sources that introduce people to Jesus, to God as Father and to the kingdom of God. Jesus remains the central figure of the gospels because he embodies the intentions of God for human beings and continues to act in their best interests. Since Jesus himself belonged to the house of Israel, he addressed audiences that were primarily members of his own group. Those members in turn presented Jesus primarily to other members of Israel. As a result, the Hebrew scriptures were commonly used to interpret Jesus and his meaning to the satisfaction of Jews. Of secondary importance to Jewish-Christians was Jesus' significance for the Gentiles ("the nations"). When that role was articulated, it was done so from the perspective of the Hebrew scriptures to ease the problems that Jewish-Christians had accepting Gentile-Christians into their groups. For that reason, the intended audience was still not Gentiles but Jews.

The advent of the third Christian millennium is marked by the erosion of patriarchy as the underlying component in some countries. The traditional perception of reality is changing. As mentioned in the Introduction, the areas that have shaped traditional Christian thought and behavior are the Hebrew epic, Greek philosophy and Roman law. Each of these three influences bear witness to the various perceptions of patriarchy that existed in the social systems in which Christianity was articulated. In addition to the shared social matrix and the Hebrew scriptures which are present in the gospels, Jesus was directly involved with nature.

The title "Son of man" establishes that the common denominator between Jesus and his audience was their shared humanity. He chose images and stories to introduce God as Father and to teach the standards of the kingdom. Through parables Jesus was able to highlight relations, actions and problems that are common to all human beings. His personal role accented the domestic activities and concerns for satisfying basic human needs which all peoples share. The miracles offer further testimony that no aspect of nature is hostile or impervious to the word of God. The words, the actions and the revelation that are embodied in Jesus establish once and for all that nature can be trusted. Children, those who are more controlled by nature than by culture, were the ones Jesus declared to be members of the kingdom of God just by virtue of their stage in life. The scripture on which Jesus chose to base his revelation of God was the "scripture" of nature that had been created by his Father.

Children: the new starting point for theology—Those writings which come to be regarded as sacred scriptures are always rooted in their initial, creative social systems. The writings are accepted by believers because they share a perception which the believer accepts as reality. For example, the main symbol which binds the members of the house of Israel together today is the belief that Israel enjoys elite status among the nations. This belief joins those Jews who believe in God with those members who do not; those who live in Israel with those other members who do not; and those who live according to Jewish law and custom with those members who do not. In Islam, the maintenance and defense of honor on all levels is the thread that links culture with religion. Reality is perceived and ordered in such a way that the honor of God, the prophet, Islam, and believers are protected and enhanced. This acceptance of honor as the central value can be seen throughout the *Qur'an*.[32] The gospels have rarely been taken seriously because the standards which they espouse are not esteemed by any social system.

Jesus linked entering the kingdom of God with becoming like children. This connection went hand in hand with his declaration that God intended to relate to people individually like a father to his child. There is no unanimous understanding of what it means to be a child or how a father should act. Jesus did not articulate his understanding of the child. It remains for those attached to Jesus to create or to adopt models that mirror nature as understood by Jesus' words and actions. The models of growth and development as well as that of parenting which have been used in this book are those advanced by Miller and Stettbacher because they are in line with gospel standards and goals. No social system gains from their image of child. Instead this model puts an effective end to the belief that children can be sacrificed for their parents, teachers, civil or religious leaders without culpability. This model allows adults who were abused as children to turn and become like children again.

Jesus' role was based on that of the first century Mediterranean wife/mother because her role bound her to the care and nurture of children. Children were expected to occupy the central position in their mothers' lives. **Only** in that central position is the infant and child able to take from his or her mother (or from one who "acts" like a mother) what is needed to flourish in all the complex dimensions which human development requires.[33] This means that the child is accepted and cared for as the central character in **his/her own** life. While the child comes from the mother and for a period of time is part of the mother, the fetus or embryo is not one of her own body parts. The child does not exist to meet the needs of the mother (or father) nor to compensate for what is missing in their lives. Instead, the **parents** exist to meet the needs of the child and to compensate for those areas which have not yet developed (thinking, problem solving, etc.).

Children and the process of "belief"—The direction of the gospel is from the personal to the social; from the private to the public. Those analogies which have been taken from the public realm for centuries must be set aside as new analogies arise from the domestic domain. The beginning and end point for all Christian theology is the child. Metaphors based on sacrifice must be set aside because they reveal a false image of God which no child could ever trust. In addition, these images and analogies impede growth and healing because they are based on intimidation and fear. Inscribed in human flesh is the inclination toward one who is good, lovable, caring, attentive and trustworthy and **away from** those who are vindictive, harmful, selfish, negligent or violent and untrustworthy. Those who are called to be children of God depend on the parenting of Jesus for all they need in order to develop their identity in relation to God. This relation with Jesus is an extension of human parenting. The central concern of those who follow Jesus is fostering belief but **only** where belief is warranted.

Despite Jesus' best efforts as remembered in the gospels, the absence of faith or the lack of belief among his disciples and followers was an ongoing problem even after the resurrection. As mentioned previously, fidelity, constancy and reliability are the qualities needed to elicit belief and trust. Either the disciples and his followers had internalized a God who was untrustworthy and therefore inspired little or no faith, or they were unable to perceive who was trustworthy and who was not, or they had been rendered incapable of faith by experiences of mistreatment and betrayal by those whom they had trusted and loved. In the first instance, the problem lies with the object (or person) who is not trustworthy. In the second instance, the problem lies in a faulty or inadequately developed perception as to how to evaluate who is trustworthy. In the third example, it is the individual who has become mistrustful and unable to believe. Usually all three problems go hand in hand.

This human process that enables one to believe provides the standards against which theology must be evaluated. Written into human nature are basic needs which must be satisfied for the growth and development of each person. When these needs are not met, relations to the self and others are impaired. A lack of belief or trust in the self is the first indication that suffering is altering nature's agenda. Eventually the ability to perceive who is trustworthy is damaged. This leads in turn to impaired relations with other people and the surrounding world. Finally, a point may be reached where the individual is unable to believe or to trust anyone. Suffering, pain and frustration distort and pervert nature's thrust toward optimal human development which necessarily includes enjoyable inter-relations.

Christian theology must build on this natural human process which results in belief. First, the individual must be able to have confidence or faith in himself. Second, the object or person in whom the individual is asked to believe must be trustworthy. Third, the process of determining who or what is trustworthy must be well-developed. The individual will be able to trust once the first three requirements are met. The "scripture" of nature shows this process of belief to be one of the earliest functions initiated in the infant. The ability to believe in the self continues its critical development in the earliest years of life. The archaic memory of each person is lodged in the body and emotions. That is where the earliest traces of mistrust are found when primal needs were not met. The direction that leads toward God resides in the satisfaction of primal needs and the honoring of those early feelings. This is the thrust of nature which theology can neither overlook nor violate. When Jesus declared children to be worthy of the kingdom **because** they were children, he did so knowing that they were basically physical bodies and emotions with continuous needs and little cognitive development.

Jesus satisfied concrete, physical human needs. Meeting primal needs enables people to trust. From these experiences with others, people develop integrity and self-confidence. The denigration of nature, of women, of natural processes and of children are continuous themes throughout Christian tradition. The theory of original sin obscured the words and example of Jesus by replicating the social world and the patriarchal view of nature. Original sin denies the inherent goodness of human beings, disdains human needs and creates distrust in the process of growth. Not only does the human image suffer but the interpersonal dynamics which are integral to human development have been perverted by this theory as well. Human nature has never been the problem. Jesus did not intend to save people from human nature. Instead he reinterpreted it, honored it and satisfied basic human needs.

Children are those who are totally dependent on others who are charged with their care. They learn how to care for others based on their own experiences of being needy, weak, powerless, speechless and with no cognitive ability that allows for understanding. Theology that disdains, ignores, denies or is ignorant of human needs and processes undermines primal integrity. This influence erodes the Christian's confidence in the inner course or direction which God places in all human beings at conception. When theology serves as the handmaiden of social systems which are at odds with the standards of the kingdom of God, and when that theology goes unchallenged and unchanged for centuries, the outcome is not individuals who can turn and become like children. The outcome is people who are unable to believe either in themselves or in others.

Peace that kills vs. healing disorder—In the world of Jesus, the family was the central social unit. Then as now, the strongest ties were not only **not** chosen, they "just happen" as accidents of birth. Similarly, the social system which shapes and controls one's perception of reality is not chosen; it too surrounds the individual as yet another accident of birth. How can human beings change when their most significant relations and creators of perception demand complete and unquestioning loyalty?

> Do not think that I have come to bring peace on earth; I have not come to bring peace but a sword. For I have come to set a man

against his father, and a daughter against her mother, and a daughter-in-law against her mother-in-law; and a man's foes will be those of his own household. He who loves father or mother more than me is not worthy of me; and he who loves son or daughter more than me is not worthy of me; and he who does not take up his cross and follow me is not worthy of me. He who finds his life will lose it, and he who loses his life for my sake will find it (Mt 10:34-39; cf. Prov 6:16–19).

This passage was addressed to those whose lives were organized around loyalty to the family as the primary social unit and to Israel as the wider social group. In this context, the cross was more than a symbol of torture and death. It was the means by which a member was expelled from the group (Deut 21:22-23). To be considered an enemy within the family and to be expelled from one's group amounted to losing one's life. For the follower of Jesus, the cross is the ultimate symbol of exile from those families which are not organized around God as Father, and expulsion from those groups which do not accept the standards of the kingdom. Because of exclusive attachment to Jesus, the outcome is a real loss of life as one has been enculturated to understand life.

Christianity is in need of a radical change in both its theology and pedagogy. The proclamation of the kingdom of God is the central concern of theology. That kingdom is the larger group which sets new social standards for believers. These standards support a household where everyone can experience the nurture and care of God which was manifested in Jesus. This kind of parenting heals people from the limitations of their own families and groups. Such healing enables adults to turn and become like children in a world where they reflect the continuity of God's love to those who are "blessed," e.g. **not** "the chosen" and the elite but instead the poor, the sorrowing, the downtrodden, sinners, those whose voices are not heard and whose basic human needs are ignored by society. The axiom of nature in the gospels was never survival of the fittest but optimal growth for everyone.

The God that Jesus reveals as Father continues to be active among human beings. His activity is not characterized by force and coercion. Instead he gives from his immeasurable abundance, from his infinite superfluity to those who have less and to those who have nothing. Power is manifested by his children through service to those in need because that is how God acts. The direction in the kingdom is always service from those who are stronger to those who are weaker and from those who have more to those who have less. All roles within the household and kingdom arise in this manner to reflect the "mothering" of Jesus and the "fathering" of God. The gospels alone provide adequate models for gender roles and parenting based on the words and example of Jesus. For two millennia these muted models have stood in opposition to society's patriarchal model. Possibly the time is approaching when changes in the public and domestic roles of the male can be more comprehensive and socially integrated than mandatory celibacy for a few who live outside common human patterns. Perhaps the muted image of Jesus that has remained suppressed and unspoken in Christian tradition will gather sound and finally be heard as the Word of God in the third millennium.

NOTES

INTRODUCTION

1. Many of the anthropological insights into the traditional roles of women were gained in personal relations with Palestinian women both in the Israeli Occupied West Bank as well as those now living in other countries. The gender expectations common to the Hebrew scriptures, the gospels and epistles reveal expectations of the domestic domain remarkably like those found in contemporary anthropological studies as well as Jewish and non-Jewish writings that immediately precede and follow the time of Jesus. (Cf. endnote 14 for additional sources.)

Based on documents from the tenth to the thirteenth century AD, S.D. Goitein's five volume work, *A Mediterranean Society* (Berkeley: Univ. of California Press, publ. between 1967-1988), provides a window on the world of medieval Jews and Arabs. His translation and commentary on these documents establishes the medieval link demonstrating the continuity of traditional gender roles among non-elite men and women from earlier times. Contemporary anthropological studies in the same regions corroborate the maintenance of that social system (more so in rural areas), except where economic necessity is moving the woman from the house to the workplace. The family is the central social institution and life is still organized around the maintenance of family honor. Thus, the domestic life, the role of women and the interpretations given to this realm retain many of their traditional features.

It is my contention that insights into the world of Jesus can be gained from later regional developments such as Islam, and contemporary anthropological studies of the Middle East and Mediterranean areas as well. While the material that is cited in the following description of the idealized woman is from anthropological studies of contemporary Greek women, other studies of Arab women present a similar picture of the traditional world of women, e.g.

Soraya Altorki, *Women in Saudi Arabia* (New York: Columbia Univ. Press, 1986).

Carla Makhlouf, *Changing Veils* (Austin: Univ. of Texas Press, 1979).

Mona Mikhail, *Images of Arab Women* (Washington, D.C.: Three Continents Press, Inc., 1979).

174

Linda Usra Soffan, *The Women of the United Arab Emirates* (New York: Harper & Row, 1980).

It should also be noted that where the family is the central social institution, patriarchal social systems around the world share much in common with the traditional gender roles and expectations found in the Mediterranean and the Middle East.

2. Goitein, Vol. III, "The Family," p. 227.

3. Jill Dubisch, "Culture Enters through the Kitchen: Women, Food, and Social Boundaries in Rural Greece," in Jill Dubisch (ed.), *Gender & Power in Rural Greece* (Princeton: Princeton University Press, 1986), p. 197.

4. Muriel Dimen, "Servants and Sentries: Women, Power, and Social Reproduction in Kriovrisi," in Dubisch (ed.), pp. 58ff.

5. Dimen in Dubisch (ed.), p. 63.

6. Dubisch, "Culture Enters through the Kitchen," in Dubisch (ed.), p. 207.

7. Dubisch, "Introduction," in Dubisch (ed.), p. 36.

8. Dimen in Dubisch (ed.), p. 54.

9. Dimen in Dubisch (ed.), p. 63.

10. Dimen in Dubisch (ed.), p. 61.

11. Dubisch, "Introduction," in Dubisch (ed.), p. 29.

12. Dubisch, "Culture Enters through the Kitchen," in Dubisch (ed.), pp. 195-212.

13. Dubisch, "Introduction," in Dubisch (ed.), pp. 15-24.

14. Additional descriptions of the woman's role in the time of Jesus may be found in:

Joachim Jeremias, *Jerusalem in the Time of Jesus* (London: SCM Press Ltd, 1976), "The Social Position of Women."

S. Safrai, "Home and Family" in S. Safrai and M. Stern (eds.) in cooperation with D. Flusser and W.C. Van Unnik, *The Jewish People in the First Century,* Vol. II (Assen/Amsterdam: Van Gorcum, 1976), pp. 728-793.

Leonard Swidler, *Woman in Judaism* (Metuchen, N.J.; The Scarecrow Press, Inc., 1976).

15. Safrai, p. 754.

16. The role of the wife of the absent husband is older than Penelope, the wife of Odysseus in Homer's epic, *The Odyssey.* Women have been left at home in charge of both family honor and property while men left to find employment, apply their trades where they could find work, travel with caravans, fight in wars and sail ships.

Eleni by Nicholas Gage, who was born in Greece and lived there until he was nine years old, describes the demands placed on his mother as the "wife of the absent husband" (*taxidimeni* Gk.). His works are significant beyond the anthropology that his accounts necessarily include. His mother was truly a hero **as a woman**, not because she acted like a man. Her son's drive to learn the circumstances surrounding her torture and death resulted in a profound insight which altered his plan for revenge. The impact of Gage's personal insight clarified the extent to which Christians have been impoverished by a tradition which devalued the domestic sphere and inadvertently overlooked the central role it played in the words and actions of Jesus. Both books deserve a careful reading:

Nicholas Gage, *Eleni* (New York: Random House, 1983).

_____, *A Place for Us* (Boston: Houghton Mifflin Co., 1989).

17. The Revised Standard Version of the Bible is used throughout this book.

CHAPTER I

1. This image was accepted by Matthew and Luke who integrated other traditions which expanded the Markan image without changing its basic contours. Likewise, many themes appear in Mark that are further developed in Matthew and Luke. These will be described in the following chapters with references to parallel passages (//) in Mark.

2. Translations of the New Testament from Greek may include shortcomings that reflect the ideology of the translators. The first bias reflects the concern of translators to keep new translations in line with earlier translations which many people have already committed to memory, e.g. "Preaching a baptism for the repentance of sins." This is a translation that has been reduced to a neat formula, easily memorized but devoid of all emotional impact. Cast as religious jargon, the words no longer resonate as a part of daily life.

The second bias appears where more common words replace obscure words despite the change in meaning, e.g. "Gehenna" is translated "hell" when in fact the concept of hell springs from different roots and obscures the images that arise with Gehenna. More will be said about this in endnote 22. Another example is the word which means one's inmost being, the self, as well as the life which animates the person. Though translated "soul," it derives nothing from the Greek perspective in which the "soul" was believed to be at odds with the body.

The third bias is interested in making translations which confirm religious doctrines arrived at independently of scriptural evidence. An example of theology radically affecting translation is to be found in the Jerusalem Bible when it translates a word to mean "brothers" but when it refers to Jesus' brothers amends that meaning in various ways throughout the footnotes. Another critical example will be given in Chapter IV. These are only a few examples of difficulties caused by translations.

3. Goitein, Vol. III, pp. 70, 116, 126.

4. Goitein, Vol. III, pp. 172ff. While the author's examples are from the middle ages, his quote from *Theseus* by Sophocles has a woman saying, "As soon as we reach our youth and our mind begins to awaken, we are sent away from home...far from the gods of our fathers, far from those who brought us into the world, to live among strangers." The role Jesus played and the image of God he revealed makes these words compatible with Jesus as portrayed in the gospels.

5. The prophets speak of Israel as a bride (Is 62:5; Jer 2:2) as well as a wife (Is 54:6; Jer 3:20). But with far greater frequency the Hebrew scriptures refer to Israel as a harlot whose actions are described as harlotry. "While Israel dwelt in Shittim the people began to play the harlot with the daughters of Moab" (Num 25:1). "And the Lord said to Moses, 'Behold, you are about to sleep with your fathers; then this people will rise and play the harlot after the strange gods of the land...'" (Deut 31:16). Other similar examples can be found in Judges 2:17; 8:27; 8:33; 1 Chronicles 5:25; Psalm 106:39; Jeremiah 3:1-6. Numerous examples can be found in Ezekiel, chapters 16 and 23, as well as throughout Hosea. Numbers 30:1-17 gives further clarification of the power of father and husbands over daughters and wives. According to the revelation of Jesus, God alone enjoyed the prerogatives of husband and father casting all males in their relation to God in the role of daughter. Despite all these analogies where Israel is portrayed as a female (wife, daughter or harlot), in terms of the gender designation for nouns, "Israel" is always masculine.

6. Julian Pitt-Rivers, "Honor and Social Status," J.G. Peristiany (ed.), *Honor and Shame* (Chicago: Univ. of Chicago Press, 1966), pp. 19-79.

7. This consistent disregard for ritual purity is noteworthy because Leviticus clearly links purity with exclusiveness. Not maintaining oneself in a state of ritual purity excludes one from the divine presence. Ritual purity was a religious ideal necessary for holiness. That Jesus touched lepers, dead people and bleeding women with no concern for ritual defilement displays an understanding of holiness and God that was not shared by his group. The fact that he knew he was at odds with the law of Moses as written in Leviticus opens the door to questioning what is revealed by God in the Hebrew scriptures and what is not.

8. According to Pitt-Rivers in Peristiany, p. 69, the woman must "refrain from actions which are proper to men, and this is possible and necessary, according to the division of labor, because women are under the tutelage of men." Using this analogy, Jesus is under the tutelage of God or in a

relation to God more **like** that of a wife to a husband than that of an adult male who was responsible for maintaining his own honor in public.

9. Max Zerwick and Mary Grosvenor, *A Grammatical Analysis of the Greek New Testament* (Rome: Biblical Institute Press, 1981), p. 108.

10. George M. Foster, "The Anatomy of Envy: A Study in Symbolic Behavior," *Current Anthropology*, 13 (1972), pp. 165-203.

11. This is a widespread phenomenon in many parts of the world, extending from Australia where the overachiever's "poppy is too tall" and will be "cut down," to Scandinavia where the rules of Janteloven admonish each member to recall:

> 1) You shall not think you are something. 2) You shall not think that you are just like us. 3) You shall not think you are wiser than us. 4) You shall not imagine you are better than us. 5) You shall not think you know more than us. 6) You shall not think you are more than us. 7) You shall not think that you are good for anything. 8) You shall not laugh at us. 9) You shall not think that anyone is concerned about you. 10) You shall not think that you can teach us anything. (Formulated by A. Sandemose in the novel, *En flyktning krysser sitt spor* (1933), trans. by Bruce Malina.)

People of the Middle East and Mediterranean employ a variety of charms to protect themselves from the effect of envy's "evil eye." For additional characteristics of strong groups cf. Bruce J. Malina, *Christian Origins and Cultural Anthropology* (Atlanta: John Knox, 1986), Chpt. 2, "Strong Group Script Elements and Meaning Fields."

12. Juliet De Boulay, "Images of Women's Nature and Destiny" in Dubisch (ed.), pp. 166-167.

13. The ongoing misunderstanding and minimization of the female role can be most recently found in David D. Gilmore's *Manhood in the Making* (New Haven: Yale Univ. Press, 1990). Gilmore, an anthropologist, reveals that his profession guarantees no more freedom from traditional, elite male standpoints that "create" reality than any other profession. He reduces the achievement of womanhood to femininity which

> ...usually involves questions of body ornament or sexual allure, or other **essentially cosmetic behaviors** that enhance, rather than create, an inherent quality of character. An authentic femininity rarely involves tests or proofs of action, or confrontations with dangerous foes: win-or-lose contests dramatically played out on the public stage. Rather than a critical threshold passed by trau-

matic testing, an either/or condition, femininity is more often construed as a biological given that is culturally refined or augmented (pp. 11-12) (emphasis is mine).

Apparently the untold numbers of women who have suffered and died in childbirth in order to prove that they are women do not fall into Gilmore's category of "traumatic testing."

14. Pierre Bourdieu, "The Sentiment of Honor in Kabyle Society," Pitt-Rivers (ed.), pp. 25-34.

15. Patriarchal tradition has long placed man on the side of culture or social order while women symbolize nature. Culture has been placed both above, as well as at odds with, nature. Sherry B. Ortner, "Is Female to Male as Nature Is to Culture?" in Michelle Zimbalist Rosaldo and Louise Lamphere (eds.), *Woman, Culture, and Society* (Stanford: Stanford Univ. Press, 1974), pp. 67-87. The parables do not reflect this antithesis. Nature is not antithetical to the kingdom of heaven whereas Jesus constantly points out that group values, expectations and goals often do not reflect the mind of God. His greatest criticism is aimed at culture, that is, the area typically attributed to males as evidence of their superior status.

16. "If a woman has a discharge of blood for many days, not at the time of her impurity [monthly menstruation], or if she has a discharge beyond the time of her impurity, all the days of the discharge she shall continue in uncleanness; as in the days of her impurity, she shall be unclean. Every bed on which she lies, all the days of her discharge shall be to her as the bed of her impurity; and everything on which she sits shall be unclean, as in the uncleanness of her impurity. **And whoever touches these things shall be unclean, and shall wash his clothes, and bathe himself in water, and be unclean until the evening.** But if she is cleansed of her discharge, she shall count for herself seven days, and after that she shall be clean" (Lev 15:25-28). Further explanation and clarification of this can be found in Swidler, pp. 130-139.

17. Dimen in Dubisch (ed.), pp. 62-63.

18. Michael Herzfeld, "Within and Without: The Category of 'Female' in the Ethnography of Modern Greece," in Dubisch (ed.), pp. 215-223.

19. Erich Neumann discusses the complex role of the mother in his book, *The Child* (New York: Putnam Publ. Co., 1973). The masculine is first experienced in the mother and the patriarchal expectations of society are first represented by her as part of child rearing according to the values, goals and demands of the society.

20. Peter Brown, *The Body and Society* (New York: Columbia Univ., 1988), p. 25.

21. "Receiving" is a formal term often used in the Hebrew scriptures which will be considered at some length in John. It means to show hospitali-

ty and to accept the ongoing relation between the giver and receiver which "receiving" initiates.

22. Gehenna is the word which is translated "hell." It appears seven times in Matthew, three times in Mark and once in Luke. When Jesus makes a reference to Gehenna, he is not talking about the underworld but a ravine south of Jerusalem where filth and rubbish was dumped in order to maintain the city in a state of levitical purity (Jeremias, p. 17). Gehenna means "the valley of Hinnom." Its dark past is spoken of in several places of the Hebrew Bible. Ahaz, the twenty year old son of David, did not follow the example of his father, but ruled as one

> who walked in the ways of the kings of Israel. He even made molten images for the Ba'als; and he burned incense in the valley of the son of Hinnom, and burned his sons as an offering, according to the abominable practices of the nations whom the Lord drove out before the people of Israel (2 Chr 28:1-3).

Jeremiah makes several references to it but the most graphic is:

> For the sons of Judah have done evil in my sight, says the Lord...and they have built the high place of Topheth, which is in the valley of the son of Hinnom, to burn their sons and their daughters in the fire; which I did not command, nor did it come into my mind. Therefore, behold, the days are coming, says the Lord, when it will no more be called Topheth, or the valley of the son of Hinnom, but the valley of Slaughter: for they will bury in Topheth, because there is no room elsewhere. And the dead bodies of this people will be food for the birds of the air, and for the beasts of the earth, and none will frighten them away. And I will make to cease from the cities of Judah and from the streets of Jerusalem the voice of mirth and the voice of gladness, the voice of the bridegroom and the voice of the bride; for the land shall become a waste (Jer 7:30-34).

Thus, Gehenna is the place where the bodies are cast because of eyes, hands and feet that continue to sin. It is the place where those who set themselves against God burned their sons and daughters; the place of slaughter and rubbish where everything is thrown that is offensive to God. This is Gehenna, a place created by human beings, a place different from Anglo/Saxon hell.

23. Elizabeth Dodson Gray, *Patriarchy as a Conceptual Trap* (Wellesley, Mass: Roundtable Press, 1982), p. 26.

24. Swidler, p. 134.

CHAPTER II

1. Bruce J. Malina, *The New Testament World* (Atlanta: John Knox Press, 1981), pp. 60ff citing Bernard De Geradon. "L'homme a l'image de Dieu," *Nouvelle Revue Théologique* 90 (1958), pp. 683-695.

2. Margaret Miles, *Carnal Knowing* (Boston: Beacon Press, 1989), p. 9.

3. John D. Crossan, "Parable," in Paul Achtemeier (ed.), *Harper's Bible Dictionary* (San Francisco: Harper & Row, 1985), p. 749.

4. John J. McKenzie, SJ, *Dictionary of the Bible* (Milwaukee: Bruce Publ. Co., 1965), "Blessing," p. 98.

5. Anna Caravelli, "The Lament as Social Protest," in Dubisch (ed.), p. 178.

6. Caravelli in Dubisch (ed.), p. 183.

7. Caravelli in Dubisch (ed.), p. 180, quoting Ilhan Basgoz, *Protest: The Fifth Function of Folklore*, 1982, unpublished manuscript.

8. Margaret Alexiou, *The Ritual Lament in Greek Tradition* (Cambridge: Cambridge Univ. Press, 1974), p. 150. She argues against the position of E. Wellesz who believes that antithesis, which was one of the characteristics of semitic poetry, added this use of antithesis to Greek thought.

9. Caravelli in Dubisch (ed.), p. 180.

10. Emil Schurer, *The History of the Jewish People in the Age of Jesus Christ,* Vol. I (Edinburgh: T & T Clark Ltd., 1973), p. 146. While this description of a despot was used to describe Antiochus IV Epiphanes who ruled over Syria from 175 to 164 BC, it shares much in common with words and actions attributed to God in the Hebrew scriptures.

11. Muhammad, Asad, *The Message of the Qur'an* (Gibralter: Dar al-Andalus, 1980), p. 247, fn. 52. In the *Qur'an*, the term which means "your neighbor" is translated by Asad as "your protector." His choice of word is derived from "the ancient Arabian principle that a man is honor-bound to aid and protect his neighbor."

12. This interpretation is largely based on the exegesis by B. Malina, *A New Testament Morality* (Typescript Omaha: Creighton Univ., 1970), pp. 91-96.

CHAPTER III

1. Ortner in Rosaldo and Lamphere (eds.), p. 78.

2. The Samaritans were also strict followers of the Torah (the first five books of the Christian Old Testament). However they rejected all the later writings as "scripture." From their standpoint (then and now), they were the

true bearers of the ancient Mosaic tradition from the earliest times when the temple was located on Mount Gerizim near modern day Nablus. Their temple was destroyed by the Judean king, John Hyrcanus, in 128 BC. This action further alienated Samaritans from their geographical and ethnic neighbors to the north and south. While the Galileans lived under a dark cloud of Judean suspicion regarding the strictness of their religious observance, the Samaritans were totally ostracized as apostates.

3. Schurer, Vol. II, pp. 388-398.

4. Schurer, Vol. II, pp. 404-414.

5. Schurer, Vol. II, p. 324.

6. Schurer, Vol. II, pp. 250-251.

7. Schurer, Vol. II, pp. 238-240.

8. S. Safrai, "Jewish Self-Government," in Safrai and Stern, Vol. I, pp. 384-385.

9. Schurer, Vol. II, p. 210.

10. Schurer, Vol. II, p. 218.

11. Sean Freyne, *Galilee, Jesus and the Gospels* (Philadelphia: Fortress Press, 1988), p. 1.

12. Cf., for example:

> The secular separateness of the Jews, their inner awareness of being a group, their outward view of themselves as in some ways apart from others—that separateness is probably all modern man can hope for socially to approximate "the holy." The archaic "holy people" have passed from the scene. In their place stands something different in all respects but the most important: the manifest and correct claim to continue as Jews, a different, separate group, and **the claim that difference is destiny**. Jacob Neusner, *Israel in America* (Boston: Beacon Press, 1985), pp. 41-42.

> In the past, the Jews were well insulated from the opinions of the Gentiles. Their social setting tended to separate them, and their theological conviction rendered them indifferent to what the Gentiles had to say about them. Jews not only knew they were different from others, but also regarded these differences as a matter of destiny. The statement in the "Alenu" prayer, "Who has not made us like Gentiles," was a matter of thanksgiving, pride, and joy, a self-conscious articulation of Israel's status as a unique people. The myth of Jews as a distinct people transformed difference into destiny. Neusner, p. 101.

The word assimilation denotes the reception of aliens by a host society and the aliens' gradual acceptance of the traits of that host culture. The history of the Jewish people is the story of how the Jews entered into one culture after another, and came to regard the cultural acquisitions as essentially Jewish. Neusner, p. 97.

13. There is a tendency on the part of Jewish scholars to minimize the strife that split the Jewish community over Jesus as well as the number of Jewish conversions to the new movement. This same tendency reduces the impact that early Christianity had on formative Judaism regarding some major areas: speculation about Moses, the binding of Isaac, the canon and role of Torah, discussion about the suffering Messiah and the future, speculation about the return and martyrdom of Enoch and Elijah, as well as the development of the oral Torah to compete with the traditions about Jesus prevalent among Jewish-Christians.

Much earlier in history, Cyrus of Persia (538 BC) had been greeted by the house of Israel with accolades of praise and rising expectations of his messianic role when he allowed them to return to the lands of their fathers (cf. 2 Chr 36:22-23; Ezr 1; Isaiah 45:1f). Cyrus never fulfilled those messianic expectations bound up with land. Centuries later, the rise of Islam impelled another group of Jews to see in Muhammad's rise to power and consolidation of the land under one God the fulfillment of their eschatalogical hopes.

The seventeenth century, pseudo-messianic movement of Shabbetai Tzevi in Turkey is a far less controversial topic because both Tzevi and his movement faded into obscurity before evolving a religious tradition which challenged Judaism. The presence of Jews as a minority group among members of Islam or Christianity has complicated Judaism's evaluation of either religion's impact on Judaism.

14. The term *minim* refers to a deviant Jew, most likely a Jewish Christian. Another term for early Christians, *nosrim*, probably derives from its cognate, Nazarene. The twelfth benediction contained in the Amidah (the Eighteen Benedictions) which the religious Jew recites three times a day currently reads,

And for the slanderers let there be no hope, and let all wickedness perish as in a moment; let all thine enemies be speedily cut off, and the dominion of arrogance do thou uproot and crush, cast down and humble speedily in our days. Blessed art thou, O Lord, who breakest the enemies and humblest the arrogant. Dr.

Joseph H. Hertz, *The Authorized Daily Prayer Book* (New York: Bloch Publ. Co., 1985), p. 143.

There is an earlier version that was part of the Cairo Geniza which is probably closer to the first century Palestinian version. The Cairo Geniza (*geniza*, room for discarded writings) stored documents dating from the tenth to the thirteenth century because they included the name "God' (which meant that they could not be burned but had to be buried). These were discovered in Old Cairo in 1890 and dispersed to libraries around the world for translation and preservation. The twelfth blessing in this collection reads:

May there be no hope for the apostates,

And speedily uproot the kingdom of arrogance in our own day.

May the Nazarenes (nosrim) and minim perish in an instant.

May they be blotted out of the book of the living,

And not be written with the righteous.

Blessed art thou, O Lord, who subdues the arrogant.

Joseph Heinemann, *Prayer in the Talmud* (New York: Walter De Gruyter, 1977), p. 28.

Reuvan Kimelman, "Birkat Ha-Minim and the Lack of Evidence for an Anti-Christian Jewish Prayer in Late Antiquity," p. 226 in E.P. Sanders (ed.), Vol. II, *Aspects of Judaism in the Greco-Roman Period,* in the three volume series, *Jewish and Christian Self-Definition* (Philadelphia: Fortress Press, 1981), is an example of Jewish scholarship minimizing the animosity that Jesus inspired within formative Judaism. He includes a bibliography of those who disagree with his conclusions.

A compilation of comments in authoritative Jewish writings that relate to Jesus, Jewish-Christians and Christians has been collected by R. Travers Herford, *Christianity in Talmud and Midrash* (New York: KTAV Publ. House, Inc., 1903).

15. Brown, pp. 39-41.

16. William Whiston, *The Works of Josephus* (Peabody, Mass.: Hendrickson, 1987), p. 477.

CHAPTER IV

1. Al-Faruqi, pp. 45-47.

2. Al-Faruqi, p. 45. Each of these points has a gender role equivalent. First, reality is composed of two kinds of beings: the male who is above all and commands all, while the female is material, human, changing and subject to male commands. Second, the male relates his commands to the woman. Third, women are created to serve their father, brother or husband

through obedience and the fulfillment of their commands. Fourth, since women are capable of obedience and male commands present what ought to be, women are held responsible for their actions. Fifth, the male plans concern the group which acts as an organic unity. Thus, the family or group is the primary unit of reality, not the individual.

3. Ortner in Rosaldo and Lamphere (eds.), pp. 72-73.

4. Henry Geo. Liddell and Robert Scott, *A Greek-English Lexicon* (Oxford: Clarendon Press, 1968), pp. 1585, 1749.

5. Wm. F. Arndt and F. Wilbur Gingrich, *A Greek-English Lexicon of the New Testament and Other Early Christian Literature* (Cambridge: Univ. Press, 1957), p. 22.

6. Asad, p. 400, fn. 45 regarding the Qur'anic doctrine that no human being has ever been endowed with "supernatural" powers or qualities.

7. Al-Faruqi, pp. 102-103.

8. Al-Faruqi, p. 171.

9. Al-Faruqi, p. 169.

10. The implications of expressing infinity and transcendence from the perspective of the semitic mind is well covered in al-Faruqi, "The Arts," pp. 162-180 with references to other sections on the same topic.

11. This is the Johannine passage referred to in Chapter I, endnote #2, that discusses the problems with translations which are bent to conform to doctrine. The Jerusalem Bible translates this passage as referring to Jesus and not to those who believe in him. This is done to bolster evidence for the virgin birth of Jesus despite the lack of evidence in early Greek manuscripts for such a translation. In the same way, whenever Jesus' brothers and sisters are referred to, the Jerusalem Bible appends a footnote variously changing the meaning of those words so as not to be understood as siblings. There is, however, more at stake in these translations than the virgin birth. The Roman Catholic declarations of the immaculate conception and assumption are based on the premise that Mary remained a virgin until death. Both doctrines were declared as infallible pronouncements. The church has considerable vested interests in controlling translations which involve defense of that nineteenth century doctrine of papal infallibility. Or, to put it another way, there will probably never be a good time to discuss how the reality of Mary's other sons and daughters affects her status in Christian tradition.

12. Zerwick and Grosvenor, p. 286.

13. McKenzie, pp. 485-489.

14. "Believe into" is used thirty-four times in John and only once in Matthew and Luke, Bruce J. Malina, *The Gospel of John in Sociolinguistic Perspective,* 48th Colloquy of the Center for Hermeneutical Studies, Herman Waetjen (ed.) (Berkeley: Center for Hermeneutical Studies, 1985), p. 10.

15. McKenzie, "Truth," p. 901.

CHAPTER V

1. Martin Hengel, *Judaism and Hellenism*, Vol. 1 (London: SCM Press Ltd, 1974), Vol. I, p. 24.

2. Jeremias, pp. 102-103.

3. Safrai in Safrai and M. Stern (eds.), Vol. II, p. 808.

4. Safrai in Safrai and Stern (eds.), Vol. II, p. 809.

5. Kenneth Cragg, *Jesus and the Muslim* (London: Geo. Allen & Unwin, 1985), p. 30.

6. Genesis 2:18ff portrays man as the one for whom the earth and women were created. The *Qur'an* portrays man in the same central role as the one for whom is meant "the enjoyment of worldly desires through women, and children, and heaped-up treasures of gold and silver, and horses of high mark, and cattle and lands" (Surah 3:14). Both reflect the social system as it existed independent of "revelation."

7. Miles, p. 155.

8. Heinemann, p. 186.

9. Foster, pp. 165-203.

10. Miles, p. 152.

11. Miles, p. 167.

12. Miles, p. 151.

13. Those readers who have no background in the development of the New Testament need an awareness that the area is as complex and elusive as it is interesting. A variety of manuscripts exist in Greek, although none before the beginning of the second century. Around the year 200 AD, Latin, Coptic and Syriac manuscripts came into use. Until the beginning of the fourth century, the text of the New Testament developed freely (Aland, 68-69). While nearly sixty-three percent of the New Testament verses have no variants, 2,948 verses (out of 7,947 verses) show differences that exist among various manuscripts (Aland, 29). The shorter ending of Mark 16:8 continued to be included in some Greek manuscripts as well as in versional manuscripts for centuries despite the fact that the longer ending (16:9-20) had been recognized as canonical or authoritative. Kurt and Barbara Aland, *The Text of the New Testament* (Grand Rapids, Mich.: Wm. B. Eerdmans Publ. Co., 1987), p. 69.

14. The following summary of Jesus' activity is based on the domestic role as found in the Introduction.

15. Dubisch, "Introduction" quoting E. Ardener, 1975, in Dubisch (ed.), p. 32.

CHAPTER VI

1. Malina, 1981, pp. 55ff.

2. Pitt-Rivers, "Honor and Social Status," in Peristiany (ed.), pp. 40-42, 44.

3. "Face" is the outward appearance of honor. Thus, one may "lose face," have one's face "blackened" or "save face." As the symbol of honor, "face" causes one to weigh words and actions very carefully so as not "to lose face." Raphael Patai, *The Arab Mind* (New York: Charles Scribner's Sons, 1983), pp. 101ff.

In classical Arabic, "face" denotes "one's whole personality, or whole being." Asad, p. 24, fn. 91; p. 206, fn. 21.

4. Ortner in Rosaldo and Lamphere (eds.), p. 72.

5. Brown, pp. 26-27.

6. Miles, p. 115.

7. Marina Warner, *Alone of All Her Sex* (New York: Vintage Book edition, 1983), pp. 25ff.

8. Warner, pp. 347-348.

9. Carol Gilligan's work evokes countless questions as to the effects of mothering when males describe in their stories of intimacy "a danger of entrapment or betrayal, being caught in a smothering relationship or humiliated by rejection and deceit. In contrast, the danger women portray in their tales of achievement is a danger of isolation, a fear that in standing out or being set apart by success, they will be left alone." *In a Different Voice* (Cambridge, MA: Harvard Univ. Press, 1982), p. 42. While moral thinking in men and women reveal different gender expectations, both reveal early experiences with the primary nurturing person who was overwhelming; extremely tricky; or too insecure to face the success of the daughter who does better than the mother. While the moral evaluation process may differ in males and females, the **treatment** of those who are powerless may show little difference. Perhaps the common denominator for both genders is poor mothering.

10. See references to Alice Miller, note 33 below.

11. Patai, p. 106.

12. Patai, p. 226.

13. Kurt and Barbara Aland, p. 64.

14. The epic is a type of literature which begins as folklore in an oral stage passed on among non-elites. There is no single author because folklore arises more like language than like literature. It becomes national property, changing slowly to remain in harmony with the people's development, discarding those aspects which are no longer fitting. In its beginning, folklore can originate as an integral part of ritual and become detached through time,

living an independent life that is written down and taken over by elites. Vladimir Propp, *Theory and History of Folklore* (Minneapolis: Univ. of Minnesota Press, 1984), pp. 5-17.

15. Bernard was also a major influence in calling for the Second Crusade. Cf. Elizabeth Hallam (ed.), *The Chronicles of the Crusades* (London: Weidenfeld and Nicholson, 1989), pp. 115ff.

16. Stephen Howarth, *The Knights Templar* (New York: Atheneum, 1982), pp. 54ff.

17. Miles, p. 55.

18. Hertz, p. 788.

19. Regina Sharif, *Non-Jewish Zionism* (London: Zed Press, 1983), pp. 12ff.

20. Sydney Ahlstrom, *A Religious History of the American People* (New Haven: Yale Univ. Press, 1972), p. 129.

21. Sharif, pp. 90ff.

22. Thomas L. Friedman, *From Beirut to Jerusalem* (New York: Farrar, Straus & Giroux, 1989), p. 436.

23. J.A. Loubser, *The Apartheid Bible* (Cape Town: Maskew Miller Longman, 1987), pp. ix-xi.

24. Loubser, pp. x-xi.

25. Loubser, p. xiv.

26. Loubser, p. 22.

27. Friedman, p. 144.

28. Loubser, p. 25.

29. Loubser, p. ix.

30. Many myths have been created about the Palestinians which minimize, deny or distort their experiences and history and replace them with others which are more in keeping with Israel's self-image. One book that quickly and clearly exposes these reconstructions of Palestinian experiences is Clifford A. Wright, *Facts and Fables: The Arab-Israeli Conflict* (New York: Kegan Paul International, 1989).

31. Alan Mintz, *Hurban* (New York: Columbia Univ. Press, 1984), p. 91.

32. Karen Jo Torjesen, "Public Roles, Domestic Virtues: The Controversies Over Women's Leadership" (Claremont Graduate School), p. 7 (citing J. Kautisky, *The Politics of Aristocratic Empires* (Chapel Hill: Univ. of No. Carolina Press, 1982).

33. There are a number of books which deal with theories of early experiences that individuals "are not allowed to remember" while they are not lost to the "body's memory":

Alice Miller, *Drama of the Gifted Child* (New York: Basic Books, 1981).

_____, *For Your Own Good* (New York: Farrar, Straus & Giroux, 1985).

_____, *Thou Shalt Not Be Aware* (New York: Meridian Book Co., 1986).

_____, *Pictures of a Childhood* (New York: Farrar, Straus & Giroux, 1986).

_____, *The Untouched Key* (New York: Doubleday, 1990).

_____, *Banished Knowledge* (New York: Doubleday, 1990).

_____, *Breaking Down the Walls of Silence* (New York: Dutton, 1991).

Daniel Goleman, *Vital Lies, Simple Truths* (New York: Touchstone Book, Simon & Schuster, Inc., 1985).

J. Konrad Stettbacher, *Making Sense of Suffering* (New York: Dutton, 1991).

Charles L. Whitfield, *Healing the Child Within* (Deerfield Beach, Florida: Health Communications Inc., 1987).

34. Pitt-Rivers, "Honor and Social Status," in Peristiany (ed.), pp. 36ff.

35. While men are reared to be concerned about their honor, women are reared with a sense of shame. That is, they recognize their inadequacy and unworthiness apart from males who embody honor. A woman reared with this sense of shame was considered virtuous and an asset to males whose honor she would not threaten. Shameful behavior is not relegated only to women but is possible for both sexes. Since female behavior in the males' public domain always implied some risk to male honor, the virtuous female "disappeared" when in public.

36. Cragg, p. 252.

37. Cragg, pp. 196-197.

CHAPTER VII

1. Annemarie Schimmel, *And Muhammad Is His Messenger* (Chapel Hill, N.C.: Univ. of North Carolina Press, 1985), pp. 4-24.

2. Hallam (ed.), p. 19.

3. Asad, p. 134, fn. 171.

4. Asad, p. 402, fn. 63. While not commenting on this surah as such, Asad writes that "the *Qur'an* states that God is utterly remote from every imperfection...complete in Himself, and therefore free from the incomplete-

ness inherent in the concept of 'progeny' as an extension of one's own being."

5. This same reference (Surah 16, pp. 402ff with footnotes) continues with references to cultural problems that accompany the birth of girls.

6. Al-Faruqi, p. 74.

7. Kenneth Cragg, *Readings in the Qur'an* (London: Collins Liturgical Publications, 1988), p. 229.

8. Norman Daniel, *The Arabs and Medieval Europe* (London: Longman Group Ltd, 1975), pp. 265-266.

9. Cragg, p. 30.

10. Gray, pp. 47ff.

11. Gray, p. 47. In addition to the lighter approach of Gray is the work of Fritjof Capra, *The Turning Point* (New York: Bantam Books, 1983). This work illuminates the specific characteristics of patriarchal perception as it has manifested itself in western intellectual disciplines. Capra further illustrates why the demise of patriarchy is inevitable.

12. Goleman, pp. 86-87.

13. Gray, p. 50.

14. Margaret Miles, *Carnal Knowing* (Boston: Beacon Press, 1989), p. 5.

15. Jeffrey M. Masson, *The Assault on Truth* (New York: Farrar, Straus and Giroux, 1984), p. 191.

16. Norman Daniel, *Islam and the West, The Making of an Image* (Edinburgh: University Press, 1980); *Heroes and Saracens* (Edinburgh: University Press, 1984).

17. Edward W. Said, *Orientalism* (New York: Vintage Books, 1979).

18. Edward W. Said, *Covering Islam*, Chpt. 3, "Knowledge and Power" (New York: Pantheon Books, 1981).

19. F. Capra explores the myth of objectivity from numerous angles. He includes many examples of how science is subject not only to the same limitations of the patriarchal perspective as other fields, but to the same patriarchal values as well (Chapters IV and V). This means that science like history and economics has been used to strengthen authorized images and to assist elites in controlling various sub-groups and out-groups.

20. Bryan S. Turner, *The Body and Society* (Oxford: Basil Blackwell, 1984), p. 155. Turner's initial insight about prejudice against women has been expanded here to encompass the wider bias in which females were declared inferior to males because of the woman's link to procreation and nurture.

21. Miles, p. 187.

22. It is important to keep in mind that the thesis of this book is not about men and women, but the idealized male and female **roles** as created

and promulgated in patriarchal social systems. There is no judgment being passed as to how well women or men approximate those idealized roles in their behavior.

23. "The Lord saw that the wickedness of man was great in the earth, and that every imagination of the thoughts of his heart was only evil continually. And the Lord was sorry that he had made man on the earth, and it grieved him to his heart" (Gen 6:5-6).

"Yet as soon as he [God] has saved them from danger, they behave outrageously on earth offending against all right" (Surah 10:23).

24. In addition to the works of Miller and Stettbacher already cited in note 33 in Chapter VI is the work of John Bradshaw, *Homecoming: Reclaiming and Championing Your Inner Child* (New York: Bantam, 1990). Bradshaw's book provides useful charts and activities which complement the theories of Miller and Stettbacher.

25. Stettbacher, pp. 5-37.

26. Whitfield, pp. 10-11.

27. Merle A. Fossum and Marilyn J. Mason, *Facing Shame* (New York: W.W. Norton & Co., 1986), p. 63.

28. Fused or enmeshed boundaries exist among those who are emotionally connected to a degree where they do not see themselves as separate individuals with distinct needs, goals and aspirations. Instead, the individual remains "locked into" or "fused" with one or more people whose lives that person needs to control and who, in turn, is controlled by those with whom s/he is fused. See Whitfield, pp. 48ff.

29. Fossum and Mason, p. 5. This is exactly what the virtuous woman is reared to feel as a safeguard to male honor. And while men are expected to feel none of this, childhood boundary violations leave adult males feeling that their honor is nothing more than a fragile shell which can be easily shattered.

30. See also A. Miller, *Banished Knowledge*, pp. 151ff.

31. See A. Miller, *The Untouched Key*, pp. 167ff.

32. Examples in the *Qur'an* include Surah 2:101 which refutes 1 Kings 11: 1-10, stating that Solomon had not been involved in idolatrous practices; Surah 3:41 which counters Luke 1:20-22 that Zechariah had not been struck dumb; Surah 7:150 which counters Exodus 32:1-5 that Aaron had not actively engaged in worshiping the golden calf; Surah 7:154 which infers that Moses did not break the tablets of the ten commandments as stated in Exodus 32:19; Surah 11:71 that Sarah laughed before she received the news of Isaac's birth as opposed to laughing in disbelief after the news in the account in Genesis 18:12-15, etc.

33. See Miller, *The Drama of the Gifted Child.*

BIBLIOGRAPHY

Ahlstrom, Sydney. *A Religious History of the American People*. New Haven: Yale Univ. Press, 1972.

Aland, Kurt and Barbara. *The Text of the New Testament*. Grand Rapids, Mich.: Wm. B. Eerdmans Publ. Co., 1987.

Alexiou, Margaret. *The Ritual Lament in Greek Tradition*. Cambridge: Cambridge Univ. Press, 1974.

Al-Faruqi, Isma'il R. and Lamya, Lois. *The Cultural Atlas of Islam*. New York: Macmillan Publ. Co., 1986.

Altorki, Soraya. *Women in Saudi Arabia*. New York: Columbia Univ. Press, 1986.

Arndt, Wm. F. and Gingrich, F. Wilbur. *A Greek-English Lexicon of the New Testament and Other Early Christian Literature*. Cambridge: Univ. Press, 1957.

Asad, Muhammad. *The Message of the Qur'an*. Gibraltar: Dar al-Andalus, 1980.

Bourdieu, Pierre. "The Sentiment of Honor in Kabyle Society." In J.G. Peristiany ed. *Honor and Shame*. Chicago: Univ. of Chicago Press, 1966.

Bradshaw, John. *Homecoming: Reclaiming and Championing Your Inner Child*. New York: Bantam, 1990.

Brown, Peter. *The Body and Society*. New York: Columbia Univ. Press, 1988.

Capra, Fritjof. *The Turning Point*. New York: Bantam Books, 1983.

Caravelli, Anna. "The Lament as Social Protest." In Jill Dubisch ed. *Gender & Power in Rural Greece*. Princeton: Princeton University Press, 1986.

Cragg, Kenneth. *Jesus and the Muslim*. London: Geo. Allen & Unwin, 1985.

_____. *Readings in the Qur'an*. London: Collins Liturgical Publications, 1988.

Crossan, John D. *Sayings Parallels*. Philadelphia: Fortress, 1986.

_____. "Parable." In Paul Achtemeier, ed. *Harper's Bible Dictionary*. San Francisco: Harper & Row, 1985.

Daniel, Norman. *Islam and the West, The Making of an Image*. Edinburgh: University Press, 1980.

_____. *Heroes and Saracens*. Edinburgh: University Press, 1984.

De Boulay, Juliet. "Images of Women's Nature and Destiny." In Jill Dubisch ed. *Gender & Power in Rural Greece*. Princeton: Princeton University Press, 1986.

Dimen, Muriel. "Servants and Sentries: Women, Power, and Social Reproduction in Kriovrisi." In Jill Dubisch ed. *Gender & Power in Rural Greece*. Princeton: Princeton University Press, 1986.

Dubisch, Jill. "Introduction" and "Culture Enters through the Kitchen: Women, Food, and Social Boundaries in Rural Greece." In Jill Dubisch ed. *Gender & Power in Rural Greece*. Princeton: Princeton University Press, 1986.

Fossum, Merle A. and Mason, Marilyn J. *Facing Shame*. New York: W.W. Norton & Co., 1986.

Foster, George M. "The Anatomy of Envy: A Study in Symbolic Behavior." *Current Anthropology*. April, 1972.

Freyne, Sean. *Galilee, Jesus and the Gospels*. Philadelphia: Fortress Press, 1988.

Friedman, Thomas L. *From Beirut to Jerusalem*. New York: Farrar, Straus & Giroux, 1989.

Gage, Nicholas. *Eleni*. New York: Random House, 1983.

_____. *A Place for Us*. Boston: Houghton Mifflin Co., 1989.

Gilligan, Carol. *In a Different Voice*. Cambridge, MA: Harvard Univ. Press, 1982.

Gilmore, David D. *Manhood in the Making*. New Haven: Yale Univ. Press, 1990.

Goitein, S.D. *A Mediterranean Society*. Vol. III. Berkeley: Univ. of California Press, 1978.

Goleman, Daniel. *Vital Lies, Simple Truths*. New York: Touchstone Book, Simon & Schuster, Inc. 1985.

Gray, Elizabeth Dodson. *Patriarchy as a Conceptual Trap*. Wellesley, Mass: Roundtable Press, 1982.

Hallam, Elizabeth ed. *The Chronicles of the Crusades*. London: Weidenfeld and Nicholson, 1989.

Heinemann, Joseph. *Prayer in the Talmud*. New York: Walter De Gruyter, 1977.

Hengel, Martin. *Judaism and Hellenism*. Vol. I. London: SCM Press Ltd, 1974.

Herford, R. Travers. *Christianity in Talmud and Midrash*. New York: KTAV Publ. House Inc., 1903.

Hertz, Dr. Joseph H. *The Authorized Daily Prayer Book*. New York: Bloch Publ. Co., 1985.

Herzfeld, Michael. "Within and Without: The Category of 'Female' in the

Ethnography of Modern Greece." In Jill Dubisch ed. *Gender & Power in Rural Greece.* Princeton: Princeton University Press, 1986.

Howarth, Stephen. *The Knights Templar.* New York: Atheneum, 1982.

Jeremias, Joachim. *Jerusalem in the Time of Jesus.* London: SCM Press Ltd, 1976.

Kimelman, Reuvan. "Birkat Ha-Minim and the Lack of Evidence for an Anti-Christian Jewish Prayer in Late Antiquity." In E.P. Sanders, ed. Vol. II, *Aspects of Judaism in the Greco-Roman Period,* in the three volume series, *Jewish and Christian Self-Definition.* Philadelphia: Fortress Press, 1981.

Liddell, Henry Geo. and Scott, Robert. *A Greek-English Lexicon.* Oxford: Clarendon Press, 1968.

Loubser, J.A. *The Apartheid Bible.* Cape Town: Maskew Miller Longman, 1987.

Makhlouf, Carla. *Changing Veils.* Austin: Univ. of Texas Press, 1979.

Malina, Bruce J. *A New Testament Morality.* Typescript Omaha, Nebraska: Creighton Univ. 1970. Unpublished manscript.

_____. *The New Testament World.* Atlanta: John Knox Press, 1981.

_____. "The Gospel of John in Sociolinguistic Perspective." In Herman Waetjen. *48th Colloquy of the Center for Hermeneutical Studies.* Berkeley: Center for Hermeneutical Studies, 1985.

_____. *Christian Origins and Cultural Anthropology.* Atlanta: John Knox, 1986.

Masson, Jeffrey M. *The Assault on Truth.* New York: Farrar, Straus and Giroux, 1984.

McKenzie, John J. *Dictionary of the Bible.* Milwaukee: Bruce Publ. Co., 1965.

Mikhail, Mona. *Images of Arab Women.* Washington, D.C.: Three Continents Press Inc., 1979.

Miles, Margaret. *Carnal Knowing.* Boston: Beacon Press, 1989.

Miller, Alice. *Drama of the Gifted Child.* New York: Basic Books, 1981.

_____. *For Your Own Good.* New York: Farrar, Straus & Giroux, 1985.

_____. *Thou Shalt Not Be Aware.* New York: Meridian Book Co., 1986.

_____. *Pictures of a Childhood.* New York: Farrar, Straus & Giroux, 1986.

_____. *The Untouched Key.* New York: Doubleday, 1990.

_____. *Banished Knowledge.* New York: Doubleday, 1990.

_____. *Breaking Down the Wall of Silence.* New York: Dutton, 1991.

Mintz, Alan. *Hurban.* New York: Columbia Univ. Press, 1984.

Neumann, Erich. *The Child.* New York: Putnam Publ. Co., 1973.

Neusner, Jacob. *Israel in America.* Boston: Beacon Press, 1985.

Ortner, Sherry B. "Is Female to Male as Nature Is to Culture?" In Michelle

Zimbalist Rosaldo and Louise Lamphere eds. *Woman, Culture, and Society.* Stanford: Stanford Univ. Press, 1974.

Patai, Raphael. *The Arab Mind.* New York: Charles Scribner's Sons, 1983.

Pitt-Rivers, Julian. "Honor and Social Status." In J.G. Peristiany ed. *Honor and Shame.* Chicago: Univ. of Chicago Press, 1966.

Propp, Vladimir. *Theory and History of Folklore.* Minneapolis: Univ. of Minnesota Press, 1984.

Safrai, S. and Stern, M. eds. in cooperation with D. Flusser and W.C. Van Unnik, *The Jewish People in the First Century.* Vols. I & II. Assen/Amsterdam: Van Gorcum, 1976.

Said, Edward W. *Orientalism.* New York: Vintage Books, 1979.

_____. *Covering Islam.* New York: Pantheon Books, 1981.

Schimmel, Annemarie. *And Muhammad Is His Messenger.* Chapel Hill, N.C.: Univ. of North Carolina Press, 1985.

Schurer, Emil. *The History of the Jewish People in the Age of Jesus Christ.* Two volumes. Edinburgh: T & T Clark Ltd., 1973.

Sharif, Regina. *Non-Jewish Zionism.* London: Zed Press, 1983.

Soffan, Linda Usra. *The Women of the United Arab Emirates.* New York: Harper & Row, 1980.

Stettbacher, J. Konrad. *Making Sense of Suffering.* New York, Dutton, 1991.

Swidler, Leonard. *Women in Judaism.* Metuchen, N,J.: The Scarecrow Press, Inc., 1976.

Torjesen, Karen Jo. "Public Roles, Domestic Virtues: The Controversies Over Women's Leadership." Claremont Graduate School. Chapel Hill: Univ. of No. Carolina Press, 1982.

Turner, Bryan S. *The Body and Society.* Oxford: Basil Blackwell, 1984.

Warner, Marina. *Alone of All Her Sex.* New York: Vintage Book Edition, 1983.

Whiston, William. *The Works of Josephus.* Peabody, Mass.: Hendrickson, 1987.

Whitfield, Charles L. *Healing the Child Within.* Deerfield Beach, Florida: Health Communications Inc., 1987.

Wolfe, Roland. *The Twelve Religions of the Bible.* New York: Edwin Mellen Press, 1982.

Wright, Clifford A. *Facts and Fables: The Arab-Israeli Conflict.* New York: Kegan Paul International, 1989.

Zerwick, Max and Grosvenor, Mary. *A Grammatical Analysis of the Greek New Testament.* Rome: Biblical Institute Press, 1981.

SUBJECT/AUTHOR INDEX

SCRIPTURE INDEX